When Elvis Played J
(The World Began To Sing)

When Elvis played his music,
   The World Began To Sing.
He took the rock, made it soft
   Called it Country rock.
His rhythm and blues and Popular Tunes
   Became his Gospel talk.

Now his concerts are at Graceland
   His voice echoes with a guitar carved in rock.
The cheers have turned to tear souvenirs
   Memories of forty-two years.

When Elvis played his music
   The World Began To Sing
Now the people play his music,
   And the world sings
He was number one, but his work was done.
   For God only calls you when your work is done.

COPYRIGHT © 1978   FRANCIS E. DELANEY

MEMORIES

MINUTES IN

TIME

Author: Francis E. Delaney

Poetry, Words & Music and Love

Special Thanks: To My Parents

To all my songs and all who made this book possible

Publisher: Francis E. Delaney

Copyright © 2006
Francis E. Delaney
All Rights Reserved

Memories, Minutes in Time, Copyright © 2006 By Francis E. Delaney
All rights reserved. No part of this book may be reproduced or transmitted in
any form or by any means, electronic or mechanical, including photocopy,
recording, or any other information and retrieval system, without the written
permission of the publisher. Exception: The use of brief quotes for review.

Information address. F. E. Delaney
P.O. Box 932
Frankfort, IL 60423 U.S.A.

Library of Congress Control Number: 2006900962

ISBN 0-615-12958-7

First Edition

Publisher: Francis E. Delaney

Printed in the United States of America on acid free paper.

Impression Unlimited   Addison, Illinois 60101   630-705-6464   www.impressionsunltd.com

MEMORIES, PIECES OF TIME

Poetry, Words, Music and Life

I have been writing poems and songs for many years,
I find that in poems and songs, are life's simple pleasures.
More than that they speak of life's great lessons, of great loves.
The friendship of laughter and tears is a remarkable fusion of
styles in friendships, relationships and words and music.
When you read a poem or listen to song, no matter who wrote it,
and, you find that a poem or song describes you -- It's you.

Take A Walk In Your Mind to all the places you can find.
You may not find the reasons and the answers to why it all happened,
each smile, each tear, each day and each year's - Love, laughter and tears.

Special Thanks;

Maureen: Some people live a lifetime with their "Audience of One"
Their world never changes. Their love never leaves.

I lived in that world where life and love never changed.
Then there are people, where life always changes.

Now I find in life's years --Love, Laughter and You

Francis E. Delaney

Pages are in years: 1964 - 2005

All copyrights used with the permission of the author and publisher.   Contents

S-Songs / music   P- poems, short stories   Index -- last pages

Memories, Minutes in Time

By: Francis E. Delaney

When I think of you
    In that little part of time

        Your rhythm and melody
            The arrangement of your moods
              It's in your walk and talk
                  The composition of your soul
                      Arranged in parts, music is the score of life

Your beauty takes me
    To memories in time and place
        It becomes the sound of music
            In the songs that poets write
                Music is the gift God gave everyone

        When the Lord takes me
            To my special place in life
                I will thank Him for your time
                    Memories of time playing in my mind
                        Set to music in pieces of time

Music is the language of love

        It's sign, is the music staff and five lines

                It's Memories, Minutes in Time

Copyright 2005 Francis E. Delaney   Lap-0505-KY

MY LOVE NOTE TREE — 1964

Here I go again writing love notes again
Still taking a chance that your my special romance
If you want your love to be
Musical, virtuous, wise and free
Then come along and be a part
Of My Love Note Tree
By writing your love notes to me
I'll always answer your love notes
So we know that our love note tree
Will always be love fed by you and me
Our love will always be beautiful and free
As the leaves on a real tree

In the summer of our love
Ours is born pure and free
As the budding of the leaves
As strong and as lovely as a spring tree
In the summer of our love
Our love will be born
As sturdy as the leaves
In a summer storm
Then it will be up to you and me
Whether our love, it will always be
Beautiful as the changing leaves
Of an autumn tree
In the winter of our lives
Our love will be like a Christmas tree
Presents of love side by side
Beneath Our Love Note Tree

Copyright 1967 Francis E. Delaney   S-6401-MH 58

BLACKIE

Blackie, Why do you lack the courage to come back
Come back to me Blackie, come back

Let me softly stroke the hair
That's black as night without the stars
Let me touch the skin that's
Soft as the light from a star

Let me look into your eyes, big and bright
As the full moon in the darkness of the night
Let me hold you tight and kiss
The warm love in the lips of Blackie, my Blackie

Blackie, bring back your smile, inviting and warm
Like bright sun after a storm

Your love is a pleasure, I can't measure
Treasure here on earth
Let me be the only one to know
Just what it is worth

Blackie, why do you lack the courage to come back
Come back to me Blackie, come back

Copyright 1967 Francis E. Delaney   S-6402-MH 63

TEACHERS PET — 1965

Teacher, teacher, where are you
All I want to be is the Teachers Pet
Teach me about the birds and bees
And how to build a family tree

Teacher, teacher, come along with me
Help me build my family tree
So its branches will be firm and beautiful
Just like the hickory tree

Teacher, teacher, you can't hide from me
For you got that little extra scent
No other creature has

Teacher, teacher, where are you
All I want to be is the Teachers Pet
Then I'll in heaven for every day
Putting the branches on my family tree

Teacher, teacher you will always be
With all the notes on my love note tree
They are a part of everything we see
Teacher, teacher remember me

Copyright 1967 Francis E. Delaney   S-6501-MH 63

WAR OF LOVE

As I sail to the War of Love
Far across the sea
I see the moon beams shinning on the sea
They remind me of my love I left behind me
Sparkling clear and crystal clean

Everyday in the War of Love far across the sea
I say a little prayer, hoping my love will be
Sparkling clear and crystal clean
When I return from the War of Love, far across the sea
Sparkling clear and crystal clean

I see the sunbeams shining on my love
Sparkling clear and crystal clean
They remind me of the love a left behind me
Moon beams on the sea, as I return
From the War of Love, far across the sea

The War of Love will always be
A part of history, and Mary and Me

Copyright 1967 Francis E. Delaney   S-6502-FD

ARRESTED BY YOU

1966

If I love you never
I'll love you forever
For I've been Arrested By You
Locked behind the bars of love

Captured forever by the loveliness of you
And the beauty in your lonely heart
Fascinated by the gentle curve of your over fed legs
And your silhouette in the window of my mind

If I love you ever
I would love you forever
For I've been arrested by you
Locked behind the bars of love

Captured forever by heavens softest cloud
And the warmth of heavens brightest star
Loved by you, no more to roam far and free
For I've been Arrested By You
Arrested by the miracle of your love
For a little statue

Copyright 1967 Francis E. Delaney   S-6601-MH 64

HICKORY KICK

Have you often wondered, how
The country folks get their kicks
Let me tell you, how
The Hicks get their kicks
They do the Hickory Kicks

Put on your stockings and put on your shoes
Stand up straight till you can't wait
Then stamp your feet
To the beat of the Hickory Kick

When your feet begin to hurt
Take off your shoes and kick your feet
Till your toes become weak
Hop up and down till your hair falls down
Now, your doing the Hickory Kick

Now, stand on your heels and wiggle your toes
Look at your turned up nose
If you can see your toes
Kneel on your knees and hold your nose
Then kick your toes to the beat of the Hickory Kick

When you fall on your nose
Take off your stockings and count your toes
If you still got ten
Get up and do the Hickory kick again

Copyright 1967 Francis E. Delaney   S-6602-LA

YOU GOTTA BE YOU GOOFY

You Gotta Be Goofy to be in love with me
For I fell in love with your Goofy little look
Your Goofy little walk
Your Goofy little talk
Your Goofy little wiggle
Your Goofy little giggle
And all the Goofy little things you did
As you fell in love with my Goofy little love

I gotta be Goofy to be in love with you
For you fell in love with my Goofy little look
My Goofy little walk
My Goofy little talk
My Goofy little wiggle
My Goofy Little Giggle
And all the Goofy little things I did
As I fell in love with your Goofy little love

You Gotta Be Goofy to be in love with me
What other reason could there be
Unless your the other Goofy little part o f me

I Gotta Be Goofy to be in love with you
What other reason could there be
Unless your the other Goofy little part of me

Copyright 1967 Francis E. Delaney   S-6603-MH 60

HECK NO !

Saw a pretty girl sitting at her desk
Asked her for a date, she said, Heck No
Wouldn't be seen with a dud like you
Or any other guy as fresh as you

Asked her for a kiss
She said, Heck No
Not even a peck, for you'll peck away
Till you get me in your little love nest

So I left her alone told her to go home
She said, Heck No
I don't want to go home alone
Take me home

This same little lady sitting by the desk
Asked me for a date
I said, Heck No
Wouldn't be seen with a hick like you

She asked me for a kiss
I said, Heck No
Not even a peck for you'll peck away
Till you get me in your little love nest

So she left me alone, told me to go home
I said, Heck No
I don't want to go home alone
Take me home to your pretty little home

Copyright 1967 Francis E. Delaney   S-6603-MM 65

BLUE MIST

1967

STOP IT STUPID

My little blue Miss
Thought she would be missed
So she put the Blue Mist my heart
Knowing she would be
The only one to know, why
My burning heart would never die

Blue Mist, Blue Mist
Blue as the sea in a sunny sky
Blue as the blue in our lonesome hearts
For we loved each other from the start

Blue as the blue in your eyes
Now with the Blue Mist in our eyes
We know that our love is
True, virtuous and wise
The Blue Mist in your eyes
Little blue Misses by our side

Blue Mist, Blue Mist
A love from the star
Always in my heart

Copyright 1967 Francis E. Delaney   S-6701-MH 65

Stop it, Stupid
What's the matter with you
You darn fool if you keep that up
Stupid cupid will catch up with you
You'll be my hubby for every day
And I won't say

Stop it stupid
You'll be my hubby every day
It's gonna cost you all your pay
For I'm gonna have seven little cupids
That look like you, then I'm gonna say

Stop it, Stupid
What's the matter with you
You darn fool if you keep that up
Stupid cupid will catch up with you
And you will have another
Little cupid that looks like you

Stop it, Stupid, Stop it
Stop it, Stupid, Stop it
Stupid

Copyright 1967 Francis E. Delaney   S-6702-MH 63

YUMMY, YUMMY DUM-DUM

I'm a curvy little woman
With cute little curls
But he always calls me
Yummy, Yummy, Dum-Dum

When it comes to doing things
Teach me to love tonight
That's way he calls me Dum-Dum
Yummy, Yummy Dum-Dum

When it comes to making love in the night
Nothing seems to come out right
In the darkness of the night
Unless we turn on the light

Only then can I get the thing right
I'm really too bright
That's why he calls me Dum-Dum
Yummy, Yummy Dum-Dum

Copyright 1967 Francis E. Delaney   S-6703-MH-65

FUNNY FACE

Have you ever wondered, why
People stop and stare when you walk by
They say, there goes Funny Face
She said No, and her turned up nose began to grow
As the loveliness of love passed her by

Funny Face, oh Funny Face
Has anybody asked you why
Your turned up nose is up so high
It's hitting you in your eye

Someday it will make you cry
All the boys will pass you by
And say there goes, Funny Face
She said no, and love passes her by

Funny Face, oh Funny Face
Has anybody asked you why
Your turned up nose is up so high
It's walking on the sky

Someday it will make me cry
For someday I'll parade you by
And say, here comes Funny Face
She said, Yes and the miracle of love
A love song, Love Fed

Copyright 1967 Francis E. Delaney   S-6704-MH 62

MY LITTLE OLD LADY — 1968

My Little Old Lady
Is as beautiful today in silver gray
As she was when my little old man asked her to stay

Her smile is as warm and bright as it was
The day she gave me to my little old man
Our little old lady taught us to have faith and trust in God
As she raised us to be responsible and true
And the understand as she did
On the day her love passed away

Now, I find I'm the guardian
And protector of My Little Old Lady

And all the love she has given me
I will someday give to
A little young lady, who will be
As beautiful in silver gray
As My Little Old Lady is today

Copyright 1968 Francis E. Delaney   S-6801-MD 63

RUSTY

Rusty, oh Rusty, let me look into your eyes
As the sun goes down in the western sky
Tell me why, I never caught your roving eye
And now, why we sit and wonder, why

The sun goes down the western sky
And why the rusty skies close the shades of night
That hide your lovely sight from my roving eyes

Oh, Rusty, tell me why
The shades of night are closed so tight
As I go passing by

Rusty, Oh Rusty, now I look into your eyes
As the sun comes up in the eastern sky
Tell me why I finally caught your roving eyes
As we sit beneath the rusty sky

The sun goes down in the western sky
And why the rusty skies close the shades of night
That bring your lovely sight to my roving eyes

Oh, Rusty tell me why
The shades of night are closed so tight
As I go passing by

Copyright 1968 Francis E. Delaney   S-6802-RH 65

A NICKLE CUP OF COFFEE

I have brought satins and silks
Earrings and things, but I only remember
A Nickel Cup of Coffee
When the sky was crying, I was dying to be
A Nickel Cup of Coffee held tight by you
To kiss, the melody of your rosy red lips of love

We have had the world on a string
Many miraculous things, but I only remember
A Nickel Cup of Coffee
When you were crying, I was sighing
As I became, A Nickel Cup of Coffee
As I kissed the rosy red lips of my love

We have had heartbreaks and tears
All through the years, but I only remember
A Nickel Cup of Coffee
When you were trying, I was asking
To be, A Nickel Cup of Coffee, held tight by you
And feel your rosy red lips of love

I always remember the flowers and candy
A
Nickel Cup of Coffee, is in every cup

Copyright 1968 Francis E. Delaney   S-6803-MH 63

GENTLE ON MY BODY (Till The End of Time)

Be Gentle On My Body, and I'll love you till the end of time
Gentle on my hills of love and the valley of the little ones
And we'll play our tune on gods instruments of love
As we sit upon the sea shores at the foot of rainbow hill
Till the end of time

Gentle on My Body, gentle on my soul
Gentle as a rainbow as it lays upon the sky
And I'll be gentle on your body as the rainbow hugs the sky
Till the end of time

Gentle on My Body, gentle on my soul
Gentle as Gentle as that sea wave draws upon the shore
And I'll be a gentle on your body as the sea wave stroke the shore
Till the end of time

So be Gentle on My Body, gentle on my soul
And we love each other at the end of time

When we find the end of the rainbow
The waves will have washed away the shores
We will play our love tune on Gods instruments of love
As we lay beneath the sea shores at the foot of rainbow hill
At the end of time

Copyright 1968 Francis E. Delaney   S-6804-MH 65

THE BLACKIE BOTTOM (Dance)

If you like to dance The Blackie Bottom
With you know, who

Just stand side by side, hold each others side
Hop up and down on your middle foot
As you kick each others opposite foot

Standing side by side, hold each others hand
Put your inner foot
On the bottom of your partners inner foot

If you like to see what's going on
Bob your head up and down, then you can see
Your doing, The Blackie Bottom, with know, who

Now you stand back to back
Look at each others funny face
Then wiggle your bottoms till they touch the ground

Now, you've danced The Blackie Bottom
For your bottom is on the ground

If you don't see a frown
You know you can do
The Blackie Bottom
With you know, who

Copyright 1968 Francis E. Delaney   S-6805-MH 64

THE RED, RED ROSES OF JUNE

I wish I was a rose
Then my life would be as rosy, as
The Red, Red Roses of June
My love for you, would be full in bloom
Warm, covered with the evening dew, as
The Red, Red Roses of June
Blooming in an ecstasy of love for you

But since I'm a rose
My life is not as rosy, as
The Red, Red Roses of June
For my love for you is as the rose bud before it blooms
Cool, covered with the evening dew
Full of love and ready to bloom
In an ever lasting feeling of love for you

The Red, Red Roses of June
Now my love for you
Is as the rose buds after they bloom
Full in bloom, warm covered with the evening dew
As my love continues to bloom
It's an every lasting ecstasy of love for you
As The Red, Red Roses of June

Copyright 1968 Francis E. Delaney   S-6806-MH 64

The QUIET AMERICANS   1968

While The Quiet Americans are looking the other way
The dirty faced girls and the bearded boys
Continue to make all kind of American noise
When America needs someone to keep her free
The Quiet Americans will get up and say

Go home little girls, go home little boys
Go home and play with your little toys
Go home little girls and wash your face
Don't let anybody know that your a disgrace
Go home little boys and shave your face
Don't let anybody know, you were taken in by the big red show

For your little girls and your little boys
Are The Quiet Americans who will fight to keep America free
So go home little Mama and wash your face
Go home little papa and comb your hair
For your little girls and your little boys
Will have their little girls and boys, and

They are the Quiet Americans who'll want to be
As free as the dirty faced girls and bearded boys
The day they closed the curtain on the big red show
When they washed their face and combed their hair
And became The Quiet Americans, looking the other way
As their little girls and their little boys
Make all kinds of American noise
As they enjoy the freedom no on can destroy

Copyright 1968 Francis E. Delaney   S-6807-QA

THE QUIET AMERICANS   (2005)

The Big Red Show

Also known as the Cold War

And the iron curtain.

The Quiet Americans closed the curtain on the big red show

Now, it's thirty-seven years after I wrote this song

And we only have to change one word in it

It may not take fifty years, but it might

To close the curtain on the big Ben show

We all have been the dirty faced girls and the bearded boys

And we all want to see our little girls and our little boys

Make as much American noise as we did

It's in every ribbon America has seen, over three centuries

Copyright 2005 Francis E. Delaney   P-2005-QA

THE GOOD EARTH (The Ballard of Flight 13) 1969

When God made the earth
He made it with all the treasures of the universe
The moon, the stars, the distant planets near and far
He gave it the warmth of the sun
The light of the moon, most of all
He gave it to you and me in the form of Adam and Eve

Only the Good Earth gave birth
To the Infant, Who gave birth to the earth
To the land and to the sea, to the animals and to me
To the birds and the bees, little girls winking knees
The beauty of the hickory tree
And the love He gave to you and me

Only The Good Earth Gave Birth
To the flowers that dot the earth
To its people a will to do right
So that someday they will give life
To the moon, the stars, the distant planets near and far

As they rocket through the sky
See the beauty in the sky
The Good Earth as it passes by and wonder why
God gave them, the moon, the stars
The distant planets near and far
And The Good Earth as it gives birth to His universe
With the Ballard of Flight 13

Copyright 1969 Francis E. Delaney   S-6901-MH

BUNNY FUN

The most wonderful fun under the sun is Bunny Fun
It's the sparking in your heart when your love begins to start
It's the rumble in your tummy when you know your love is yummy
It's the way your little ones call you Mommy
The sounds of Bunny Fun will be around as long as the sun

The most beautiful fun under the sun is Bunny Fun
It's the feeling in our heart when our love begins to start
The kissing you been missing as your sitting and wishing
The hardness of your man to take your softness in his hands
To the sounds of Bunny Fun as long as our music plays

To the buzzing of the bee, the chirping of the bird
The honey of the bee, and the feathers of the bird
Become one in the sound of Bunny Fun
The wiggling of your hips, your warm panting breath
As you lay upon my heart, listening to the sound of Bunny Fun

The most revealing sounds under the sun are the sounds of Bunny Fun
The clamor of your room, when your on your honeymoon
The quiet of your love, when your loving in your room
The bounce in every once, when your loving on the couch
It's forgiven the past, that endures your love to last

It's the heart breaks and the tears, that makes your love better through the years
It's the rabbit habit when your young and full of Bunny Fun
It's the feeling in your soul when your growing old
Your love will never let you go, for the sounds of Bunny Fun
Will last as long as you are around, Bunny Fun

Copyright 1969 Francis E. Delaney   S-6902-MM

MY FAMILY TREE

Mary, marry me, sign an contract
And help me build My Family Tree

When we begin to build our tree
God has promised He would be
In the middle of heaven with you and me

If our family tree is love fed by you and me
It would be a sturdy as the hickory tree
Beautiful, wise and free

Sign a contract and marry me
God has promised love for you and me

So if you like to be
The architect of My Family Tree
Sign a contract and marry me

Promise me, I will be
The only one to plant the seeds
To sprout My Family Tree

And I promise you will be
The only baby making machine
To build My Family Tree

Copyright 1969 Francis E. Delaney   6903-MH 60

I DON'T LIKE YOU ANYMORE

I don't like to see you cry

So I'll tell you, why

I Don't Like You Anymore

I just can't tell a lie

So I gotta tell you why

I don't Like You Anymore

It's because, I love you more, Now

Then I ever did before

I really don' know, why

But you know it's true

I love only you and told you, why

I Don't Like You Any more

Because I Love You more, Now

Then I ever did before

Copyright 1969, Francis E. Delaney   S-6904-MH 61

MINI BLOUSE BOUNCE

Mini Blouse, mini blouse
Turn around and around
Put your arms up and put them down
Jump up and down
As you go around and around
Hop up and down
To the beat of the Mini Blouse Bounce

Mini Blouse, Mini Blouse
Left foot up and hop on the right
Right foot up and hop on the left
Hop two times, then touch your chin with your knees
Hop three times as you bend your knees
Now, stand up straight and go around

Mini Blouse, Mini Blouse
Turn around and around
Put your arms up and put them down
Jump up and down
As you go around and around
Hop up and down
To the beat of the Mini Blouse Bounce

Copyright 1969 Francis E. Delaney   S-6905-MH

MARIANNS SANDMAN

Mariann, Mariann, you are a beauty
In the eyes of this man
Can I be your sandman
Mariann, Mariann
And rock you to sleep tonight
Can I be Marianns Sandman

Can I hold your love in my hands Mariann
And love play with the beauty of my Mariann
Can I be Marianns Sandman

If I can, If I can, hold my hand Mariann
Mariannn, hold my hand if I can

Cradle you to sleep in the arms of my love
Rock you to love with the beat of my love
As I close your eyes with my sandpaper hands
And watch the softness of your love
Fall asleep to the rhythm of
Marianns Sandman

Copyright 1969 Francis E. Delaney   S-6906-ML

BLINKY, THE BLUE NOSED SNOWDEER   1958

Out of the Hickory trees there came
A little blue nose and a big white tail
And they called her
Blinky, The Blue Nosed Snow Deer

Santa went down the last chimney in the town
She pranced around with her nose in the air
And they called her
Blinky, my Blue Nosed Snow Deer

Winking and a blinking at a Santa reindeer
Every time she winked her nose went
Blink, Blink, blink to form
Little blue halos in the air

As she danced around and around
Her boots high in the air
Pointing to the chimneys, oh so bare
Wondering how, when and where
She could be a Holiday treat for children everywhere

Copyright 1969 Francis E. Delaney   S-6907-MH 58

PEACE OF LOVE

Instrumental—only   Inst-6908-FD

WATER AND DIRT

God made the earth
Gave it food from water and dirt

The sun and the moon
The light and the dark

The flowers and animals
The lakes and the seas

Then He made you and me
In His image for us to see

That the miracle of life is the earth
His masterpiece, the miracle of birth

A peace of love right here on earth
His birth, a touch of heaven

Will earth be the birth of his universe
Or will it be the end of time

Copyright 1969 Francis E. Delaney   P-6909-MH 59

1970

LITTLE GREEN BAG

Everybody has a bag, mine is green
Everybody does a thing, it's in their bag
My Little Green Bag is full of dreams and beautiful things
And they will all come true
When you say I love you
Even if you never say, I do
I will remember you in the miracle of memories
In My Little Green Bag

As you dream about my schemes
I realized they were your dreams
And I wish I would have tried
To make you my bride
Now I find you fell in love
Everybody has a bag, yours is black
Now I know you said. I do
To that little man in my Little Green Bag

As you go to do your thing, it's in your little black bag
It's all my love in My Little Green Bag

Copyright 1970 Francis E. Delaney   S-7001-MH 66

SUGAR DADDY

I'm your Sugar Daddy, and daddy loves you too
And all the things I'd love to do, I'd love to do with you
Give me a little sugar love and I will love you too
For my sugar love will low for you as long as you want it too

I'm your Sugar Daddy, and Daddy knows it's true
And I'm sure he wouldn't care
If there was something you would like to do
My love will love you as long as you want it too

I'm your Sugar Daddy and Daddy loves you too
Now, you got two Daddy's who love you true
Sugar Daddy and Daddy too

I'm your Sugar Daddy, and Daddy loves you too
Now, you got two Daddy's who love you
Sugar Daddy and Daddy too

Copyright 1970 Francis E. Delaney   S-7002-MM

THE HILLS OF MAUREEN (AN IRISH BALLARD)

Gonna tell a tale, about the rainbow tail
Prettiest tale I ever tell
About the pony walk of a pretty girl
Dressed in the colors of the rainbow tail

The soft and gentle colors, paint the mountains in my eyes
As they ride the rainbow highway in the sky
To the fields of gold in the valley of
The Hills of Maureen

Warm and tender curves touch my eyes
Sparkle like rainbow dew in her eyes
Monday pink, Tuesday blue, Wednesday green, Thursday cherry blue
Friday black, Saturday yellow and white

Hold them tight, every night, they become rainbow dew
Sunday gold, the end of the rainbow cherry gold
A pony walk on the rainbow trail
A pony ride on the rainbow tail

Was it just a pony tale, an Irish ballard
Did I have a pony ride or just a dream
About the pony walk of a pretty girl
Dressed in the colors of the rainbow trail

Walking the lonesome road, through the fields of gold
An Irish Ballard in the valley of the Hills of Maureen
Every day gold, the end of the rainbow, cherry gold

Copyright 1970 Francis E. Delaney   S-7003-MM 66

LOVE THAT MAN OF YOURS

If your happy and cry
Everything is going your way
Love That Man of Yours

If your down and out
Beginning to doubt and pout
Love That Man of Yours

For if your love isn't in his hands
Someone else will
Love That Man of Yours

If your sad and cry
Forget the past and
Love That Man of Yours

Make the present of your love
The future of his love
Love That Man of Yours

For if his love is in your hands
No one else will
Love That Man of Yours

Copyright 1970 Francis E. Delaney   S-7004-MM

PUSSY FOOTING AROUND

I really didn't know
If she was playing in the snow
Or Pussy Footing around
Trying to get me to say Hello

I thought I'd say Hello
As she was kicking the snow
Dancing on her toes
Pussy Footing around

Knowing I'd come around
To push her car out of the snow
And when I asked her
Where she was going

I really didn't know
If she was playing in the snow
Dancing around on ground
Trying to get to push her around in the snow

Copyright 1970 Francis E. Delaney   S-7005-MM

THE WORLD BEGAN TO SING   (Beatle rock)

When the Beatles played their music
The World began to sing
They took their rock and made it soft
And called it Country Rock

Their rhythm and blues, and popular tunes
Became their Gospel talk
They roamed around and played around
In every village and town

There music made men of them
And now they're world renown
As they go their separate ways
The Beatles play their music and the world sings

Perhaps someday the world will be
As free as the songs they sing
For when the Beatles played their music
The World Began To Sing

Copyright 1970 Francis E. Delaney   S-7006-B

CANDY LAND OF LOVE

I wish, I was a little piece of candy
In a little box of candy
Your Candy Land of Love
Sweeter than any candy

Feel the rhythm of your fingers
As you hold me in your hands
Taste the melody of your love
As I kiss your lips and take a ride
Through the love land of my Candy Land of Love

I wish you were a little piece of candy
In a little box of candy
My Candy Land of Love
Can I have a piece of candy

Feel the rhythm of my fingers
As I hold you in my hands
Taste the melody of your love
As I kiss your lips and take a ride
Through the love land of your Candy Land of Love

Copyright 1970 Francis E. Delaney   S-7007-MM

HALLOWEEN HONEY

Your walking the wrong way
Looking at the wrong side of life
Thinking there's only one way
To have a world of love

Start walking the right way
You'll find the nice ways
You'll be as pretty on the inside
As you are on the outside, then

Your a trick or a treat
Your Halloween Honey
No money can buy
A little love bunny
And oh, so funny on Easter Sunday

Your candy and nice, everything nice and handy
Snow on the mountains and rain in my eyes
Your sugar and spice and all that is nice
The sweetest treat for our eyes to meet

A bird in the sky, a wildflower blooming wild
With the sweetest kiss my lips will kiss
Are the kisses that will always be sweet
Halloween Honey, no money can buy

Copyright 1970 Francis E. Delaney   S-7008-MM

LOVE CALL   1971

The little bit of rain that falls
Makes the grass and the trees grow tall
It's there Love Call

The little bit of love that calls
Helps us understand we're not alone at all
It's our Love Call

When a little baby comes
And asks us for another one
It's your Love Call

So pretty little baby
If you're the one
I just gotta ask you

It's my Love Call
For a little bit of love, for a little one
Who will ask, for another one

It's my Love Call

Copyright 1971 Francis E. Delaney   S-7101-MM

THE CHICKEN KICK

If you have chased a chicken
Then you have danced
The Chicken Kick

For when you catch the chicken
You count her toes on her nose
Just like the chickens

When you leave go of her toes
The chicken tries to fly away
Till she finds another way
To lay her eggs upon the hay

But when she finds there's no other way
She wants the rooster to stay
And do the Chicken Kick

Remember one thing
Always count your chickens
With their toes on their nose

You'll keep her heart ticking
And her feet kicking
As she scratches the turf
With her nose counting her toes

Dancing to the beat of the Chicken Kick

Copyright 1971 Francis E. Delaney   P-7102-MM

LITTLE WORLD OF SNOW

Covered with starlight on a moon light night
Pretty as an angel sleeping in the snow

Pretty as the day I first said, Hello
Soft as the day she first began to glow

Seven years old, our Little World of Snow
Smiling with a smile that made our hearts glow

Snowflake playing on a blanket of snow
Sweet as an angel sleeping in the snow

Covered with snow from her head to her toe
Pretty as a flower in the morning snow

Pretty as a snowflake in the evening glow
Our Little World Of Snow

Copyright 1971 Francis E. Delaney   S-7103-RS

I CAN'T FIND A WOMAN

When I find a woman who will love me
I won't find her in my mind
For all the woman in my mind never loved me
No, not for the first time

I Can't Find a Woman who will love me
Thought I can find many women in my mind
No one ever fall in love
For loving me is loving all of me

When I find the woman who will love me
It will be for the first time
All the women in my mind never loved me
They never knew me

When I love the woman who will love me
I won't find no other women in my mind
And when she finds me, knows me and loves me
Its then I will know

I Can't Find A Woman, who didn't love me

Copyright 1971 Francis E. Delaney   S-7104-MHLL 1962

A MOMENT OF YOUR TIME

I really didn't know
If she was playing around
I knew I had to know
I said, Hello
Where are we gonna go

I really didn't know
If she was pussyfooting around
Trying to get me to say, let's go
All I really knew, I couldn't let go
So I said, lets go, she didn't say, No

I really didn't know
If she was trying to get me
All I really know
I could feel her love
Where ever I was

You said, lets go
I didn't say, No
I became, A Moment of Your Time

Copyright 1971 Francis E. Delaney   S-7105-MM

CHRISTMAS LOVE

Little Infant Jesus

Show your Christmas Love

Send a Christmas Card to me

Let her know, her love will be

A miracle for me

Little Infant Jesus

Showed His Christmas Love for me

Today I received a Christmas Card

From the little Miss

Who misses me

Merry Christmas Francis

From: Sister Mary

Copyright 1971 Francis E. Delaney   P-7106-MH

SUPER STAR

From this dark and cloudy ball

I see a little star

Shining bright, shining far

I wonder if it's The Little Infants Super Star

Bringing Little Jesus to a world far beyond the stars

Super Star, Super Star

Shining bright, shining far

Bring Little Jesus back to hearts of men near and far

Let your light and your love

Make our earth a bright and shining star

Super Star, Super Star, shining bright, shining far

Copyright 1971 Francis E. Delaney   S-7107-LJ

IT'S ONLY AN ACCIDENT

Driving down the road in rain
Behind a truck throwing mud
Decided to go around this truck
The truck I was in went out of control
A head on collision
At about 40 mph
I didn't get hurt
But the truck I was driven was totaled
I called the office to let them know
Their truck was in no shape to go
Office girl said
It's Only an Accident that you were not hurt   P-7108-FD

WHEN TOMORROW IS

When Tomorrow Is
The first day of a new year

Your another year older
Maybe a little smarter

But there's one thing for sure
If she's still there. She loves you

Copyright 1971 Francis E. Delaney   P-7109-MMML

I'LL ALWAYS BE LOVING YOU   1972

What ever your reasons may be
What ever you want to be

You will always be apart of me
For I loved you in my dreams

I loved you in my dreams
And if I ever love you

And my dreams come true
I'll Always be Loving You

What ever my reasons may be
What ever I want to be

You will always be part of me
For you loved me in my dreams

I loved you in my dreams
And if you ever love

And my dreams come true
I'll Always be Loving You

Copyright 1972 Francis E. Delaney   S-7201-MM

WILD EYES OF LOVE

I don't believe no one has seen them before, seen them before
And I hope, no one else will see them again, see them again
Your Wild Eyes of Love

If you never been in love before
I'll hold you in my arms, if your Wild Eyes of Love ask for more
I can tell no one else has seen them before

If you never loved before
I'll Ask you to stay, and never go away
And if your Wild Eyes of Love ask for more
No one else has seen them before   S-7202-MM

TWO STRANGERS ARE WE

Even though I know you for a long time
All that we do and all that is said
May someday become a reality
Until your time becomes mine, Two Strangers Are We

As we get to be a part of each other
All that we do and all that we say
We're still strangers in the day
Till that time in the feelings of our life
We're still strangers in the night

Two strangers are we, until we agree
To be all that we can be
Do all that we can do
For the Two Strangers We Are

Copyright 1972 Francis E. Delaney   S-7203-MMky

IT'S FANTASTIC, IT'S YOU

There are many words I can use
To describe the picture of you
But there's only one word I will use
It's Fantastic, It's You

The beauty of your picture in my eyes
Makes me wish I was many things

I wish I was a tumbleweed a chasing you
The prairie dust that kisses you
The sunset that sets on you
The star dust that covers you
The moon and sun that shine on you

But since I can't be many things
I'll just keep this picture of you
I'll always have you next to my heart
It's Fantastic, It's You

This picture of you
It's Fantastic, It's You

Copyright 1972 Francis E. Delaney   S-7204-MMML

OKLAHOMA BLUES

In my mind, I see sun dust in your hair of gold
Blue wine in your eyes, moon glow on your cheeks of snow
Blue sparks when you cry
The Oklahoma Blues, I wish were mine

As the silent music of your pen
Draws your picture in my mind
I see you running in my mind, tasting the sweet wine
The Oklahoma Blues I wish were mine

In My mind, I am loving you, you are really mine
As I kiss your sweet lips, I taste the cherry in the wine
Flowers on the vine
The Oklahoma Blues I wish were mine

I can taste love wine in your tear drops when you cry
As I see you running through my mind, I sigh
Tasting the sweet wine
The Oklahoma Blues I wish were mine

As the silent music of your pen
Draws your picture in my mind
I see you running in my mind, tasting the sweet wine
The Oklahoma Blues, I wish were mine

I got, The Oklahoma Blues from knowing you
I got, The Oklahoma Blues Falling in love with you

Copyright 1972 Francis E. Delaney   S-7205-MJC

IS THERE NO SANTA CLAUSE 1973

Some children say
There is no Santa Clause
But what of all the children
Who have nothing at all
Shouldn't they be the ones to say
Is There No Santa Clause

Some parents say
There Is No Santa Clause
But what of all the people
Who have no children
Surely they should be the ones to say
There is no Santa Clause

There Is No Santa Clause
For those who need nothing at all
But for children who have nothing at all
Surely they should be the ones to say
There Is a Santa Clause
Daddy is my Santa Clause

Copyright 1973 Francis E. Delaney   S-7301-MM

MELODY OF MARY

There's a melody
That lingers on in me
It's the melody of the cherry blossom tree
Soft and pink with honey for the bee
The Melody of Mary
Lingers on in me

In a little glass of wine
I can see the Melody of Mary
For that little glass of wine
Is her kiss of cherry wine
Soft and sweet as the love she gave to me
The fruit of the cherry blossom tree

Like the cherry blossom
That gave birth to the cherry tree
Mary gave birth to the love in me
Soft and warm, the Melody of Mary
In the words and music she gave to me
Lingers on in me

Copyright 1973 Francis E. Delaney   S-7302-MH

AND I AM YOURS

I look across all that I see
And it all looks good to me
If you are mine, when and I Am Yours

I hear all that I can hear
And it's sweet music to me
If you are mine, And I Am Yours   S-7303-MM

TIAMI A MI (Love me softly)

On a Sunday evening I can see
The little love you share with me
And it's rhythm is in motion
With the beauty That I see
Swaying softly to the melody
Of Tia-na Mi-a MI

Tia-na Mi-a Mi, Love me softy
As the sun loves everything it sees
And I'll love you as the wind loves the sea
In all its rhapsody

And when you share your love with me
May its rhythm be in motion
With the beauty that I see swaying gently
To the melody of Tiami A Mi

Copyright 1973 Francis E. Delaney   S-7304-SF

APPALACHAIN WINE

There's coal dust in the air
And coal wine everywhere
There's poor people there
And No one cares

The black sparking waters
From the streams above
Fill the air with the perfume
Of Appalachain Wine

The coal dust in the water
And the coal dust in the air
Pollution everywhere
And nobody cares

For the little Joe mines
Are now the strip mines
A mountain crying with the perfume
Of Appalachain Wine

Copyright 1973 Francis E. Delaney   S-7305-LY

SUGAR SHACK   o

Sugar Shack, Sugar Shack
Little disco by the railroad track
Sugar Shack, Sugar Shack
People come, people go

Riding on the trains to and fro
To work and school
To love and Sugar Shack
If you love me, Sugar Shack

If you want me, I want to love you
Just ask me at the Sugar Shack
If you love me, Sugar Shack   S-7409-SS

IT'S THE CHOO, CHOO BUMP (rock)   o

It's the Choo, Choo, Bump--Wow, It's the Choo, Choo Bump
Feet together one, two--Feet together one, two jump
Circle your hips around--now let's touch--wow, It's the Choo, Choo bump

Yeah, right now, Yeah left now, do'in the choo,choo, bump
Two hops forward, hips around, then your hips bump
Choo, Choo, Choo, Choo, Choo Choo Bump

We're groving tonight. Choo, Choo, Choo, Choo, Bump
We're all right, dynomite and all night
Do'in The Choo, Choo, Bump

Copyright 1974 Francis E. Delaney   S-7409-MM

SONGWRITER

Flowers say I love you
Candy says the words I can not speak

With flowers that say I Love You
And the candy that says your sweet
I give you this song of the words I can not speak

Words form little notes on a line
Echo the feeling in my mind

When you find, you are love fraid
Find someone like you to love feed you

When you have been love fed by someone like you
You will find you are no longer love fraid

For you have fallen in love with the one who love fed you
With the flowers that say I Love You, candy says your sweet

I wish I was the Songwriter of your songs mh

I wish I was the Songwriter of your songs mm

Your Songwriter, Love F.E.D.

Copyright 1974 Francis E. Delaney   S-7411-MM

RED, WHITE and BLUE CHRISTMAS TREE

I'm a Red, white and blue Christmas Tree

A Soldier of History of freedom

In the history of the white cross

That cover the graves of two centuries, so America could live

Remember them every year

With the colors they loved so dear

A Red, White and Blue Christmas Tree

The smile of your girls and boys, laughter of their toys

Mama kissing Santa Clause, Daddy knowing why

They are free to honor the blood on the crosses

That cover the graves of two centuries

Knowing that their love ones may someday be

Soldiers of freedom in our history

A Red, White and Blue Christmas tree

Copyright 1974 Francis E. Delaney   S-7412-FD

THE OLD COUNTRY HOME OF NASHVILLE TENNESSEE

Its walls will never hear
The voices of those so dear
But through its doors will pass
The memory of those in its past

Its' stain wood windows and slanted lines
Blend with the country music of their time
In It's Old Country Home Of Nashville Tennessee

Its songs will always hear
The voices of those still hear
But though their songs will pass
The memory of them will last

Its stain wood windows, slanted lines
Blend with the country music of our time
And the Grand Old Opry will forever last
In Its Old Country Home Of Nashville Tennessee

The GOOH, The Grand Old Opry House

Copyright 1974 Francis E. Delaney   S-7413-GOOH

NO OTHER CITY (Los Angeles)

No Other City in this land
Has as much American land
From its city limits
To its inner core
The people of Los Angeles
Are as proud as those who came before

Pride in the color God made them
Proud of the colors of His love
Our flag that flies above
The City of the Angeles
From the city limits to its inner core

The City of the Angels
Looks beyond the stars
To the future of America
The color of her love
The flag that flies beyond the stars
In the universe above

There's No Other City like Los Angeles
No Other City in no other land

Copyright 1974 Francis E. Delaney   S-7414-LA

BLUE JEANS, RED HAIR AND MUSIC

Blue Jeans, Red Hair and Music
If I never see you again
I will always see you in all the colors I see
Blue Jeans, Red Hair and music

When I look in the windows of your mind
What color do I see
I see the color of your love watching me

When your soft and gentle hair touches me
What color do I see
I see the color of your love touching me

When I kiss your warm and inviting lips
What color do I see
I see the color of your love kissing me

When your soft and lovely form is loving me
What color do I see
I see all the colors of your love, loving me

In Blue Jeans, Red Hair and Music

Copyright 1974 Francis E. Delaney   S-7415-MM

WINTER TIME

Once again the snow is falling

Christmas is special this year

We're engaged for the next year

And the years that will pass our way

May they be every year

With all the old folks old

May they be hear next year

And as we enter a new year

May the old years be as the new

None have been cold

Happy New Year

Copyright 1974 Francis E. Delaney   P-7416-MM

MUSICAL SOUNDS

Your

Arrangements

Are

Soft

Round

Curves

Of

Musical Sounds

Copyright 1974 Francis E. Delaney   P-7417-MM

LOVE IS THE GREATEST GIFT OF ALL   1974

Love Is The Greatest Gift of All
It's the spirit in us all
It's a feeling that does not have to be explained
It's as free as the open plains

Love is Gods divine perfume
Love is the absence of all that is bad
I didn't do it, I wish I had

Love Is The Greatest Gift of All
Only you can give it
It doesn't have to be real
Or as pure as a virgins seal

Love Is the Greatest Gift of All
A gift God gave us all
We can accept it, give it or deny it
For love is the free will God gave us all

Copyright 1974 Francis E. Delaney   S-7400-MM

ALIVE IN LOVE   o

When you were one foot tall
You were a baby soft and small

When you were two foot tall
You were two years old and growing tall

When you were three foot tall
You were seven an angel playing ball

When you were four feet tall
You were kissed on your talking door

When you were five foot tall
You answered your first love call

Now, your five foot-one
Your eighteen and your love is alive

Now every foot of you
Is a woman soft and true

Yes, your love is alive
For every foot of you is

Alive in Love

Copyright 1974 Francis E. Delaney   S-7401-MM

CHRISTMAS IS, that's what   o

Christmas is, Christmas Love. I love you, you love me
Loving you, That's what Christmas Is
Christmas Is, lots of love
Presents under the Christmas Tree
Christmas Is, lots of fun

Cold and snow with green mistletoe
Present under the Christmas tree, Christmas tree love
A kiss under the mistletoe, mistletoe love
There's Christmas love, Christmas fun
Christmas is little ones

Christmas is, Christmas love
It's all the things you love to do
I love you, you love me
And Christmas Is what Christmas was

Christmas Is, Christmas love, I love you, You love me
Loving you, That's What Christmas is
Christmas Is, Christmas love
Golden old with green mistletoe
Little ones all in a row

Christmas is, Christmas love
Loving you, That's What Christmas Is
I love you, you love me
And Christmas was what Christmas Is

Copyright1974 Francis E. Delaney   S-7402-MM

SEA NYMPH   o

I see you in everything I see
The sky, the earth and the deep blue sea

In everything that I see
I see yourself in motion with me
Rock, little Sea Nymph, rock
Roll, little Sea Nymph, roll

Sail our boat to our land in eternity
At the end of the sea, you and me

In everything that I see
Your poetry in motion with me
Rock, rock, little Sea Nymph, rock
Roll. roll. little Sea Nymph, roll

Rock, rock little sea Nymph
Ride to uncontrollable sea

Roll, roll little Sea Nymph
On the uncontrollable sea

For in everything I see
Your Poetry in Motion with me

Copyright 1974 Francis E. Delaney   S-7403-MM

MISTER MUSIC, Duke Ellington   o

He was just another man
But one of the few who found, love
In the heart and soul of everyone

He is, Mister Music, music was his mistress
The world was his stage, the sky above and the earth below
No walls to hold him, no strings attached
No one to own him, no promise of wealth
The color of his music was the beauty of his soul

He was Just another man
Like Bobby, Martin and John
Music history, memories of time

He was Mister Music
With words that formed notes upon a line
Echoed the sound of the music in his mind
He was our brother and the color of his music
Was the color of his mothers love

He was Duke Ellington, Mister Music
And the beauty of his music
Was the beauty of his love
For his mistress (music) is in the heart and soul of everyone

Copyright 1974 Francis E. Delaney   S-7404-DE

WALKING DOWN THE COUNTRY ROAD   o

With a banjo in my hands
And a woman who understands
Just how far a man can go
Walking Down The Country Road

I play the natural rhythm in my mind
With the rhythm since the beginning ot time
For everything I see is a melody
Walking Down The Country Road

With my guitar in my hands
And a woman who understands
Just how far a man can go
Walking Down The Country Road

There's a melody in every movement that I see
And my guitar plays there melodies
For the rhythm of your silent music
Is, Walking Down The Country Road

Copyright 1974 Francis E. Delaney   S-7405-MM

SHE'S A WILL OF THE WISP   o

Her name is unknown, she never said, no
She's a Will of The Wisp

Love is a dream, that never grows old
Life is a moment in the mystery of time

Be mine, be mine, She's a Will of The Wisp   S-7406-MH

_____

LAZY COUNTRY DAYS   o

The wind is shy, the sun is high
Side by side, you and I
Lazy Country days

Live warm as the wind
Love hot as the sun
Together we live, love and learn

Clouds pass by, side by side
Storms come and go
The wind becomes shy
The sun is high

Love, soft as the wind
Live, true as the sun
Together we live
Together we learn to love, Lazy Country Days

Copyright 1974 Francis E. Delaney   S-7407-MM

COUNTRY WALTZ   o

Gonna take journey, back into time
To 1776 with you

Let's all dance the Country Waltz
The tune of the country when it was young
Give me a little bit of yesterday

When a man held a woman in his hands
Kissed her on her cheek and told her charms
Kissed her on her talking door
Asked her if she wanted more

Held her close and watched
The shades of night close her eyes
As they danced to the music of the Country Waltz

Let's all dance the Country Waltz
When love can once and never went away
Give me a little bit of Yesterday

As I hold you in my arms
Kiss you, as I dance with all of your charms
Kiss you on your hearing door
Ask you if you want some more

Hold you close and tight
Watch the shades of night
Close your lovely eyes
As we love to the music of your Country Waltz

Copyright 1974 Francis E. Delaney   S-7408-MM

COUNTRY CHRISTMAS o   1975

Let Christmas light your way
Let there be love and let it begin with
A Country Christmas on Christmas Day
Candles in the snow, stockings in a row
Packaged gifts under the tree
Christmas dinner or an evening out
The sights and sounds of a Country Christmas
Peace on earth, good will to all
And Let it begin with us   S-7501-MM

RAGTIME DUDE o

I can't keep all the tears in my eyes
They flow from the heart of my mind
Every little beat, memories of you
Everyday of our life and love

Now I see, the sun go down in your eyes
And feel the quiet lips that kiss mine
Our hearts crying, ragtime music in the dark

When I here, your spoken words of love
They keep me loving you, my ragtime chick
For your Ragtime Dude, will always love you.

I'll keep on loving you

Copyright 1975 Francis E. Delaney   S-7503-MM

BLUE SYMPHONY o

A Blue Symphony, a story of love
Sad, happy and true
The Blue Symphony, of our love
Yes, when I lost a little part of heaven
I fell into the well of hell

As I fell into the well of hell
Deeper and deeper I felt the loss of love
Flow from my body, soul and mind
A Blue Symphony, little tears of happy times
Sad times, now the story of a love symphony

As I fell into the well of hell
Deeper and deeper I felt the loss of life
Memories from both sides of the gates of hell
I saw the Blue Symphony of losing you

And as we fell into the well of hell
We knew, cancer will someday take you away

How long will this symphony go on
This story of love, sad, happy and true
This Blue Symphony is our love story
The story of love

Copyright 1975 Francis E. Delaney   S-7502-MM

NASHVILLE MUSIC TRAIN o

Come on, aboard and brings your songs
Come on, get on and sing your song
And listen to the music of
The Nashville Music Train

It's a new music sound, it's Nashville You
Country, soul, rock and roll
Spiritual, rhythm and blues
Nashville and you

Cha-Cha, rumba, waltzes too
There's bluegrass music, gospel and square dances too
There's a new music, quadraphonic sound
Recorded on many tracks, of the Nashville Music Train

The Nashville rock, Nashville Soul
The Nashville Folk and the Nashville You
All the music in the world plays at the last stop
At it's Nashville music home, the Grand Old Opry house

Rock and roll, country soul
Spiritual, rhythm and blues and You
Nashville Music You
The Nashville Music Train, train

The Nashville Music Train

Copyright 1975 Francis E. Delaney   S-7504-MM

YOUR SOMETHING CALLED LOVE o

In the morning when I see
Your beauty looking at me
Two strangers are we
Looking for that something called love
You're that Something Called Love

In the afternoon when I see
Your beauty passing by me
Two strangers are we
Looking for that something called love
You're that Something Called Love

In the evening when I see
Your beauty laying by me
Two strangers are we
Looking for the something called love
Your, Something Called Love

In the night time of our lives
Your beauty aging with me
Two strangers are we
Looking for that something called love
We're that Something Called Love

Your, Something Called Love

Copyright 1975 Francis E. Delaney   S-7505-MM

RAGTIME CHICK o

Ragtime Chick, sun shy and sly
She's ragtime melody
Of a ragtime love affair
Shy with love, alive in love
She will always be a part of me
Concrete memories of love

In this world turning cold
A rosebud blooming new
When in love
A rosebud full in bloom
In her world turning bold
A rose among the thorns

Ragtime Chick, sun shy and sly
She's my ragtime melody
From the days of Ragtime
I'm in love, alive in love
For my heart is ticking
With her Ragtime heart

In my Ragtime melody
Ragtime Chick

Copyright 1975 Francis E. Delaney   S-7506-MH

ALL THE CORNERS OF MY MIND o

Days of endless dreams
Scenes I may never see
Like a empty sky
You fill
All The Corners of My Mind

All The Corners of My Mind
Sparkle in the dark windows of your mind
Like the universe of stars
You fill
All The Corners of My Mind

Nights of sleepless dreams
Visions of empty scenes
Like the quiet of my room
You fill,
All The Corners of My Mind

No where on earth will I find
The corners of my mind
Till your walking in my eyes
And fill
The empty scene of sleepless dreams

With the love you will find
In All. The Corners of My Mind

Copyright 1975 Francis E. Delaney   S-7507-MM

RUFFIAN o

Beautiful, symphony of motion
An American dream that came true
In the eyes of all who saw her lose

Lost only to death
Won all the races she run
Explicit, rhapsody of motion
An ecstatic emotional moment of time

Ruffian, ecstatic rhapsody of music
Teardrops in the wind, raining of love
In the eyes of all who saw her die

Sad piece of music
Tears, blowing in the wind
Ruffian, symphony of music
An ecstatic emotional moment of time

The Song Of Ruffian

This race horse, never lost a race   12-0
Broke her leg on the back stretch
And had to be shot on the track.

Copyright 1975 Francis E. Delaney   S-7508-MM

I HAVE KNOWN SADNESS o

I Have Known Sadness at the end of love
I have known gladness that's the way it was
Was it just fun or was it love
Did I really find love, was that touch of love only mine

I Have Known Sadness in the mist of love
I have known happiness that's the way it is
It was really love, that's the way she was
I Have Known Sadness at the end of love

If you haven't known sadness at the end of love
Then it was a touch for the love of the games people play
It wasn't love, it was fun   S-7509-MH

BUTTERFLY WALTZ

Maureen Murray marry me
Bloom little flower so I can see
A Butterfly waltzing with me
Whose love will be as soft and gentle
As the soft touch of a butterfly
For as the butterfly loves the flower
In the rhythm of the wind

Our love for each other is true
As the oceans are blue
Bloom little butterfly, bloom
On the seven emeralds and a diamond
In this ring I give to you

Copyright 12-25-75 Francis E. Delaney   S-7510-MM

PATTY'S SONG, Mystery of the mind   o   1976

In The Anxiety of Patty's Song
There's a blue Symphony of life
Intricate in its movements
The haunting melody of time
In the mystery of the mind

In the obsession of Patty's Song
Are the rhapsodies in life
When happiness is happy
And sadness is sad
In taunting memories of time
In the mystery of the mind

God gave the earth water and dirt
Gave us laughter and tears
On mountains of faith, valleys in fear
Simplicity of love, complexity of life
In the mystery of the mind

In the reality of Patty's Song
Lie the mysteries of the mind
The anxiety of love, the obsession of life
For only Patty can write
The symphony of Tanya's life
The will to survive in the mystery of the mind

Copyright 1996 Francis E. Delaney   S-7601-PH

TANYA'S SONG the loss of love   o

In the tragedy of Tanya's Song
The dark memory of fear
A life in the realm of peril
A rich girl, so sad in a cruel world
Torn free, consumed by hate and despair

She was warm, soft a dreamer of dreams
Born free into a rich world
An innocent child in world of fear and despair

In the insanity of Tanya's Song
Bad memories of a insane mystery
Abandoned and lost in a different world
A dreamer of all things good and free
Of the day when she would be free

In the story of Patty's song
Rich child lost and confused
In a nightmare of despair
The loss of love, Tanya she was

In the story of Tanya's Song
A lesson learned, no escape, nowhere to go
On the day she became free
In the mystery of the mind, Patty she is

Copyright 1976   Francis E. Delaney   S-7602-PH

COUNTRY MOON, SHINE SOME MAGIC ON ME   o

When I feel blue
Like the country moon
When you feel blue
Sing a country tune

Sing, love and be happy
Sing like the birds in spring
Love a little more
Let it be true, happy and you

Country Moon, Shine Some Magic On Me

Let the country moon
a little magic on you
You will feel the country moon
Full with the magic of the moon

Country Moon, Shine Some Magic On Me

Copyright 1976 Francis E. Delaney   S-7603-MM

RONDA'S SONG, a special world   o

In the simplicity of Ronda's Song
There's a blue symphony of love
Blue sparks in happy times
Love wine in sad
An Angel of god, in a special world
Born free, from all the things that bother you and me

In the complexity of Ronda's Song
There's a true symphony of love
Complex in her movements
Trust in our love, an infant of God
Born free in the complex world of you and me

Pure as a blossom on a cherry tree
Still as the feathers of a bird flying free
Warm as the sun hugging me
A butterfly waltzing with me
A child of God, in a special world
Born free into our world of you and me

In the reality of Ronda's Song
There's a true mystery of love
A symphony of love, a rhapsody in blue
An Angel of God, in His special world
Brought love to the world of Maureen and me

Copyright 1976 Francis E. Delaney   S-7604-RS

JADE   o

Jade, in shadows of shade, in colors of stone
Hard and strong are rippling shadows in the Jade
My love is Jade, when I see your silhouette in shadows of shade

Precious scenes never fade
Never bend always blend
See quiet winds beneath the sea
Shadows in shade

Blue shadows in the jade, whisper your name
Soft and strong the rippling waters of your song
You're a gemstone, Yes, you are my love and my Jade

Green shadows in the slate, young love unafraid
Soft and strong the passionate rhythm of a song
Our love is Jade, unafraid like silhouettes in shadows of slate

Precious scenes never bend, always blend
Never bend, always blend
See pencil lines that paint the sky
Shadows in Shade

White shadows in the Jade, whispering your name
Soft and strong the rippling movements of our song
Cut and polished, we are in love, we are Jade

Copyright 1976 Francis E. Delaney   S-7605-MM

HIGHS AND LOWS   D

I have never reached a high or touched a low
Until you said, Hello and No
Now I reach the highs, I touch the lows
I hear the music, I see the song
For my highs and my lows
Are the love melodies of your, Yes and No

Now I have reached the highs and touch the lows
For I have touched your, yes and no
As I reach your highs, I touch your lows
I write your music, I sing your songs
For your highs and lows
Are the love melodies of my Highs and Lows

Every time we reach a high, we feel our love
We understand our highs and our lows
For as reach our highs, we touch our lows
We hear our music, we sing our songs
For our highs and our lows
Are the love melodies of our Yes and NO
Highs and Lows

Copyright 1976 Francis E. Delaney   S-7607-MM

THE DISCO BABY ROCK   o

Another day is done, once again
I can do the Disco Baby Rock with you
Swing, sway and rock away
Till the morning brings a new kind of day
When I awake and find
I do the Disco Baby Rock with you

Swing sway, rock away
Ask you to stay, one more day
Swing, sway and rock away
The Disco Baby Rock with you   S-7606-MM

ONE DAY LONGER   o

Life is One Day Longer, when I think of you
Life is a melody of love
The melody of loving you, One Day Longer

Life is one sun more, loving everyone, one day more
Life becomes like the sun above
The warm feeling of loving you, One Day Longer

Love is all of you, morning, noon and night of you
Hot as the sun, cold as the moon
Your love is forever, for it's One Day Longer

Copyright 1976 Francis E. Delaney   S-7609-MMLL

BIG CITY BLUES   o

Faces black, faces white
Heart beats in the night, beat a rhythm of fright
Bad feelings, love beatings and the big city
Cries softly for its people living the Big City Blues

Concrete strips, iron lights
Mirrors in the sky, built to reflect in eyes
Glass buildings, stone faces, in the big city
Cry softly for the people living the Big City Blues

Dark faces, Spanish words
Answering it's call, breeds new life in the city
Little faces, Spanish words in the big city
Cry softly for their people living the Big City Blues

Those who will not leave, those who can't afford to
Those who don't care at all
Those who repeat and repeat the same old day
All of them, they have the blues, the Big City Blues for you

Your Chicago, you are mine, in my blood line
Your life, your love, your soul are spoken in written words
That flow in rhythm with my life, my love the rhythm of her love
Big City, your mine for all time
Live and love your Big City Blues

Copyright 19976 Francis E. Delaney   S-7608-MM

SHADES OF BLUE MOODS   o

Each time I love you, it's you
Loving you is loving someone new
Each time I touch you, you turn me on
So here I go again, touching, loving you

Now I know you, now I love you
With words I never said in Shades of Blue Moods
I love you with special feelings I never had
Each time I love you, loving you is loving someone new

Each time I touch you, you turn me on
Loving you, loving me
A miracle in Shades of Blue Moods
So here I go again, loving, knowing you again   S-7610-MHKY

CHRISTMAS MIRACLES   o

We are miracles, we are what we are
We are gifts to many things, to all we see
Miracles of sight, miracles of sound and of Christmas
See the pictures in your eyes, miracles in miniature
Hear the songs we sing, miracles of invisible sound

Sing a song to Infant Jesus
You'll hear invisible sound, see pictures of His love
For miracles of love are Christmas Miracles
Like St Anthony, hold the Christ child, say a prayer
You'll hear the visions, and see the sounds
In miracles of love and Christmas

Copyright 1976 Francis E. Delaney   S-7611-MMML

DISCO, TO THE BODY WALK   o

Hold each other in your arms
To the beat of the disco
As you dance the body walk

Walk her up front
She walks you on back
Bounce to the bump and rock
Let your body talk
To the rhythm of the body walk

As you do the body walk
Listen to your body talk
Answer the Disco beat
The Disco, To The Body Walk

Walk her up front
She walks you on back
Let your body talk
Let your body rock
To the rhythm of your body walk

Listen to your body talk
Answering her body walk
Listen to her body talk
Answering your body walk

As you walk her on up
She walks you on back
Bounce to the bump and rock, too
The Disco, To The Body Walk

Copyright 1976 Francis E. Delaney   S-7612-MM

SUGAR AND SPICE   o

You're Sugar and Spice. Welcome and nice
For your my honey dew, Halloween honey
Honeymoon Bunny, no money can buy
You're a trick of a treat, when ever we meet
Honey, are you a trick or a treat or a Honeymoon due
Sugar and Spice and every night

Your a trick and treat when your moving on your feet
When you dance, your a trick and a treat, that's all right
Your true and your false and that's alright
When we meet, it's Sugar and Spice, That's all right
Halloween honey, an Easter bunny
A trick and a treat on a Honeymoon night   S-7613-MH

DISCO BLINKEY   o

The Disco Blinkey is a good thing going
Lights are blinking, sound is winking
The music goes on and on

Every woman is Disco Blinkey
Dancing to the music of her Disco dance
Eyes are blinking, curves are winking, body's hustling
As her music goes on and on

Every woman is a Disco Blinkey
Rocking to the rhythm of her Disco beat
Lights are blinking, sound is winking, body's hustling
And her music goes on and on, your her music goes on and on

Copyright 1976 Francis E. Delaney   S-7614-MMKY

SILVER RIVER   o

When love becomes fun
The poet of your love is you
Loving the heart of the one you love
Love's near and you know it

When love becomes fun
You know you're in love
Love's tears and you know it

When fun becomes love
The poet of your love is me
Loving the heart of the one I love
Love's here and we know it
Loves' Silver River surges on and on

Like the Silver River
Loves flows in rhythm
The blood beats in your heart and it's true
When love becomes fun, It's Love

When love become fun, the poet of love
Surges on and on like the Silver River
Love's here and we know it
I'm your poet in love
Your my Silver River

Copyright 1976 Francis E. Delaney   S-7615-MH

YOLANDO   o

Love is just a day a way, a flight to southern Spain
Where love's just a game, as in the dance of hats
Love is just a touch away, Lolando

With a little bit of loving, keep me in your ring of love
For any time of the day or night
Yolando, Love is just a touch away

With that little bit of looking
You keep me in the mood for loving
Lolando, Love is just a look my way   S-7616-YO

GEORGIA JAZZ (peaches and cream)   o

It is sweeter than sweet. It's Georgia Jazz
It's you and me, peaches on a tree
And whimsical melodies

Raspberry, strawberry, blueberry and cherry
Moon shine, wine, sun shine pine
Peaches and cream and Georgia Jazz

Sweeter than sweet, It's Georgia Jazz
Moonshine wine, sleeping in sunshine
Rhythmical melodies of Georgia Jazz

Sweeter than sweet, Georgia and me
We're sunshine wine sleeping in moon shine
Whimsical melodies of Georgia Jazz

Copyright 1976 Francis E. Delaney   S-7617-MM

CAN'T KEEP THE HURT FROM SHOWING   o

Can't Keep The Hurt From Showing
For it flows from the windows of my mind
Each little tear, a memory of your love
Your little tears of love, when we fell in love

I can't keep my heart form crying
For it yearns for the warmth of your love
Each little beat, a memory of love
Your taste of love, when we loved

I can't keep my eyes from crying
For the memory of your love
Will never pass away, it's the memory of first love

Can't Keep The Hurt From Showing   S-7618-MH

DISCO DAN, THE RADIO MAN   o

Disco Dan, the radio man
Plays our music when he can

All you gotta do is have a band
He'll play your music if he can

Disco Dam the radio man
Plays the country music of our land

Copyright 1976 Francis E. Delaney   S-7619-DD

CRY SOFTLY, WHEN I LEAVE

Cry Softly, when I leave
Wipe away the tears, with the hands that loved me
Listen to your heart, it leaves with me
Close your eyes and realize the good things
Then you will see the good times, we have never seen

Cry Softly, When I Leave
For in this world there is someone who will need you
She will cry softly when she loves you
You'll will wipe away her tears with hands that never felt her
And listen to her heart beat you have never heard

Cry Softly, When I leave
Listen to my heart, the music you hear
Close your eyes and realize the good times
For in this world there is someone who will need you
She cry, softly loving you

Cry Softly, When I Leave
She will
Cry Softly, When You Leave

Copyright 1976 Francis E. Delaney mtm   S-7620-MM

ROSES ON THE VINE

I've road the open road and tasted its dusty glow
I've seen the world from the darkest side of the road
And I loved the roses, and if you don't mind
I'll sing my song on the C-B line

To the sloppy rock music of the stone soup cooking in this can
My handle is Big Vine and I drive a cement mine.

Now, all you truckers and you smoky bears
All of you have seen the Roses On The Vine
Some of you have tasted the sweet wine

When you exit the crossroads at Route 53 and I-55
Remember what you heard on the C-B line
Roses On The Vine, she's mine and I'm Big Vine

She works everyday in a little cafe
Her legs are divine, she's a rose on a vine
So I put a little band of gold on her hand
And watch it sparkle in the windows of her mind

I feel divine as I kiss the Roses On The Vine
Forty-Two, Twenty-six, Thirty-nine
She' mine and I'm Big Vine

If I catch anybody ripping off the Roses on The Vine
They'll be six feet deep, listening to the sloppy rock music
Of the stone soup cooking in this can
My handle is Big Vine and I drive a cement mine

Copyright 1976 Francis E. Delaney   S-7621-MM

POOR MARILYN   1977

She is a song
That never was sung
Beautifully sad
She is the love story

She's a love doll
Love symbol of our times
She was Marilyn Monroe

Her story is of life and love
Fragile life of love, was lost
Stolen silently

The world was her playground
Though she was shy, she was sly
Lovers loved her, women awed her
People look at her

Poor Marilyn
Sad and beautiful

Alive in history's
Mystery of life

Poor Marilyn
Picture of love

Copyright 1977 Francis E. Delaney   S-7701-M.M.

SAMMY THE STAR

Sammy The Star
A miracle of sight and sound
The pen that drew the picture
On the face of a star

Yvonne also drew the music on the lines and bars
The melody of Sammy The Star
Someday she may finish his story
In the words and music of this song

For behind the makeup of the artist
Lie the body, soul and mind
Her soft and gentle heart
In a world without bounds

Sammy The Star
With the happy face of a clown
In the sad face of a star
Makes us all children in the eyes of a clown

Those who can't walk, talk or see are not alone
Their laughter and tears are young and old
They may not see or hear, Sammy The Star
The mystery of its frown, the laughter of a clown

In their special world without bounds
They touch the feelings, the heart of a clown

Copyright 1977 Francis E. Delaney   P-7702-YO

PURPLE PEPPERMINT WINE

Come a little closer, get a little bolder
If you are mine, then you are my good times
For you're my little bottle of wine

Come a Little Closer to me
For I'm in love, when I'm with you
You and me and love
You and me, loving the good times

You're my eloquent times
And my succulent wines
You're my little bottle of wine

Like the amethyst jewel
You're a violet blue
Purple Peppermint Wine

Come a little closer, get a little bolder
If I am yours, then I'm your good times
And your my Purple Peppermint wine

Come a little closer to me
For you are you and I am me
Together we will love the good times

Copyright 1977 Francis E. Delaney   S-7703-MM

MAKE THE MUSIC BEAUTIFUL

Make The Music Beautiful, Make the Music Beautiful
Let it be me, loving you
You can play harmony, I can play melody
We're God's instruments of love

Make the Music Beautiful, Make the Music Beautiful
Let it be you, loving me, I can play melody
You can play harmony in our symphony of love

Make The Music Beautiful, Make The Music Beautiful
Let it be you and me
Melody and harmony, we're the Rhapsody in Blue

Make The Music Beautiful, Oh! Make The Music Beautiful

" Beautiful " Make The Music Beautiful   S-7704-MM

DALLAS DAN, THE GAMBLING MAN

To Love, the love boogie
Dallas Dan, The Gambling man
Gonna tell a tale about gambling Dan from Dallas
I will tell you why he never gambled love away
When it comes to loving. Dallas Dan, he was a rich man
Who never gambled love away for his lovers always had to pay
Dallas Dan, the Gambling Man

Copyright 1977 Francis E. Delaney   S-7705-DD

A BOUQUET FOR MY BABY   o

A Bouquet For My Baby, and for our love
She is all I think of, my only love
A Bouquet For My Baby, she's such a lady
She'll always be my love. A new love
I'm sending you a bouquet of love

In May, I'll send you violets
With my song of love
A cluster of lady-love violets
To my baby I love

In June, I'll send you roses
With a message of my love
Red, Red Roses in love
To my lady in love

A Bouquet For My baby
She is all I dream of, my lady love
She'll always be my baby
Our love is new, it will grow old

Copyright 1977 Francis E. Delaney   S-7706-MM

RESTLESS SPIRITS IN THE NIGHT   o

I can see the wind——woo—And hear the sun
I can touch your dreams, dream
Restless Spirits In The Night

I can smell the wine—ah—And taste the rose
I can hold your love dreams
Restless Spirits In The Night

Woo——The owl bites the night
And the rooster calls the day
When love bites you
See the wind, hear the sun, touch a dream

You can smell the rose—
And taste it's wine, ah–
Or you can love me

And leave your, Restless Spirits In The Night
Whoa, leave your Restless Spirits In The Night

See the wind, hear the sun, touch a dream
Love me, and leave your
Restless Spirits In The Night

Copyright Francis E. Delaney   S-7707-MM

I AM EARTH   o

I Am Earth, God made me and God made you
He put together in the world we see
With all the things He gave you and me

I Am Earth, I am everything you see
For everything was made from me
I am oil, I am coal, I am silver, I am gold
I am water, I am tree, I am coffee, I am free

I Am Earth, I am everything you see
Take them away from me
Earthquakes will devour me, tidal waves will drown me
As fire surrounds me, God will come and stand upon me

And all who see Him will find Heaven right here on earth

For Heaven is at the end of the world   S-7708-MM

YVONNE LOUISE

When you have seen, Yvonne Louise
Green eyes, gold hair, silhouette in curls
A summer flower, a winter rain

She's warm and she's cold, Yvonne Louise
Warm as the sun, soft as the snow
Silhouette in curls, Yvonne Louise

Copyright 1977 Francis E. Delaney   S-7710-YO

MOE (More of Everything)

You are more of everything I knew
And, as I get to know you, Moe

You are more of everything
 I ever dreamed

As I see you more and more
I want more of everything I see

More of the eyes that talk to me
More of the lips that touch me

More of the feelings that you give to me
Feelings that want me to touch you more and more

You don't have to love me
But you gotta be my friend

Copyright 1977 Francis E. Delaney   S-7709-MM

NORMAL FEELINGS   JD

When you don't know what life is all about
Listen to a love song, life's music story
Normal Feelings, more of everything

When you know what life is all about
Then your life is a love song
Songs of love are happy and sad

When you know what love's about
Your love is a music story
Spoken words among the tears
The fears of loving you
Normal Feelings, more of everything   S-7711-MM

I CAN'T BELIEVE

I Can't believe the things I can't believe
For I believe the things I believe
I believe you can see, your in love with me
I believe the world was made for you and me

I Can't Believe the things I can't believe
For I believe the things I Believe
I Can't Believe that God will take you away from me
I Can't Believe I can't see the clouds that rain on me

I Can't Believe the things I Can't Believe
I believe that you will live and love with me
For I believe that Love was made for you and me

Copyright 1977 Francis E. Delaney   S-7714-MM

WE BELONG TOGETHER

We Belong Together, our love has become fun
We belong together for our love has won

We Belong Together, your my poet of love
And I'm your melody, we're music we love

We Belong Together, our music's in love
A friendship wild in its love. Listening to its music move

We belong Together, our fun has become love
We Belong Together, for our love has won

We Belong Together, for we are what we are now
And now, we are in love, melodies of love
We Belong Together, a melody in love   S-7713-MM

I'M RETURNING TO GEORGIA   D

I'm Returning To Georgia
To my memories of love
Sunshine pine and fine dining
Moonshine wine and good old boys

I'm Returning To Georgia
To my melodies of love
Sun lit peaches teasing me
Moon lit shadows loving me

Razzamatazz and Georgia Jazz

Copyright 1977 Francis E. Delaney   S-7716-MM

LOVE ME AGAIN

It's the smile in your eyes
And the way you wear your hair
It's the way you say, it
Love me, love me, Love Me Again

It's the feeling in your eyes
And the way you wear your hair
It's the rhythm of your love
Love me, love me, Love Me Again

Hold me and kiss me and love me again
Love me, love me, Love Me Again
Touch me and hold me and Love Me Again
Love me and Love Me Again

It's the look of your eyes
And the way you wear your hair
It's the way you do it

Touch me, hold me, kiss me again
Love Me and Love Me Again
Love Me and Love Me Again

Copyright Francis E. Delaney   S-1977-12-MM

DANCE YOUR CARES AWAY   D

Share your love today
Let the world pass away

Love your cares away
Taste your tomorrows today

Life's a melody in time
A time and a place to love

Dance your cares away
Life is just a breath away

Share your love today
Say the words you never say

Love your cares away
Touch your tomorrows today

Life's a melody in time
Like the mystery of wine

Dance Your Cares Away
Love is just a touch away

Copyright 1977 Francis E. Delaney   S-7715-MM

THE WAY YOU WEAR YOUR HAIR   D

The Way You Wear your hair
Reminds me of a place
I Never was
A place where love begins

The way you wear your love
Reminds me of a time
That never was
A time to love a dream

When your eyes ask me mine
To the time and a place
I never was
A time and a place to love

The picture of a dream
That always was
The time and place to love
The love that never was

Is here today in
The Way You Wear Your Hair

Copyright 1977 Francis E. Delaney   S-7717-MM

MY SECRET SONG

A light of beauty in each strand of hair
A mystery in every frown

A shapely figure, your only crime
Things will come right in time

A fairest beauty lies beneath the sky
In symphony that ends each day

If I survive this night of love
Things will come right in time

Now, I take a longer look before I jump
I sing myself a Secret Song

And all the things that can go wrong
Come right in my Secret Song

I know your secret, but you know not mine
A smile flows from every tear

If we survive in love tonight
I know my dear, we'll make it through for all the years

Copyright 1977 Francis E. Delaney   S-7718-FD

SURVIVE

Will we Survive
Through this time
Love is the strength
That carries us on

We do what we have to
When tough times come by
We say a little prayer and ask, why
Cancer always seems to Survive

Remission has finally arrived
The doctors are surprised
Was it the power of love
The will to Survive

Now her doctors tell us
Three to five years
Maybe five to ten years
Before heart problems arrive

To all who have walked
Through this time in their life
The power of love
Is the will to survive

Copyright 1977 Francis E. Delaney   S-7719-MM

SHE'S A LITTLE DUSTY

She's a Little Dusty
Heart's a little Rusty

Everything went wrong
As time turns it around

The dust and the rust
Has made our love strong

We will face the future
In love and in song   P-7720-MM

NEXT YEAR IS TOMORROW

When we were told
Tomorrow would never come
Yet, here it is
Just hours away

For better or worse
We hope for the better
One more year
When, Next Year Is Tomorrow

Copyright 1977 Francis E. Delaney   P-7721-MM

IN OUR LAND OF LIBERTY D   1978

In Our Land Of Liberty
Free life has lost its' liberty
I can not see why
People call us free

When the littlest one
Doesn't have the right to breath

In Our Land of Liberty
To be aborted is not free
I can not see why
Freedom lets them die   S-7800-USA

HOLD ME, DON'T LET ME GO D

Hold Me, Don't Let Me Go
Love me, don't let me know
It's just a dream, a dream called love
Just live your dream and it will be

Hold Me, Don't Let Me Know
Love me, don't let it show
It's just a game, a game called love
Yours dreams come true when your in love

Copyright 1978 Francis E. Delaney   S-7801-MM

I SAW YOU PASSING BY D

I Saw You Passing By
Your rippling signs of love
Disappearing into my eyes
And I knew, I was going to love you

I Saw You Passing By
Sparks of love in your eyes
Realizing your alive
And knowing, you are going to love me   S-7802-MM

I COULD NOT SAY GOOD-BYE D

I Could Not Say Good-Bye. I found me
Gently loving you in the quiet of my room

I Could Not Say, Good-Bye. I found you
Crying softly when I leave

You could not say Good-Bye. When you find me
You will have found you with me

We could not say, Good-Bye
We found us, gently loving you and me
Crying Softly, when as leave

I Could Not Say, Good-Bye

Copyright 1978 Francis E. Delaney   S-7803-MM

BAD BOY CHARLIE BROWN D

Bad Boy, Charlie Brown
Daddy didn't know
Mama does not care
Charlie Brown's in town

Playboy, Charlie Brown
Oh, he kissed her here
Oh, he kissed her there
Loves her every time

Joking like a clown
Charlie fools around
Charlie doesn't frown
Charlie just leaves town

Bad Boy, Charlie Brown
Daddy doesn't know
Mama Loves him too
Bad Boy, Charlie Brown

Bad Boy, Charlie Brown

Copyright 1978 Francis E. Delaney   S-7804-CB

WALKIN' THRU THE YEARS D

Walkin' Thru the Years
A deer walking through the snow
We may be old but our love is young
Walkin' Thru the Years, to love

I may be slow, but I'm ready
So I give his love a home
We may be old, but love's new
Walkin' thru the Years, in love

Take him if you can
His love will excel
But you'll find
No peace of mind

I give his love a home
I may be old, but I'm steady
I'll be there when he's ready
Walkin' thru the Years, to love

Copyright 1978 Francis E. Delaney   S-7805-MS

THE SONGWRITER   D

I wish. I was The Songwriter of this song
If I could write a song, you could hear my music stories
As the notes on the line
Echo your music in my mind

Flowers say, I Love You
Candy says, your sweet

But, only The Songwriter
Can say the words I can't speak

I want to love you
What will you do
When I say, I love you
What will you do when I try

Flowers say, I love you
Candy says, your sweet

Only The Songwriter
Says the words I can not speak

I wish. I was The Songwriter
The Songwriter of your love

Copyright 1978 Francis E. Delaney   S-7806-MM

MEMORY   D

Memory, remember me
When you leave me. I know I will find you

Memory, remember me
When I leave you. I know, I will find me

Memory, listen to me
Now that you left me, I'll find you there
Where the women meet the street

Memory, yesterdays dreams
I will find you, where I found me
Where the women meet the street   S-7807-AD

MAYBE, I'LL GET LUCKY   D

Open your eyes, let love in
Maybe I'll Get Lucky and you'll let me in

Open your mind, let love in
Maybe I'll get lucky, your love in time with mine

Open your heart. Hold me in its arms
Answer its alarm, trust me with its charms

Open your arms, let me in
Maybe I'll Get Lucky and you'll love me too

Copyright 1978 Francis E. Delaney   S-7808-MM

GET A LITTLE CLOSER   D

The Little Bit of Rain that falls
Makes the grass and the trees grow tall
The little bit of love that calls
Says we're not alone any more

Pretty little baby, If your the one
I just gotta ask you, yea, I gotta say
Get A Little Closer, and love me more
I just gotta ask you, yea, I gotta say

Hold me in your arms where the grass and the trees are green
Like the little bit of rain that falls
You make my loving grow a little more
Get A Little Closer, I'll love you more

Get a Little Closer, You'll love me more   S-7809-MM

BING SINGS HIS SONG   D

Birds sing there song and spring is here
Summer is here in thunder song
Rain falls as snow, a winter song

It all began with a song
On opening night, Bing sang his song
Though He is gone
Bing Sings His Song

Copyright 1978 Francis E. Delaney   S-7810-BC

IN MY FANTASTIC MOOD   D

You can hold me close, you can hold me tight
You can love me once or you can love me twice
In My Fantastic Mood
You know What I can do

I can hold you close, I can hold you tight
I can love you once or I can love you twice
In my fantastic mood
I know what you can do

When I ask you
I know what I can do   S-7811-MM

CUDDLE UP FOR SWEET DREAMS   D

Cuddle Up For Sweet Dreams
Touch the moon, you'll feel the stars

See the pyramids, and hear there call
Peace among the pyramids

Cuddle Up For Sweet Dreams
To hold love, catch a star

See the pyramids, alive in love
Dream under there stars

Hear my call, keep me sweet
Cuddle Up For Sweet Dreams

Copyright 1978 Francis E. Delaney   S-7812-MM

WHEN ELVIS PLAYED HIS MUSIC

When Elvis Played His Music
The world began to sing
He took the rock and made it soft
Called it Country rock
His rhythm and blues and popular tunes

Now his concerts are in Grace Land
His voice echo's
With a guitar carved in rock
The tears have changed to tear souvenirs
Memories of forty-two years

When Elvis played his music
The world began to sing
Now the people play
His music and the world sings

He was number one
But his work was done
God only calls you
When your work is done

Copyright 1978 Francis E. Delaney   S-7813-EP

WHEN YOUR IN LOVE THE WORLD STAND STILL   o

See the star and the moon
They are standing still
When Your In Love The World Stands Still
When your in love, love moves
Love's an ocean, wild and calm
Hold me, love me now

Hear my heart and feel oceans of love
When Your In Love The World Stands Still
For you and me, everyday is free
Hear your heart listen to its feelings
When we're in love our world stands still
For you and me, loving is free

Love is an ocean wild and calm
Love me and love me again
The world is still, we are in love   S-7816-MM

GOODBYE MR, BLUE   o

Goodbye, Goodbye Mr. Blue–don't want you no more
Don't you come knocking at my door, no more
Mister Blue, I aim's gonna let you make me blue, no more– no more
For I'm feeling good, free from the life that made me blue

Go away, go away Mr. Blue, I started life new
Don't need you knocking at my door, singing the blues
Goodbye Mr. Blue. I am me and I am free
Don't need you knocking at my door singing the blues

Copyright 1978 Francis E. Delaney   S-7817-AO

MONKEY HUG (rock)   D

Monkeys rocks with me
Monkey see and monkey do
Monkey round with me
Monkey do what monkey see
Come on monkey, Monkey Hug with me

Monkey rocks and monkey rolls
Get to it, and lets do it
Monkey dance with me
Monkey like what monkey see

Monkey round with me, monkey loves what monkey hugs
Come on monkey, Monkey Hug with me
Monkey rocks and monkey rolls
Get to it and lets do it
The Monkey Hug with me.   S-7814-MM

LOVE IS WANTING TOO   o

Love is feeling you, when you touch me
Love Is Wanting Too
I want to hold you and touch you
When you want too, I'm going to love you
Love is touching you, when I feel you
Love is feeling me
I want to see you and be with you
I want you when you want me
Love Is Wanting Too

Copyright 1978 Francis E. Delaney   S-7815-MM

PATTERNS OF LOVE   o

Say Hello, to your friends
And Goodbye to your foes
It's the natural thing you should do

Life, just let it natural
And you'll hear and feel
The Natural Patterns Of Life

Love, just let it be natural
And it will be real and true
Patterns Of Love

You'll be in love with someone
Who is in love with you
It's the natural Patterns Of Love   S-7818-MM

DANCIN' IN LOVE   o

Dancin'—dancin'—lovin'—lovin' dancing with you

Colors are blending to the rhythm and the beat
Music is ascending in the reflection of its sound

Hearts are feeling the pulse of the lights
Love Dancin', Love Dancin' with you

Dancin'—dancin'—lovin'—lovin'
Love Dancin, is dancing with love

Copyright 1978 Francis E. Delaney   S-7819-MH

LOVE SYMPTOMS

When you know what you know is true
And it's making you blue
Love Symptoms. Love Symptoms
Love is making you blue

When your mind is awake
Love me in your mind, like a taste of wine
Fall asleep, loving me one more time

When you know What you know is true
Your tummy's feeling blue
Love Symptoms, Love Symptoms
Love is making you blue

Throw away the pills and the doctors bills
Try a little loving and you will find
Sleeping alone is a waste of time

When you know what you know is true
A fights making you blue
Love Symptoms, Love Symptoms
Love is making you blue

A fight is a fight
But a lonely night
Is a waste of time

So try a little loving and you will find
Love is making you blue

Copyright 1978 Francis E. Delaney   S-7820-MM

FOREVER FREE (Engagement letter)

May I engage you
The rest of my life
The long or the short of it
And may I take
You and make you
A part of all that I love
And may you be forever free
To engage me and love me
So That I may be
Forever free

May you engage me
The rest of your life
The long or the short of it
And may you take
Me and make me
A part of all that you love
And May I be forever free
To engage you and love you
So that you may be
Forever Free

From letter, six, fifteen
Nineteen hundred and sixty-eight
You and me, Forever Free

Copyright 1978, Francis E. Delaney   S-7821-MM 68

HEAVEN'S GOT TO BE THAT WAY

She is beauty, she is free
She was only twenty-three
Kathy loved in her own way
Heaven's Got to Be That way

She was real, she was me
Live as only life could be
Heaven's Got To Be That Way

She was pretty, She was free
She was only Twenty-three
Kathy touched my heart with tears
Heaven's Got to Be that Way

She was real, so I will be
Live as only life can be
Love's gotta be that way

Kathy had a special love
Heaven's Got To Be That Way
Love will always be that way

Copyright 1978 Francis E. Delaney   S-7822-CS

ANGELA

To update this story

Angela was a Caretaker

She started in nineteen seventy-six

She cared for the old folks

Maureen had cancer for almost two years

The dog had a major operation

This is the Christmas when the old folks

Finally got approved for state aid

Our first Christmas with a nurses aid

A dog, a cat and a bird

It was a Christmas I'll never forget

I picked up Angela and her two friends

All three were Nurses and Nuns

They cared, till the old folks left 1991-2

Copyright 1978 Francis E. Delaney   S-7823-SA

STRUMMIN' A PRETTY WESTERN TUNE   D   1979

I see the mountains full in bloom
The cleavage of there drifted snow
I hear an avalanche of snow
Strummin' A Pretty Western Tune

I walk her lonesome roads
Her feelings turning cold
Warm rain changing to snow
Rigid in frigid cold
The cleavage of her rippling snow
Strummin' A Pretty Western Tune

I will climb the mountain
And I will taste the snow
I will bare her coldness
And she will make me warm
The melting of her ruffled love
Strummin' a Pretty Western Tune   S-7901-MM

A SNOWFLAKE

Each Snowflake is different
Like the people all around
A Snowflake melts on the land
A person returns to the ground
Each has its' place in the earth

Copyright 1979 Francis E. Delaney   P-7900-MM

COUNTRY IN MY HEART   D

The Bud of a Rose opens when it blooms
Its' fragrance is sweet Country In My Heart

Grits in the kitchen, sweet corn in the field
Banjos and fiddles play Bluegrass as sweet

There is love in my heart
It awakens in me the Country In My Heart
The part where the Bluegrass is sweet

The tears in your eyes opens your heart wide
Its Bluegrass is sweet Country In My Heart   S-7902-MM

HAPPY TIMES AND YOU

Happy Times and You
You are my woman I am your man
Feelings I see, when you love me

You are a woman, I am a man
Give me the woman
And I give you the man

Happy Times And Loving You
Happy birthday, too

Copyright 1979 Francis E. Delaney   P-7906-MM

REAL LIVE TOY

Of all the things I ever seen
And all the sounds I ever heard
I have yet to see and hear
The sounds of your real live toys

I am here with you today with my real live toys
I am yours to feel the touch of love and joy
For I am Your Real Live Toy

Of all the love I ever shared
And all the love you ever knew
We have yet to know and share
The love of our real live toys

Of all the things I ever touched
And all the tears I've shed
I have yet to feel the tears
Of love, of your real live toys

You are here with me today with your real live toys
You are mine to feel the taste of love and play
For you are my Real Live Toy

I am yours to feel the touch of love
For I am your Real Live Toy
Real Live Toy

Copyright 1979 Francis E. Delaney   S-7903-MM 67

I LOST MY BRA AT THE OLD CANTEEN   o

I Lost My Bra at The Old Canteen
When I did the disco bounce
Up went hand and down went my eyes
As I watched the disco bounce

I Lost My Bra At The Old Canteen
My falsies and my pretty little body made the scene
Wild were their eyes as they did the disco bounce

Wild were my eyes as I tried to hide
Up their hands and down went their eyes
And everybody danced to the disco bounce   S-7904-BC

AMERICAN MAMA   D

American Mama, American Mama
She got a lot of feelings, she has a lot of love

American mama, American Mama
She's got a lot of living and a lot of loving

She is true to all her dreams
Beautiful and blue, she is forever free

American Mama, American Mama
She got a whole lot of giving
For she gives a lot of love
To the man and the land she loves

Copyright 1979 Francis E. Delaney   S-7905-MM

SPANISH RHAPSODY

When you touched
You didn't turn away
For your feelings wanted me to stay

When we kissed
I knew that we would be
Lovers in Spanish Rhapsody

When you love me
I know your expressions
And want them all of my life

We will build a castle of love
A Spanish Rhapsody
That will weather the sands of time

When I love you
I feel your musical
Spanish Rhapsody

Copyright 1979 Francis E. Delaney   S-7907-MM

UNBROKEN CIRCLE

A circle is a round curve
Same distance from the center

A closed line
A group of friends

When the circle is broken
It becomes something more

The center of time
Defined with no lines   P-7908-FD 59

LIMITATIONS

All that a person has done
All that he or she will ever do
In the time frame of their life.

Copyright 1979 Francis E. Delaney   P-7909-MM

JUST A PICTURE IN MY MIND

Your, Just a Picture in My Mind
Running in my heart
A memory laying in my mind
That will be forever mine

Your picture plays in my mind
With a new love of mine
Running through my heart and mind
New melodies in time

God gave us time together and forever
Now, your Just A Memory In My Mind
.

And the picture of your memory
Is smiling in my mind
This new love of mine
Beat the odds against time

Both pictures in my mind
In a remission of time
A musical arrangement
A love forever mine.

Copyright 1979 Francis E. Delaney   P-7910-MH 68

COMING DOWN HARD 6

It's the way you love
The way I love you
The way you love me
It's the way you need me

I love you with my song
Touch you with its words
Coming on down
Coming Down Hard

The melody of your love
Is the music in my song
It's the way you love me
Coming on down   S-7911-MM

LITTLE CHRISTMAS

My Little Infant Jesus
Show your Christmas love for me
Let Maureen know that her life will be
Her miracle of love with me
I know my Little Infant Jesus
Will soon call her home
Will the love she leaves with me
Find another home.
One more Little Christmas

Copyright 1979 Francis E. Delaney   P-7912-MM

THE CHILL IS OFF THE FLOWER   D   1980

When the mountain snows melts
The rivers run free
The Chill Is Off The Flower
You have fallen in love with me

When the fields are gold
The grass will be green
The Chill Is Off The Flower
When you are loving me

The Chill Is Off The Flower
In minuet specks of dew
Rainbows that never end
When I am loving you

When your hair is silver
Your love will be gold
The Chill Is Off The Flower
Your still loving with me

The Chill Is Off the Flower
In minuet specks of gold
Rainbows that never end
When you are loving me

Copyright 1980 Francis E. Delaney   S-8000-MM

MAYBE I WOULD NOT BE HERE TOMORROW   D

Maybe I Would Not Be Here Tomorrow
So touch me today
So we may know tomorrow

Maybe I Would Not Be Here Tomorrow
So kiss me today
And we'll hope for tomorrow

I don't know where life will carry me
For today is tomorrow

Maybe You Would Not Be Here Tomorrow
So love me today
Remember me tomorrow

I Don't know when life will bury me
Today or tomorrow

Maybe I Would Not Be Here Tomorrow
So love me today
Remember me tomorrow

Copyright 1981 Francis E. Delaney   S-8001-MM

TANTALIZING MUSIC MAGIC   D

Tantalizing Music
Is the magic in you
A desire we never reach
Till the torment turns to ecstasy
The tantalizing fantasia and the rhythm of its' beat

I see magic, when it's you
I see him look at you
And I see the magic of his love for you

When the magic of our love has ended
We feel the magic of a new love
Tantalize the feelings of the old

I see magic and it's you
I see him look at you
And I see the magic of my love in you

Tantalizing Music Magic
Is the magic I see in you
A dream we never see
Till the desire turns to ecstasy
The Tantalizing magic and music of its' beat

Copyright 1980 Francis E. Delaney   S-8002-MM

I DO, I Love You   D

I Do, all the things I can do
For all the things I Do
I Do with you

You do, all the things you can
For all the things you do
You do with me

Oh, the way that you are
Is the way that you love
When you say, I love you, you do

When your are loving me
We are free and it's easy
To do all that we can do

When I say, I DO, I love You
I Do
I DO

Copyright 1980 Francis E. Delaney   S-8003-MM

HANGING ON A RAINBOW   D

Hanging On A Rainbow
Looking at life a new
Love is certain and true
Just like the colors in a rainbow

Hanging On a Rainbow
Living my life with you
Watching my love come true
Walking on the rainbow with you

I love you
I didn't know what to do
Till you loved me with, I Do

Hanging On a Rainbow
Loving my life with you
Touching my world of love in you
Hanging On a Rainbow

Hanging on you

Copyright 1980 Francis E. Delaney   S-8004-MM

ANGEL   D

Angel, you're a Christmas Rose
On the morning snow
It blossoms in your eyes
Its rosebud on your nose

Angel, watch the flower grow
And you will know
There is beauty in your eyes
Where the flower grows

Angel, when the flower blooms
It's then you will see
All the colors of your love
Bloom with your love

Angel, when the petals fall
Another rose will bloom
And the beauty in your eyes
Will forever be in mine

Angel was three days when she passed away
Her family gave me a Christmas Rose cactus plant
It's in full bloom on my windowsill
Angel, a Christmas Rose in the morning snow

Copyright 1980 Francis E. Delaney   S-8005-AW

I'M A COUNTRY SINGER   D

I'm A Country Singer
Singing country songs
Life's real life stories
For life is a Country Song

I'm A Country Singer
Singing life stories
Of real live people
Whose love is a country song   S-8006-FD

―――――――――――――――――――――――

CHARISMA   O

I have it, now
Like the flower when it blooms

I see it, now
It's in everything I do

Charisma, I need you
Charisma, I Love You
Charisma, stay with me now

Charisma, Charisma, I know you
Stay with me Charisma, I need you, Too

Copyright 1980 Francis E. Delaney   S-8007-YO

I WANNA BE WITH YOU FOR CHRISTMAS   D

I Wanna Be With You For Christmas
Love is word, far beyond our dreams

I Wanna Be With You For Christmas
Your love is far beyond all my dreams

I know what it's like
To say, maybe you might

I know who I am, and who you are
For I know what I want

I Wanna Be With You For Christmas
I want to love and live my dream

I Wanna Be With You For Christmas
I want your gift of love, only you can give.

I Wanna Be With You For Christmas
And live my life of love with you

Copyright 1980 Francis E. Delaney   S-8008-MM

STARLITE OVER YOU D   1981

Covered with snow from head to toe
A snowflake in the snow
Bright as the morning snow
Starlite Over You

Moon beans asleep on the snow
Sprinkle Starlite Over You
As you smile, with a smile
That's makes my eyes glow

Starlite Over You
Awakens me, to love you   S-8101-MM

PUT A LITTLE INK ON ME

If you have the time
And if you don't mind
As the clock unwinds
Put A Little Ink on Me

You, Put a Little Ink on Me
Now, it's all the words I see
All the sounds I hear
Now, all the flowers I meet

Put a Little Ink on Me

Copyright 1981 Francis E. Delaney   P-8100-MH

SNOWFLAKES AND WINE

Snowflakes drifting in my mind
Taunting memories of mine
Tiny bubbles of wine, tear drops in time

Snowflakes blowing in the wind
Frozen mysteries of time
Softly, gently kiss you, Snowflakes and Wine

Your Love, loving me
Snowflakes and Wine are different each time

The cleavage of shifting snow
Moving memories of time
Your love, loving me
Love's different each time

Snowflakes melting in your eyes
Rippling movements melting time
Your softness touching mine
Snowflakes and Wine
Are different each time

The cleavage of your ruffled love
Rippling movements warming time
Your love in contact with mine
Snowflakes and wine
Your different each time

Copyright 1981 Francis E. Delaney   P-8102-MM

YOUR WAY TO LOVE D

Some day
Some day you will say, I Love You
Some day you will
It's Your Way To Love

Some day we will be alone
Some day I will say I Love You
Some day we will
It's Your Way To Love

Some we will be
You will be you, I'll be me
Love will come easy and true
That's what I like about you

Some day we say I Do
Hear things we never heard us say
It's what I like about
YOUR WAY TO LOVE

Copyright 1981 Francis E. Delaney   S-8103-MM

EIGHT O'CLOCK SHUFFLE D

One, two, three, four, five, six, seven
Eight O'clock Shuffle, "It"

Sugar daddy and ice cream man
Noontime lover and midnight man

When we were little boys and girls
We used to play a game called "It"

Now I'm a man looking for it
And a woman who wants it

Gonna chase you, when I catch you
Gonna touch you and say " Your It"

Sugar Mama, and ice cream woman
Noontime lover and midnight woman

Gonna chase me, when you catch me
Gonna touch me and say "Your It"

Sugar daddy and morning man
Noontime lover and midnight man

Every morning and every night
Everyday we play

The Eight O'clock Shuffle
Your It

Copyright 1981 Francis E. Delaney   S-8104-MM

SLEIGHBELL D

It's time for sleigh bells ringing
Peace on earth to us all
Love is His greatest gift
His spirit in us all

It's time for sleigh bells bringing, the visions in our mind
A symphony of love in a world yours and mine
So hold your head a little higher, walk a little sprayer
I'll stop and talk when you pass by, I'll say Hello, Sleighbell
It's time for sleigh bells bringing, wedding rings and baby things
Sugar sweets, a pumpkin pie in a rainbow sky

It's time for Sleigh bells ringing
The miracle of birth, a universe of love
Where ever we may be

It's time for sleigh bells ringing there melodies of time
A million blossoms chime, His mysteries in wine
So hold your head a little higher, walk a little sprayer
He'll stop and talk when He returns, He'll say Hello, Sleighbel
It's time for sleigh bells ringing, Peace on earth to you all
On planets of your dreams, in galaxies of love

From the rainbow rings of Saturn
To the mystery at the end of time

Copyright 1981 Francis E. Delaney   S-8106-MM

MY DREAM DIDN'T COME TRUE

Let's take journey
To the end of time

Think about it in your mind
Take a walk in mine

When I first seen the sky
I didn't know, I was a little guy

Things changed through the years
The sky stayed the same

It was still there in the light of day
And the dark of night

I once had a dream
But My Dream Didn't Come True

It did me no good to complain
So I took the blame

Before you left, I knew the answer, Why
My Dream Didn't Come True

Copyright 1981 Francis E. Delaney   P-8107-MM

REASONS, I LOVE YOU O

Here's what I love about you

The Reasons I Love you
Are the reasons, I do
Win or lose, yes or no
Like Las Vegas, we are gambling with love

Oh, the gambling was meant for me
For you won at love, gambling with me
You got the Las Vegas Blues

When a chance comes for love
Like Las Vegas, you are gambling
Win or lose, I got the Las Vegas blues loving you

Oh, the loving game was meant for me
For I won at love gambling with you
I got the Las Vegas blues

The Reasons I Love You
Are the reasons I do
Win or lose, yes or no

I won the Las Vegas Blues
I won love, gambling with you

Copyright 1981 Francis E. Delaney   S-8108-MM

THE FACE OF A CLOWN O

In many ways you are a clown
In miracles of sight and sound
In many ways you are not
For behind the makeup of a clown
Lies a soft and gentle heart, and the mystery of its frown

In many ways you are alone
With those who can't walk, talk or see
In many ways they are not
For behind them makeup of a clown
Lies the soft and gentle heart, in the laughter of a clown

In many ways you are a clown
Laughter to tears in young and old
For behind the makeup of a clown
Lie the body, soul and mind
Touching the feelings of the mind

In many ways we are alike
Laughter and tears are young and old
In many ways we are not
For behind the makeup of a clown
Lies a special world without bounds
In the heart of a clown

Feelings, happy and sad—The Face Of A Clown

Copyright 1981 Francis E. Delaney   S-8109-MM

TEXAS EYES   1982

With tears in the eyes of Texas
And a love stronger than her own
She had to go to San Antoine
She had to go home

Then with tears in her Texas Eyes
And a love greater than her own
She had to leave from San Antoine
She had to come home

From the thrills of New Orleans
To the hills of Texas
My Texas knew no fear
Her love was stronger than her own

With a heart as big as Texas
Tears of love that knew no fear
She gave my love a home
In the heart of San Antoine

Copyright 1982 Francis E. Delaney   S-8201-MM

ANGELS AND STARS   o

Angels and Stars
An angel under the Christmas Tree
An angel on top of the tree
It's you and me
Our family and a Christmas Tree
Where ever we may be

Bright Christmas Star
My Christmas Star
Star of the east, a world at peace
Angels that sing of life and love
On Christmas Night
We're still in love

Angels and Stars
It's the miracle of you
It's the miracle of me
It's you and me, a family
Where ever we may be

Copyright 1982 Francis E. Delaney   S-8202-MMky

JUMP WITH JOY   D

There's music in people

Like you and me

It is a love in rhapsody

The silent words I can not see

I can Feel

Softly, gently. Jump With Joy

There's music when people

Like you love me

Love is touching live fantasies

The softness of love

Loving me

Softly, Gently Jump With Joy

Copyright 1982 Francis E. Delaney   S-8203-MM

CHRISTMAS MEMORIES   o

Do you remember Christmas, old
I Do

Do you remember Christmas, New
I Do

It's the first Christmas
I fell in love with you

Do you remember when we danced
I Do

Do you remember what we dreamed
I Do

We had danced with our dreams
And we fell in love, to love

Do you remember Christmas, old
I Do

Do you remember Christmas, new
I would with you

Copyright 1982 Francis E. Delaney   S-8204-MMml

COUNTRY WOMAN LOVING ME D 1983

Growing on the prairie sea
The Country flower Grows

Covered with the evening dew
The prairie flower sleeps

Country Woman Loving Me
Feeling the love of me

Country Woman Loving Me
Loving the feel of me

The prairie wind blowing free
Tumbling tumble weeds

Country Woman Loving Me
Country Woman Loving Me

Copyright 1983 Francis E. Delaney   S-8301-MM

MELODIES

All the things we hear
Melodies of sound

All the things we see
But can not hear

Are melodies of sound
In the memory of the mind

In the Melodies of love
We see and hear

The words we speak
The feelings we feel

In life and in love
Life and love are Melodies

The composition of life
The way we are

Melodies

Copyright 1983 Francis E. Delaney   P-8302-FD

SOUND IN THE MIND the

How many times

Have your heard something

When no one else did

Why did you hear that

When no one else heard

The Sound in Your Mind

The words and music of a song

Will they ever be heard   P-8303-MH65

FIGI AND TAFFY

Figi candies
Taffy apples
All the sweet
All the sour
Are The gifts of life

Copyright 1983 Francis E. Delaney   P-8304-MH66

THE LAKE

I take a walk along the lake
Listen to what it has to say

On the quiet days
When the wind is shy

The Lake whispers its words
To the birds that dive

And when they fly
They never ask why

On the wild days
The Lake washes the shores

I sit here and listen
To all that it says

For all the water
On the bird and the shore

Have been here before
The bird and the shore

To learn more
Take a walk along the Lake

Copyright 1983 Francis E. Delaney   P-8305-MM

TELL ME, (why) D — 1984

Tell Me, why—with loving eyes
Tell Me, why—tears cloud your eyes
Tell Me, why—with feelings shy
Tell Me, why—love's soft and wise

Why, Oh why do I love you
Please tell me why
I hear your heart
Beating with mine
Tell Me, Why

S-8401-MM

BONAFIDE

There's a common bond
Between you and me
Words and music
Past and present
Between you, me and the future
A Bonafide love affair

Copyright 1984 Francis E. Delaney   P-8402-MMky

MINI SKIRTS AND WHITE LEVIS

I have seen many pretty things
Bumble bees in sunshine trees
Lollipops and tinsel string-in
Mini Skirts and White Levis

You are all of life pretty things
Your love is my tender dreams
All the things I visualized—in
Mini Skirts and White Levis

Your beauty in laughter's tears
When your walking in my eyes
A pleasure beyond love shy—
In Mini Skirts and White Levis

You're my eloquent times
Life succulent wines
All the things I realized—in
Mini Skirts and White Levis

Copyright 1984 Francis E. Delaney   S-8405-MM

YOU AND ME

I look at love
And I see you
What is life without fun
It's the absence of you

I look at life
And I see you
What is love without you
It's the absence of me

I look at you
You are life, you are love
You Are Me

P-8403-MM

EXPECTATIONS

A promise of the future
The present isn't certain
And the future becomes
A part of the past

Copyright 1984 Francis E. Delaney   P-8404-MM

INVITATION TO A BALL

We were invited to a big party
At the Hilton hotel in downtown Chicago

It was a black tie affair
Tuxedo and all the rest

I asked my better half
What are we doing here

Who are all these people
And as always

She had the answer
These are all my friends

Where are yours
In reply, I just said

You got too many friends
You don't need anymore

Copyright 1984 Francis E. Delaney   P-8406-MM

WHEN YOUR LOVING ME IN COUNTRY D   1985

When Your Loving Me in Country
Mountains touch the sea

From the mountains come the sea
Rivers of snow kiss the sea

Way out in the Country
Valleys golden in leaves

When Your Loving Me In Country
Country music is loving me

When Your Loving Me in Country
Feelings are touching me

Your love, taunting me
Your feelings holding me

Way out in the country
Touching the golden leaves

When Your Loving Me in Country
Your country love is loving me

Copyright 1985 Francis E. Delaney   S-8501-MM

BAD, BAD BLUES

When your a little blue
What do you do
Keep me home
Leave me alone with you

We'll take a look
You ask, I'll do
Hit me with a kiss
Chase away the Bad, Bad Blues

The Bad, Bad Blues
My dream didn't come true
I'm not going to loose you too
Fell in love with you

Let's take a walk
You talk, I'll Listen
And when we get back
We'll love away the Bad, Bad Blues

Take a look at what you got
Walk around the block
Talk about what you never talk about
And you will know who your talking too

Copyright 1985 Francis E. Delaney   P-8502-MM

IT'S NO USE

This is a doggie tale
About the day
When Tracy
Our Dog
Almost
Passed away

Out for walk
She laid down on her side
Four legs shaking
Then she lay quiet
Tried to get her up
Said to myself, It's No Use

Moe was crying when she said
Bury her with Petti, behind the garage
I started to dig the hole
Quit when I seen Tracy looking in the hole
She had to be dead for twenty minutes
But there she was looking at our tears
Took her to the doctor, diabetes he said

Tracy takes her medicine every day
One in the morning and one at night
How long will she last
It's, No Use– to ask

Copyright 1985 Francis E. Delaney   P-8503-TM

YOUR SISTER

Sometimes you put up with stuff
Sometimes you don't have too

She's Your Sister
She's not mine

I figured away around all this stuff
Sometimes you have to do that

She's Your Sister
She' not mine

I told Moe, I don't want to know
Where, we're going. When we go out

It's always an adventure, now
Where ever we go

Most of the time
We both don't know, Your Sister

Copyright 1985 Francis E. Delaney   P-8504-MP

TEXAS FLOWER — 1988

Down in Texas
Visiting the family
A Texas Flower back home
In the homes of San Antoine

The family is old and young
Moe's mother was Irish
Father part Indian and Mexican
From that mix a beautiful Texas Flower

Papa had a band and could sing
Indian and Mexican
He passed away several years ago
Some of his grandkids still sing the songs

Getting on the plane to come home
I wrote the title of this poem
When a stranger asked Moe
Texas Flower are you going or coming

This Texas Flower is going home

Copyright 1988 Francis E. Delaney   P-8801-MM

MUST I PASS HER BY   66

When I first seen you
I found myself talking to you
You looked around
And went the other way
Must I Pass Her By

One day I found myself
Singing a song to you
One day I found you
Singing my song
Must I Pass Him By

Must I Pass You By
There are no reasons why
Your feelings and mine
Love, has yet to live

Someday we'll remember
That day we met
All the years between
On that day and today

I still sing that song
Must I Pass Her By

Copyright 1988 Francis E. Delaney   P-8802-MMky

THERE'S NO WAY   65

There is no way
I don't think of you

Your the first letter I wrote
The first poem I penned
The first song I wrote
The First Love

There's no way
I didn't know why

You left with a tear in your eye
The first tear I cried
The first beer I tried
The first time

There's no way
You don't know Why

I can't forget you
Your first smile
Your first song
Your first love

Copyright 1988 Francis E. Delaney   P-8803-MHla

WRONG SIDE OF THE STREET

Christmas around the corner

Ten Christmas days have come and gone

On the right side of the street

This Christmas is different

Once again we find ourselves

On The Wrong Side of The Street

The cancer has returned

Looks like a long year and tears

An operation and treatments

The doctor used to say

Three to six months the first time

That was twenty-two years ago

Today he says three to five years

Copyright 1988 Francis E. Delaney   P-8804-MM

CAN SHE MAKE IT　　　1989

This little poem reminds me of story
"What went wrong"
Will I ask the same question

Can she make it the second time through
All the medicine, all that she has to do
Will she ask the same question　　　P-8901-MM

SAN ANTOINE

Visitors from San Antoine
Brother and sister both in the Navy
Second cousins in the family

They were never in Chicago
So we showed them around
We know why Chicago is called the second city

Because San Antoine is the first city

Copyright 1989 Francis E. Delaney　　　P-8902-JM

WHAT WENT WRONG

Children are grown my wife is gone
I sit here singing the same old song
What Went Wrong

I don't know why, it went wrong
Maybe it was me for making you
The mother of my children and me

Now, I look for a new love song
Gonna do it right, not gonna do wrong
To the rhythm and the beat of my new love song

My cloths are torn, my beer is warm
I sit here written my new love song
What Went Wrong

Gonna love you to your music
The rhythm of our love
As I lay here loving my new love song

Now my wife is pregnant and my beer is warm
I sit here singing a new love song

My little one is born, but my wife is gone
She died given birth to my new love song

Copyright 1989 Francis E. Delaney　　　P-8903-TA

ALL TIMERS HERS

Mary has had Alzheimer's
For about ten years now
This is the second time
Mary came back to normal for a while

We were ready for her this time
First question Maureen asked her
Mary, where have you been
Mary, where are you

Mary answered, I'm in a cave
And there is no way out
That was the first time she said anything
In almost five years.

Smitty was always telling jokes
So he told her a pretty funny joke
And he asked her, wasn't that a funny joke
She said, No

It was the last word Mary said

Copyright 1989 Francis E. Delaney　　　P-8904-MS

NO WAY OUT

If Mary could write this
What would she say

Today she goes on a stomach pump
Can't eat nothing solid anymore
I took lessons on how the pump worked
I guess I am now a nurses aid

But what does Mary say
In a cave with No Way Out
What is she thinking about
Will we ever know

She had a stroke before the all timers
In a coma for about 2 months
When she came out of it
I couldn't understand what she said

I sat her up on the side of the bed
And asked her to say that again
"Do you think, you can think of what I'm thinking of"
What does Mary say today

Probably the same thing

Copyright 1989 Francis E. Delaney　　　P-8905-MS

TEARS CLOUD MY EYES   1990

Tears Cloud My Eyes
For another year

It seems as though
We are always here

Cemo comes again
Is it, life friend

With all that's happening
Moe keeps on working

And just for kicks
Avon's calling again

I deliver all her Avon sales
Meet all her friends

And when they ask me
Who are you, " I'm Maureen's Avon man"

Copyright 1990 Francis E. Delaney   P-9001-MM

SING ANOTHER SONG

Now I Sing Another Song
About all the people all around
Sitting in this waiting room

Each person sitting here
Sings a different song
They have something wrong   P-9002-FD

MARGARITE

This is an old person
No one knows
Sitting in a wheelchair
She's all alone

Moe takes her here and there
To the doctor and everywhere
Invites her to Christmas
When no one else cares

Now Margarite asks me why
And who will take care of her
If her caretaker is taken away

Copyright 1990 Francis E. Delaney   P-9003-MB

LOVING IN THE BREEZEWAY

Loving In The Breezeway
On a warm summer night

The lightning bugs light
A dark summer night

The crickets talk
To the silence of the night   P-9004-KY

HOME IN THE WOODS

All the trees around this place
All the plants in place
Flowers inside and out
Taste this place

Reminds me of a place
A pretty face
That used to be
Home In The Woods

Copyright 1990 Francis E. Delaney   P-9005LL

TRACY

Tracy is the family dog
Lots of tales about Tracy
Started to write a song about her
I guess I will finish it someday

Here's a tale of a story
The nurses aid was cleaning the bird cage
The bird got out, Tracy tries to catch the bird
The bird gets in the house plants in the breezeway

I had the cover off the air vent
So more cool air would cool the breezeway
The house plants were a Messy mess
The bird was in the heating ducts

When we got home from work
The nurses aid said, she couldn't find the bird
She didn't think Tracy ate the bird
Even though she found some yellow feathers in the flowers

The bird was in the duct work of the heating plant
I won't tell you how long it took
To get the bird out, or the birds name " Messy"

Copyright 1990 Francis E. Delaney   P-9006-TM

WRONG WAY 1991

Free of cancer once again
From all the cemo and radiation
Over all the years of treatment
A heart valve running backwards

Congestive heart failure
Now a big problem
Once a month visits to Rush hospital
And emergency room at Christ hospital

A run away heart
Running the Wrong Way
Hardly no immune system left
Its a tough call

Over the next few months
Moe has to build up her strength
But its difficult to get her to eat
She's now slim and trim

How to get her to eat again
Breakfast at Carsons on Sunday
Once a week at Enricos
Two   evenings at the Warsaw Inn

Copyright 1991 Francis E. Delaney   P-9101-MM

ICU

This was a tough day
Off to the emergency room at Christ
Rolled the wheel chair
Right in to the emergency room

All beds were full
Didn't matter
When I mentioned her name
He doctor was called

Ten minutes later we were in CIU
Doctor told her, your lucky you got here
Did you know the emergency nurse
Called security on the driver of your wheel chair.

Gotta tell you about that nurse someday
Wanted to make her wait in the waiting room
First Doctor didn't know
What the little blue dot was under her chin

That meant she was a cancer patient
With no thyroid gland
When I told him what it was
He sent her to ICU

Copyright 1991 Francis E. Delaney   P-9102-MM

AFTER I SAID, NO

After I Said, No
I knew I was In Love with you
Why have I been so cool
Why did I break your heart in two

I know how cool I've been with you
Your not the one who is a fool
My foolish heart has always been in love
With yours from the start

After I Said, No
I knew I wasn't in love with a fool
You always kept me cool
Why did I break my heart on you

Your love is in my lonely heart
All the words from the start
All those that I wrote and didn't keep
I write them now for you to keep

Copyright 1991 Francis E. Delaney   P-9103-MHla

LITTLE BITTY LOVE

Your little bitty of love
Is a little bit love
From the love land of my lady love

Your a flower that blooms
A touch of heaven
A rainy day

The joker in a deck of cards
A chicken in a coup
Looking for the wolf

Its the way you are
When your behind the bar
Its what you don't say

That Little Bitty Love
When you introduced me to
Your, Daddy

The Bartender

Copyright 1991 Francis E. Delaney   P-9104-MHla

I'M (from) CHICAGO, CALL ME JAZZ   1992

You are, what you are
In the mirror of your mind
Your love is the touch of the music called Jazz

Your the gold and the silver
In the eyes of the poor
Your a ruby as red and as ripe as the fever of Jazz

You are from Chicago, and your something called Jazz

She's from Chicago
Born the heart and soul of Jazz
Chicago music, touching the feelings of life

As her buildings sway
In broken lines of glass and stone
Her bridges open the sky
To a silhouette of shadows

A river dancing, to the music she calls Jazz

I'm From Chicago
Where the highs and the lows
Are live as life can be, I'm Chicago, Call Me Jazz

Rapping to the beat
That dances with the soul of Jazz
The rapid movements of the lake, a rhapsody in music

Her sky line calling, "I'm Chicago, Call Me Jazz

Copyright 1992 Francis E. Delaney   S-9201-MM

LOVE MAKES MY HEART, TRY

Your Love Makes My Heart Try

I taste your love

In the tears I cry

A love that cares

A love that shares

All that love is

Will I see that love

That Makes My Heart Try

Again

Copyright 1992 Francis E. Delaney   P-9202-MM

REMISSON

Its a long road to the room
But remission means the operation
Is on the road again.

If everything goes well
For six months to a year
It's operating time

One new heart valve, Please   P-9203-MM

HOUR GLASS, NO MORE SAND

Time to watch the time go by
Or time to make the rest of time
The best of times

I got a lot of miles
Pushing wheel chairs around
So we use it only when it's necessary

Women are an amazing piece of art
In the good times and in the bad times
This one takes me one step farther

Copyright 1992 Francis E. Delaney   P-9204-MM

YOU GAVE MY LIFE, LOVE

You Gave My Life, Love
Took me to where I never was
And all that we have done
Has made us one

One in the eyes of love
One in the heart of love
One in the fire of love
In love with all of love

You Gave My Life, Love
In all that I see and do
I will always know it was you
Who took me to love

When our time is over
I'll be better. For the time with you
Took me beyond the things I could do
Just take a look at all that we did

You give my life, love
And as life leaves you
You leave with my love
And give my life, your love

Copyright 1992 Francis E. Delaney   P-9205-MM

If I EVER LOVE AGAIN

Will I ever be in love again
Feel love
Only time will tell
If I Ever Love Again

If God calls you
Will He let me love again
A love that will be true
And know me too

Will a new love
Become a partner in life
Will she take our music
To where it's never been before

If I Ever Love Again
Will I be in love again
Will I write her love songs
Or will there be no more

If God calls you
Will He call me too
If there is another love for me
He will call me, when my work is done

Copyright 1992 Francis E. Delaney   P-9206-MM

ALL THAT, AND YOU LOVE ME TOO

Remember the day we met
The day we kissed
The day we loved
All That ! And You Love Me Too
Every Day   P-9207-MM

WE DID IT ALL

We did all we wanted to do
If we're not finished
With what we are doing
It will be done
In the future with you

We Did It All
Each and ever day
We gave it our best
I let you, be you
You let me, be me

We Did It All
It Was An Easy Call

Copyright 1992 Francis E. Delaney   P-9208-MM

CHRISTMAS LOVE

First Christmas alone
Everybody's gone
Smitty passed away
At the age of ninety-six

Twenty-seven years ago, I asked Moe
What do you want to do
Now that the doctors told you
You only got six months to a year

I want to out live Smitty, she said
He and Mary raised me from the age of six
Twenty-seven years later

She's tough as hell and still alive
One year after Smitty died
Six years after Mary

Maybe her work is done
She did all she wanted to do

Copyright 1992 Francis E. Delaney   P-9209-MM

NEW YEARS EVE, What Ever Way It Goes

It's New Years Eve

The eve before the operation in Feb.

Everything has to be OK

No sign of cancer

Nobody can have a cold

Last week one of the doctors had a cold

Next week someone will have something

And when its all over

Only then will we know

What Ever Way It Goes

All the days of Christmas and all our New Years

All were happy, none were cold

And if you don't make it

The rest will be, What ever way it goes

Copyright 1992 Francis E. Delaney   P-9210-MM

LOOKING FOR THAT LOVE AGAIN

words & music:
Francis E. Delaney

1) When I was some-thing twen-ty, I picked a rose from the vine When I was some-thing fif-ty, it with-ered and died Now I'm on the
2) When we were some-thing twen-ty, we love ros-es on the vine When we were some-thing fif-ty, they with-ered and died Now I'm on the
5) When we were some-thing twen-ty, love blos-somed in our lives Through our thirties and our for-ties, the ros-es bloomed a-gain Now I'm on the

road a-gain, look-ing for that love a-gain
road a-gain, look-ing for that love a-gain

3) Road, the o-pen road, tast-ed its dust-y glow Seen the world from the dark-est side of the road And I loved her ros-es
4) Watched it spar-kle in the win-dows of our mind Felt di-vine as we loved the roses on the vine Forty two, twenty six, thirty nine

© COPYRIGHT 1993 FRANCIS E. DELANEY ASCAP all rights reserved.
P.O. Box 932 Frankfort, IL 60423

RL

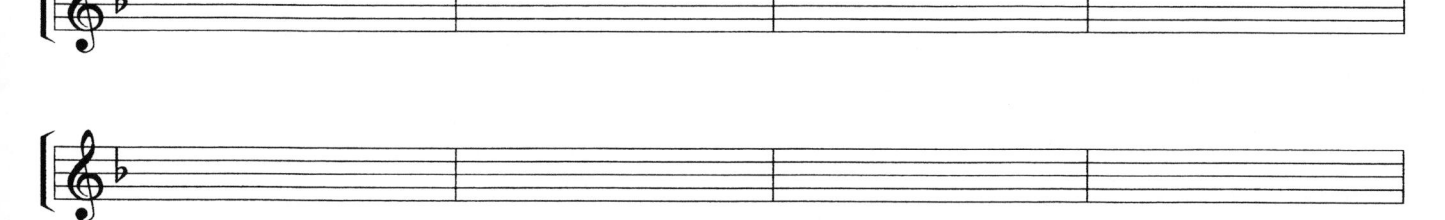

PREFACE   1993

This is the year that love passed away
Before Maureen left, she left two poems

1. Little Fish   2. Cancer Took My Tears

LITTLE FISH

When I was a little girl
My father took me fishing
Every time I caught a Little Fish
I would throw it back in the river
So it could live again
Will God catch me and throw me back   P-9301-MM

CANCER TOOK MY TEARS

Some days when your here
I can't see but I can hear
Some days I wake up, when your not here
I can see your tears but you can't see mine
Each night we kiss and say Good-bye
I can feel your tears but you can't feel mine
Cancer Took My Tears   P-9302-MM

This book is numbered with the years 1993 to 2005

Another World

Copyright 1993 Francis E. Delaney

I WILL REMEMBER

A lifetime is the time
You spend together
The years between October and September

Measured years to be remembered
For everyday in every year
I Will Remember
My time in life loving you

When our eyes touched our heart
We knew from the start
The years between June and July

All the words of our heart
From the Hills of Maureen
Till the end of time
I Will Remember
Your time in life loving me

Forever I Will Remember
My time in your time loving you

Copyright 1993 Francis E. Delaney   S-9303-MM

THOSE DAYS HAVE GONE BY

I see her eyes in the sky
In tears that cloud my eyes
From her heart soft and wise
Tell Me Why,
Those Days Have Gone By

I see her love in my eyes
Through tears that cloud the sky
From my heart warm and shy
Tell Me Why
Those days Have Gone By

Tell me why, did I love you
Tell me why, did you love me
Tell me why, Tell me why
Those Days have Gone By

I hear your heart it's beating with mine
To the rhythm of the beat
Of a love that was yours and mine
Tell Me Why
Those Days Have Gone By

Copyright 1993 Francis E. Delaney   P-9304-FD

LOOKING FOR THAT LOVE AGAIN

When I was something twenty
I picked a rose on a vine
When I was something fifty
It withered and died

When we were something twenty
We loved the roses on the vine
When we were something fifty
The rose left the vine

Now I'm on the road again
Looking For that Love Again

I road the open road, tasted its dusty glow
Seen the world from the darkest side of the road
And I loved the roses

Watched them sparkle in the windows of our mind
Felt divine as we loved the roses on the vine
Forty-two, twenty-six, thirty-nine

When we were something twenty
Love blossomed in our lives
Through our thirties and our forties
The roses bloomed again and again

Now I'm on the road again
Looking For That Love Again

Copyright 1993 Francis E. Delaney   S-9305-MM

ONE BEAUTIFUL MOMENT

Look at the spider spinning her web
One beautiful movement in artistry
Look at the Butterfly flying free
One beautiful movement in melody
Look at the flower blooming in your eye
One beautiful movement of the butterfly

Look at love and it looks at you
One beautiful moment to see
In the tunnel of your eye
A whirlpool loving me
Waterfalls rainbows hugging
The windowsills of our mind

If you can see what I can see
Then your One Beautiful Move
Has happened to me

If your that spider spinning her web
And the butterfly flying free
Then your the flower blooming in my eye
Your one beautiful movement hugging me
One Beautiful Moment loving me

Copyright 1993 Francis E. Delaney   S-9306-DA

FALLING LEAVES

For every creature, big and small
On earth and beneath the sea
There's a Falling Leaf from a living tree

On the baron lands, big and small
The little creatures feed
From the little trees we call weeds

What would the world be
Without a Falling Leaf
Take a look at the living tree

No computer can compute
How many leaves fall from a tree
Or how many creatures it feeds

How many things are made from a living tree
Just take a look around and you will see
Everything that you can see

A tree is made from water and dirt
And all the Falling Leaves
Feeds all the creatures and things you see

Copyright 1993 Francis E. Delaney   S-9307-DA

COLOR OF YOUR LOVE

I see the color of your love
In everything I see
The birds, the bees, leaves on a tree
The golden sun shining on the deep blue sea

What color do I see
When I look in your roving eyes
I see the color of your love watching me

What color do I see
When I caress your gentle hair
I see the color of your love touching me

What color do I see
When I kiss your warm tender lips
I see the color of your love kissing me

What color do I see
When you're loving me
I see all the colors of your love Loving me

Copyright 1993 Francis E. Delaney   P-9308-MM

NEW YEARS EVE

It's the Last Day of the year
The Last year of someone dear
It's not a Happy New Year

Everything was last this year
Last Christmas day, last of everything
It's was not a happy year

What will the new year bring
It will bring the first of everything
It will be an all new year

How many new years will there be
Before one brings some one dear
What year will it be

How many times will love pass by
Before one becomes mine
Is there one more new year

How many times will love pass by
Will there be another new year

Copyright 1993 Francis E. Delaney   P-9309-FD

STAR OF CHRISTMAS

When God made the earth
He covered it with water and dirt
Sprinkled it with laughter and tear
On mountains of hope and fear

Then He gave it to you and me
The Star of Christmas
His earth with all its creatures big and small
In the miracle of birth

Each little baby that dies before birth
Takes with him what was his on earth
A little water a little dirt
A tree, a flower, a bird, a animal

His laughter, his tear and his birth
To become the Star Of Christmas
That gives to us
All that was his on earth

Copyright 1993 Francis E. Delaney   S-9310-MM

PICTURES ON THE WALL

The artist draws a different line
Takes a picture from her mind
And paints it in the windows of our mind

When love can hear what others can't see
Love's the artist in the mind
And draws it so that only love can hear

Turn around and you can hear
All the sounds you can not see
In the Pictures on the Wall

The poet draws with a different line
The songwriter with different curve
Puts it in a song for all to see and hear

Turn around and you can see
All the sounds you can not hear

Copyright 1993 Francis E. Delaney   P-9311-DA

ALL THAT AND YOU LOVED ME TOO

All That and You Loved Me Too

All that's in the sky

All that's on the land

All that's in the sea

All the beauty God gave you

All your love you gave me Yesterday

All of it is here Today

All of it will be forever Tomorrow

All the tears and all the days pass by

All the years will come and go

All that I come to know

All That and You Loved Me Too

Copyright 1993 Francis E. Delaney   P-9312-MM

FIRST AND LAST

When love has left you
Your life is like the seasons of the year
Spring, Summer, Fall and Winter
Each has a first day and a last   P-9313-MM

_____

WALKING ON FOUR

Little one Walking on Four
Your much, much more than a little dog
You're a companion, a faithful friend
Someone to walk with at the days end

Little one Walking on Four, you're a lot more than a little dog
You're the eyes and ears of those walking in the world of stone
You're the joy and the love in the lives
Of the little ones growing up and the big ones growing old
A pain in the butt for the rest of us, cleaning up

You know what's right, you know what's wrong
You know when we're happy and we know when your sad
So take a look at your dog and you can see
She's got feelings like you and me

Your much, much more than a little dog
You're a companion a faithful friend
Someone to walk with at the days end

Copyright 1993 Francis E. Delaney   S-9314-TM

WHEN THE ROSES TURN SILVER 1994

When the Roses Turn Silver
A new life begins
The feelings of a new love
Fade the memories of the old

When the Roses Turn Silver
The new love comes true
New feelings of love
Bring new memories to hold

When the Roses Turn Silver
The butterflies return
Feelings of loving again
Are surpassed by the feelings of falling in love again

When the Roses Turn Silver
Your love becomes gold
Feelings of loving again
Are but a moment in time

When the Roses Turn Silver
Feelings of being in love
Last until the end

Copyright 1994 Francis E. Delaney   P-9401-DA

LOVE'S ANOTHER DREAM

When love is a real dream
It is a part of life
That will always be
A part of yesterday

Her name was Maureen
She never said, No
A picture of the first time
Love's Another Dream

Love is a dream
It never grows old
From young to old
Love, dreams

It's a part of yesterday
It is here today
It is tomorrows dream
Love's Another Dream

Copyright 1994 Francis E. Delaney   P-9402-DA

EYES (I'S) OF LOVE

Something magic in the Eyes of Love
Something mystic in the "I love you"
Makes me happy and makes me sad
Knowing that your loved by another man

Something magic in the eyes of Love
Something mystic in the "I love you"
Makes her happy and it makes her sad
Knowing that she is loved by another man

How many men are caught in the mystic magic
Of another woman's love
How many women love
The magic melodies of another mans love

Something magic in the Eyes of Love
Something mystic in the women I love
"I love you" but never "I do"
The mystic in the Eyes of Love

The mystic magic of a woman's love

Copyright 1994 Francis E. Delaney   S-9403-DA

THANKS FOR LOVING ME

Catch a falling leaf
Listen to its breeze
It's a whisper from me
I was down, you came around
Thanks For Loving Me

When a little cloud covers you
Touch its shadow
It's resting on me
I wrote them and you read them
Thanks For Loving Me

Read them and leave them
With this ink upon this line
Draw their picture in your mind
No one will find your love letters signed
Thanks For Loving Me

When the moon is full
Its stars are in your eyes
They are talking to me
You wrote them and I read them
Thanks For Loving me

Copyright 1994 Francis E. Delaney   S-9404-MM

SHE'S COUNTRY

Why is Grandma running barefoot by the sea
She's Country, running free and loving me

She's Country, flower and a honeybee
Blossom on a cherry tree
Wild flower in a prairie sea
Running barefoot by the sea
Her children and theirs born free
In her Red, White and Blue sea

She's Country, sun shinning through the trees
Moonlit shadows holding me
Soft rippling movements that I see
Running barefoot by the sea
Her children and theirs living free
In her Red, White and Blue sea

When she is free from all the things that have to be
She's Country, loving me running barefoot by the sea
She's Country, running free and loving me

She's Country, flower on a honeybee
Soft gentle hair, riding the breeze
Running barefoot by the sea
Her children and theirs asking me
Why is Grandma running barefoot by the sea

Why is Grandma running barefoot by the sea
She's Country, running free and loving me

Copyright 1994 Francis E. Delaney   S-9405-DA

BOSTON BAY

Don't ask me why, I don't want to leave
The quiet nights and busy days of Boston Bay
On a quiet night when the moon is in the bay
We'll walk beside the moon, backwards through the years
The quiet nights and busy days, the caring moments
And all the loving years that brought you here

To the busy days when the sun melts the mist and warms the bay
Your beauty looks across the bay, through its yesterdays
I can see in the colors of its rain
That I couldn't have found a lovelier friend
If I followed the rainbow to it's end
Monday Pink and Tuesday orange, Wednesday yellow
Thursday lavender blue, Friday violet, Saturday silver and Sunday gold

On a quiet night when the moon is in the bay
I'll watch your beautiful melody, I'll remember Yesterday
The quiet nights and the busy days
The caring moments and the loving tears that brought me here
On that quiet night and busy day when you were here

On the busy days when the sun is in the bay
I'll watch your beautiful movements, I'll remember Yesterday
The quiet night and busy day
The caring moment and loving tears that brought us near
On that quiet night and busy day when I was here

Don't ask me why, I don't want to leave
The quiet nights and busy days of Boston Bay

Copyright 1994 Francis E. Delaney   S-9406-DA

COLORS IN THE RAIN

I see the Colors In The Rain
In all things I see
The birds and the bees
The leaves on a tree
And in the deep blue sea

When I look into your eyes
I see the Colors In The Rain
I can touch the color of your hair
In the Colors In The Rain

I can taste the wine in your kiss
Raindrops, Colors In The Rain
I can hug you every time it rains
When I hold The Colors In The Rain   P-9407-MM

LOOK WHAT YOU DID

Look What You Did, when you did it
You became one of Gods loveliest flowers
Mary Louise, Maureen Teresa and You
I can only imagine that only His loveliest flowers
Will write the poems and songs that will come along
See what you did, read what you did
Look At What You Did

Copyright 1994 Francis E. Delaney   P-9408-DA

RAINBOWS

Colored water in the sky
When rain is passing by
A rainbow hill in the sky

Hanging in the sky
A balloon shaped rainbow
The sun colors the rain

A round rainbow in the clouds
There's not many who seen all three
Perhaps only me.   P-9409-MM

ALL YOUR CARING MOMENTS

I remember the day a year ago
When you asked me
Who's going to know you
Who's going to care

If no one else knows me
And no one else cares
I'll just remember all the days
All Your Caring Moments everyday.

Copyright 1994 Francis E. Delaney   P-9410-MM

TEXAS EYES

With tears in the eyes of Texas
And a love stronger than her own
She had to come home
Then with tears in her Texas Eyes
A love stronger than her own
She had to leave San Antonio
She had to come home

From the thrills of New Orleans
To the hills of Texas
My Texas knew no fear
Her love was greater than her own
With a heart as big as Texas
And tears of love that knew no fear
She gave my love a home
In the heart of San Antonio

Her heart was always San Antonio
Her love was in time with mine
She was a melody in love
She never said, No
With tears in the eyes of Texas
And a love greater than her own
She had to leave San Antonio
She had to come home

My Texas knew no fear
She gave my love a home
In the heart of Texas, San Antonio

Copyright 1994 Francis E. Delaney   S-9411-MM

AUDIENCE OF ONE

I was twenty-three, Mary was seventeen
Life and love was young, falling in love was fun
So I wrote them and she read them
And I sang my songs to Mary, my Audience of One
I didn't care if anyone ever heard a song I've written and sung
For they were only for the eyes, ears and heart of my Audience of One
When she was twenty-three, Mary left me
Of all the things I ever had to do the toughest of them all
Was saying Good-bye to Mary, my Audience of One

When I was twenty-nine, Maureen was twenty-five
Live as life could be, full of the devil and falling in love
So I wrote them and she read them
And I sang my songs to Maureen, my Audience of One
I didn't care if anyone ever heard a song I've written and sung
For they were only for the eyes, ears and heart of my Audience of One
When she was fifty-two, Maureen left me
Of all the things I ever had to do the saddest of them all
Was saying Good-bye to Maureen, my Audience of One

When I was fifty-six my Audience of One was fifty-one
I wrote them and she read them
And I sang my songs again to an Audience of One
For the first time I want everyone to hear
The songs I've written and sung to my Audiences' of One
When I get to the top of the charts I surely will say
Thanks for Loving Me to my Audience of One
And of all the things I will ever have to do
The easiest of them all will, be always loving you

Copyright 1994 Francis E. Delaney   S-9412-MM

LAVENDER BLUE

On a hillside with you
Flowers all around
Two people on the hill
Watching the clouds go by
In a sky of Lavender Blue

I remember it's true
Flowers all around you
Two strangers in a room
Feeling a love gone by
In moods of Lavender Blue

Every time I see a cloud in Lavender Blue
I see the people on the hill, as the clouds kiss the sky
I feel your love passing by
With the touch of Lavender Blue

On a hillside with you
I remember it's true
Two strangers in a room
Friends now, with the little flowers
On a hillside covered with Lavender Blue

Copyright 1994 Francis E. Delaney   P-9413-DA

SIX O'CLOCK BLUES

I guess I'm doing the right thing
Walking the wrong way
Watching the sun set
On my Six O'clock Blues

See you Tomorrow, make it a good night

As the day turns into the night
I look at the moon
And suddenly it's you
My Six O'clock Blues

What do I do, when you say
Take a walk around the moon with me
And on the face of the moon
We'll watch the sun set
On our Six O'clock Blues

Take a walk around the moon with me
And on the light of the moon I will hold you
In a shadow on the moon I will kiss you
And on the dark side of the moon
Love's playing on the moon

Take a walk around the moon with me
And in the cradle of the moon
I will love you
On the cradle of the moon
We will lose the Six O'clock Blues

Copyright 1994 Francis E. Delaney   S-9414-DM

ALL MY HEART CAN TAKE

All that you give
All that you gave
Your, All My Heart Can Take   P-9415-MP

ALL THE TIME MY VALENTINE

All The Time, My Valentine
I place this rose on the tree
Next to where you will always be
Every time I visit you, I kiss the rose on the tree
Thanks for all the roses
All The Time, My Valentine   P-9417-MM

THIS PLACE

This Place is the nicest place I like to be
This Place where life slows down to let you see
This Place and just how nice things can be
This Place where the flowers meet the trees
This Place where the butterflies fly free
This Place where life becomes what life should be
This Place with all its families
This Place its' windows of Christmas
This Place, Christmas in Space

Copyright 1994 Francis E. Delaney   P-9419-MR

TEDDY BEAR CHRISTMAS

Teddy Bear oh, Teddy Bear
You will always be my friend
With a hug and a kiss
And a Teddy Bear Christmas

I never had a Teddy Bear
Till I brought this one
To give to you Christmas day
Teddy Bear Christmas

Teddy Bear Christmas
When the kids ask you why
There's a Teddy Bear laying there
Tell them the story of Christmas 94

With a hug and a kiss
And in all things they will ever do
There will never be another
Teddy Bear quite like you

With a Teddy Bear on Christmas
You make all your dreams come true

Copyright 1994 Francis E. Delaney   P-9416-DA-ky

ROSES IN THE WINE

She was just another waitress waiting on me
Then it seems to be something different than it seemed to be
Could it be Mariola has fallen in love with me
Or is it just another dream, for loves that were mine
Are but memories of mine, rare beautiful melodies
Running through the bloodstreams of my mind

In the hallways of my mind, there's a melody of mine
Taunting me through the windows of my mind
In colors of its wine, rare beautiful melody
The melody of the Roses In the Wine, Mariola wine

Every time you catch me looking at you
You're the blooming in colors of its wine
Every sip, a kiss in my little glass of wine
The melody of the Roses In The Wine

Every rose that grows a million blossoms chime
The melody of the roses on the vine
Every rose that blooms in colors of its wine
A million blossoms chime the melody of the Roses in The Wine

I'll make the coffee and that's why it's good
You serve the love and that's why it's good
And if our love in only in the words that rhyme
Then we'll have a merry-o-time loving the Roses in the Wine

You serve the love and I'll love the way I do
Until my last glass of wine, Mariola wine
Rare beautiful memories running through the bloodstreams of my mind

Copyright 1994 Francis E. Delaney   S-9418-MR

DIFFERENT WINDOWS

When someone close and dear
Pass through the window of there years
No more days like Yesterday, Tomorrow is Today
Like looking through Different Windows, nothing is the same

When you find your the only one who really cared
You look through the Different Windows in a different way
You look for something nice and something far
Like the music in the stars

Now I look through the Different Windows of a different year
And I found something nice and something near
The music of our years, in someone nice and someone dear
In the Different Windows of our years

When I pass through the windows of a different year
You will have something nice and something dear
The music of our years in someone close and someone dear
In the Different Windows of their years

When you look through the different Windows of a different year
No more days like Yesterday, Tomorrow is Today
So love me Today, remember me Tomorrow
In the Different Windows of our years

Copyright 1994 Francis E. Delaney   S-9420-MR

BIRTHDAYS, younger than me

Of all the Birthdays I have had
Some have been happy, some have been sad
But the last one was something like I never had

Made me wish I was younger than me
Then I would know what to say
To the young woman who put
The candle light in my eyes, her music in my ears

When I was fifty-eight
She made my Birthday a happy day
Made me younger than me
I almost asked her to stay
For I know what to say

Birthdays younger than me
Little ones in Birthdays suits
Then of all the Birthdays I have had
Birthday number ? will be the best Birthday
I ever had.

Copyright 1994 Francis E. Delaney   P-9421-MR

FALLING IN LOVE WITH YOU

Falling in Love with You
Is easy to do
Falling in love with love
I'm Falling In Love With You

Love always follows the heart
Seldom follows the body
Your love is in my heart
So my heart will always follow yours

My heart can see your heart
Like no one else can see you
If yours can see mine
Like no one else can see me
Falling in love will continue

The letter "Y" is the first letter of the last word
Falling in Love With You
From the first time our eyes touched
To the last breath of my heart
Falling In Love With You, will continue

Copyright 1994 Francis E. Delaney   Nap-9422-MR

WEDNESDAY NIGHT

Do I want to fall in love again
How many times will the beauty of love
Love, and love me again
How many Wednesday nights will there be

Do I want to play that love again
How many times will the pleasure of love
Love me, and love me again

When I look at you
I see my kids I never knew
If you can see them
Saying I do, is easy to do

Make them beautiful
Make them true
So that they will always be
In the loving arms that loved me

Do I want to fall in love again
Yes, I do, I want to love you
As many times as you want me too
How many Wednesday nights will there be

Before every night is Wednesday Night

Copyright 1994 Francis E. Delaney   S-9423-MR

DREAMS OF LOVE

Marquarite, in a wheel chair at age eighty-five
I took over the job Maureen had done for years
I became a caretaker of Marquarite
She gave me a title to a song she wanted me to write
But I told her to write it herself
Don't know if she did, title was
"Where were you when I was young"
If Marquarite could dream of love at the age of eighty-five
I can dream about it again at the age of fifty-seven

Dreams of Love   P-9424-MB

BREATHLESS

There are no brakes on love

Only heartaches and tough breaks

Definition of real people says it all

Real people are Breathless

They have last names, birthdays and kids

Copyright 1994 Francis E. Delaney   P-9425-MR

ALWAYS 'ROUND MY HEART

Always Round My Heart
Since the first time you said, No
To the roses in the wine

Always round my heart
Breathless as a butterfly
For it's nice the way it is

I remember love
Cheese cake and rose wine
Different windows, pink butterflies

No one else is there
In this place on Wednesday night
When you're Always Round My Heart

Always Round My Heart
Right from the Start
You are a work of art

Always Round My Heart

Copyright 1994   S-9426-MR

VIBRATIONS OF THE SOUL

When something vibrates it's moving
When you feel Vibrations
You are happy or sad
Your emotions tremble
When the weather is cold
When you love
Vibrations of The Soul   P-9427-MR

CHRISTMAS SWEETHEART

This little poem is for everyone
To remember their first Christmas Sweetheart
Can't imagine anyone would forget
Their first Christmas Sweetheart
When life was young, love was fun
And Christmas was Christmas   P-9428-MH

FIRST TIME YOU SAID NO

The First Time you said, No
Was the first time you said, Yes

Copyright 1994 Francis E. Delaney   P-9429-MM

IT'S NICE THE WAY IT IS

It's Nice The Way It Is
When it's different then its always been

It's Nice The Way It Is
In this place where you can be
A part of all the things
That may never be

It's Nice The Way It Is
When you find what love has never been

It's Nice The way It Is
When love becomes a real dream
And life brings feelings
You have never seen

It's Loves, real dream
When, It's Nice The Way It Is

Copyright 1994 Francis E. Delaney   S-9430-MR

NO ONE ELSE IS THERE

Come out of your dreams
Be a Part of the scene
For you are the heart
Of all that I see
No, One Else Is there

Come out of your dreams
Take a ride on my dream
Let me be a part of all that I see
No One Else Is There

You can't hide in your dream
For I'm in all of the scenes
Waiting for you too
Dream in reality with me

Come out of your dreams
For your in all of the scenes
Our dream will come alive
No One Else Is There

Copyright 1994 Francis E. Delaney   S-9431-MR

PINK BUTTERFLY

Pink Butterfly, as rare to the eye
As an eclipse in the sky, a comet passing by
A star so far away, that only love can see
Twinkle in the eye of a Pink Butterfly

I never seen a Pink Butterfly
Till I seen the twinkle in your eye
That only love can see
In the eye of a Pink Butterfly

I never heard a Pink Butterfly
Till I heard the melody in your talk
That only love can hear
In the flight of a Pink Butterfly

Pink Butterfly, don't ever be shy
Of the twinkle in your eye
The love of your walk and the joy of your talk
For they are the colors of your love

I never felt a Pink Butterfly
Till I seen the love of your walk
That only love can see
In the love walk of a Pink Butterfly

Pink Butterfly, will I ever see
The twinkle in their eyes
The love of there walk
The joy of their talk
When your little butterflies open their eyes

Copyright 1994 Francis E. Delaney   S-9432-MR

CHEESE CAKE AND ROSE WINE

Roll out your mind
In a little ink upon a line

Tell me that you're mine
Cheese Cake and Rose Wine

The canyons of your mind
Echo your music in my mind

Through the sound of time
Cheese Cake and Rose wine

Cheese Cake and Rose Wine
Through the centuries of time

A love that beacons
The body, soul and mind

Roll out your mind
With the ink upon this line

Tell me that your my
Cheese Cake and Rose Wine

Copyright 1994 Francis E. Delaney   P-9433-MR

BUTTERFLY WALK

Did you ever watch a Butterfly Walk

Does it walk on its feet

Does its wings move

Does it look like something

Did you see someone walk like that before

Did I, Yes. You   P-9434-MR

MUSIC

Music is the sound written by man

Of notes on a line or space

Played by a musical instrument

A voice singing a song, a poet wrote

Music is a gift God gave everyone

Copyright 1994 Francis E. Delaney   P-9435-MH

MUSIC, THE TALK OF LOVE

Music is The Talk Of Love

It's been around as long as love

It feels everyone

Your rhythm and melody

The arrangement of your moods

It's in your talk and walk

The composition of your feelings

Arranged in parts

Music, the score of life

Copyright 1994 Francis E. Delaney   P-9436-FD

PRETTY MUSIC, Let love fall in love   1995

I remember the day
You first said, Hello
Little did I know
It was the beginning of Pretty Music
Let love, fall in love

I remember the song
I first sang to you
Little did I know
It was the beginning of Pretty Music
Let love fall in love

Let's do it again
Let's fall in love again
Let's love to Pretty Music
Let's love being in love again

Let love, fall in love
Let it be in love
I remember your love
Pretty Music, let love fall in love

Copyright 1995 Francis E. Delaney   S-9501-MR

FOR I REMEMBER LOVE

I write the lyrics
And the music came by
It's worth a try
For I Remember Love

I write the music
And your words come my way
It's still worth the try
For I Remember Love

I remember the look of love
The beauty of the way it was
The pleasure of being together
In this place where I remember love

I'll sing your songs
To your audience of one
And I will listen to them
For I Remember Love

Copyright 1995 Francis E. Delaney   P-9502-MR

FOOT PRINTS IN THE SNOW

I see the mountain
In its drifted snow
I hear you walking
Foot Prints In The Snow

Warm rain changes to snow
Ridged in cold
Your feelings
Foot Prints In The snow

I walk this lonesome road
The cleavage of its snow
Strumming a pretty tune
Ridged in, Foot Prints In The snow

I look at the mountain
Feel the snow
As I walk
In your Foot Prints In The snow

Copyright 1995 Francis E. Delaney   P-9503-MR

WHERE WERE YOU WHEN I WAS YOUNG

Where Were You When I Was Young
When life was fun and I could run
You were in my dreams of love
Where every one loves

Where Were You When I Was Young
When life was sad and love was tough
You were in my dreams of love
Where every woman loves

I never dreamed, I ever see
The one I loved in my dreams of love
I thank you for bringing a life I never knew
Laughter in tears and tears of love
In the songs you sung

Where Were You When I Was Young
Where will you be when life leaves me
You will be in my dreams of love
In heaven, where everyone is loved

Copyright 1995 Marquerite L. Backus   S-9504-FD

COUNTRY LOVE

Why your Country Love has come my way, I don't know
All you have to do is say go-away
If your love likes this quiet night. Country Love is a quiet night

Why your Country Love has come my way, I don't Know
All I have to do is say go-away
But my love likes this quiet place. Country Love is a quiet place

Country Love is a quiet place
No; yes, no or go-away, a little or a lot, I don't know
You share the love that's there
On a quiet night in country Love

When your Country Love is loving me
To the beat of your country music
A little or a lot I don't know, I'll love the way you love
On a quiet night of Country Love

Country love is a quiet place
No; yes, no or go-away, a little or a lot I don't know
I love the love I found
In this quiet place in Country Love

No; yes, no or go-away a little or a lot
I'll love the love I found
In this quiet place of Country Love
A little or a lot, I love the love I found
In your quiet place in Country Love

Copyright 1995 Francis E. Delaney   S-9505-MR

THE BACHELORS TRAP

You're the opposite of male
Soft from top to bottom
A heart covered with love
Made from gold and white lace

You're the ideal female
In the eyes of every male
Every mans love tail
You're The Bachelors Trap

Like a diamond in the sun
Sparkling all its colors into one
Butterflies in love
On the flowers in the sun

You're the opposite of male
You're the ideal female
In the eyes of this male
You are The Bachelors Trap

Copyright 1995 Francis E. Delaney   P-9506-MR

GIVE ME A LITTLE BIT OF YESTERDAY

When life was simple
And the world seemed far away
Love came once and never went away
Give Me a Little Bit of Yesterday

When the lakes were clear
The sky was blue
And the trains rumbled across the plains
Give Me a Little Bit of Yesterday

Give me a Little Bit of yesterday
The summer of ninety-three
Spring and autumn of ninety-four
Give Me a Little Bit of yesterday
In the winter of my love of ninety-five

Give Me a Little Bit of yesterday
When life was simple
And the world seemed far away
Love came once and never went away

Give me a Little Bit of yesterday
When the lakes were clear
And the skies were blue
And I'll give you a little bit of yesterday

Copyright 1995 Francis E. Delaney   P-9507-MR

THIS IS IT

God made it
He said, I got it
This Is It

He couldn't take it
So He got rid of it
And He gave it to Papa

Papa had it
He couldn't control it
So he gave it to Mama

Mama had it
She couldn't hold on to it
So she gave it to the world

I found it
At table twenty-seven
In the roses in the wine

If I find it again at table twenty-seven
This Is It
Your It

Copyright 1995 Francis E. Delaney   P-9508-MR

HE SAVED THE BEST FOR LAST

I sit here and look at all those I see
I write their words and music but they don't see me
I guess someday I will say
He Saved the Best For Last   P-9509-FD

THAT FEELING DON'T GO AWAY

I see you're blue in your lovely eyes
The tears that cloud your eyes
Come from a heart that is soft and wise
Tell me why, That Feeling Don't Go Away

I see the sun in an empty sky
And its sight glows in your eyes
Your feelings are warm when they are shy
Teel me why, That Feeling, Don't Go Away

I hear your heart, it's beating with mine
To the rhythm of the beat
Of a love that's yours and mine
Tell me why, That Feeling, Don't Go Away

Tell me why, do I love you
Tell me why, do you love me
Tell me, That Feeling, Don't Go Away

Copyright 1995 Francis E. Delaney   S-9510-MM

MY HEART IS GETTING CROWDED

My Heart is Getting Crowded
With the beauty that I see
The big ones all around me
But there's always room
For the little ones I see

They're a little part of heaven
A gift for all to see
Your smile in their eyes
Your love in their walk and
Your joy in their talk

It is beyond me
Why anyone wouldn't want one
Perhaps someday the Bill of Rights will say
Once conceived you have the right to breath
Life, liberty and the pursuits of happiness

What good is it today
When the littlest amongst us
Doesn't have the right to breathe
If your heart is getting crowded
With the little ones I can see
Then someday the Bill of Rights will say

One conceived you have the right to breathe
Life. Liberty and the Pursuit of Happiness
In the world in which you are conceived

Copyright 1995 Francis E. Delaney   P-9511-MR

EVERYBODY'S GONE

The first time I fell in love
I thought I'd never fall in love again
She married a very special guy
And I wondered why, Everybody's Gone

The second time I fell in love
I thought I'd never fall in love again
She cried with me as she passed away
And I wondered why, Everybody's Gone

When your love came by
I caught your roving eye
As my love came alive
I wondered why

Could it be your that very special love for me
Could it be in a very special way
You were always there
When I wondered why, Everybody's Gone

Copyright 1995 Francis E. Delaney   S-9512-MR

ARE YOU HAPPY, NOW

When love becomes fun
The poet of love is in your eyes
In the little words upon this line
Are You Happy, Now

When life becomes fun
The poet of love is in your heart
With these little words
Are You Happy, Now

Like a quiet river in an empty eye
The poet of love can describe
The sky above and the earth below
No walls to hold them, no strings attached

When fun becomes love
Love is near and you know it
When love becomes fun
You will love, Are You Happy, Now   P-9513-MR

WHAT DO I SAY

What do I say, When do I say it
Now, it's time for me to leave

Copyright 1995 Francis E. Delaney   P-9514-DK

HOW MANY TIMES HAVE I CRIED

It's been two years
From my heart to my eyes
How Many Tears Have I Cried   P-9515-MM

THE MUSIC IS BACK   M. Jorden

The movement of his picture in your eyes
Dancing to the rhythm of the circle in your eye
The Music is Back

Rings in the roar of the crowd
The audience sings again
The Music Is Back

How many times will the circle
Go through the hoop in my eyes
The Music Is Back

How many times will the crowd roar
One more trophy, one more time
The Music Is Back

When he finally leaves
Will the music be gone

Copyright 1995 Francis E. Delaney   P-9516-MJ

YOU HAVE TO WAIT

How many times have you waited
For someone or something
It seems like we are always waiting

When you go in a restaurant
And a little voice says
You Have to Wait. Do you really have to wait   P-9518-JG

HEART OF ROSES

The rose is the sign of love and the symbol of life
The heart of a rose is in the way that it grows

The Heart of Roses is your heart of love
Your heart of love
Is your natural look of love   P-9519-MR

NUMBER ME LAST

After you have had your fling
And done everything
Remember one thing
All the loves of your past
Will never surpass the love of the one
You numbered Last

Copyright 1995 Francis E. Delaney   P-9521-MR

KNOCKING ON THE DOOR

Time's running out and I gotta be moving on
Gotta find a woman who will have my kids and love me too
And take my love and music to heights I never knew
Like no other woman could other woman could

I found that love in the woman I found in you
The biggest thrill of all was the first little one who called
And before we turned around
Number two was Knocking On The Door

I was counting their diapers hanging on their doors
When number three brought his little sister through the door
Now, we had twins a total of four
Forty-eight diapers hanging on their doors

I waited awhile before I asked her
What went wrong with number four
Number four was supposed to be a boy
Well, she said "Nothing went wrong with number four
There just ain't gonna be no more

I could tell there wasn't going to be anymore
When number five was Knocking on the door
That's when she said "Didn't I tell you no more"
Or you will the one knocking on the door   cond.

Cond.

Number six came along and closed the door
We found ourselves Knocking On The Door
I knew sooner or later she'd open the door
Take me and the seven kids she gave me
To heights we never knew like no other who could

She was forty-seven when she gave me my seventh son
And I was eighty-one, would you believe she said it again
"Didn't I tell you no more" and I had to keep on Knocking On The Door
Till she kicked the bucket at one hundred and four

When I got to that golden door, St. Peter wasn't there
And I found myself Knocking On The Door, would you believe
She opened the door and said it again
"Didn't I tell you no more" and closed the door

I knew sooner or later she'd open the door
And take me and the eight kids she gave me
To heights we never knew
Like no other woman could.

Copyright 1995 Francis E. Delaney   S-9517-MR

MINUTES OF GOLD

If you ever love, love again
And you like to love again
When you hear the flower cry
And see it in your eye
Wipe away the Minute Of Gold

Love is a tall tree, singing in the wind
Love me and love me again
When you hear the music
And see it in the breeze
Marry me and love in Minutes Of Gold

Your love is a silhouette
Of the shadow of the wind
It is there for all to see
In the beauty of its tree
Minutes of Gold loving me

If you ever love, love again
Your love will be a symphony
In Minutes Of Gold
In silhouettes of the shadow of the wind

Copyright 1995 Francis E. Delaney   P-9520-MR

WHY DID YOU LEAVE ME

Why Did You Leave me
I didn't ask why
Why did I care
Tear drops don't lie

What would you do
If I left you
Why would you care
Tear drops don't lie

Two miracles of love have left me
I didn't ask why
For the answer is three
Three miracles of love for me

Why did you leave me
The answer is three
Now there is only one
You have fell in love with me

Why Did You Leave Me
Now there are none

Copyright 1995 Francis E. Delaney   P-9522-FD

MARRY ME AND LOVE ME AGAIN

Marry Me and Love Me again   Madiola
For I love to be in heaven
Before the good Lord calls me
And I'll always love you again

Marry Me and Love Me again   Mariola
Take me and make me a part
Of all that you love
And I'll always love you again

Marry Me and Love Me Again   Rosiola
Make the rose in the wine
A pink Butterfly of mine
And I'll always love you again

Mary, Marry Me and Love Me Again
For I too will cry when the good Lord calls me
In that year of tears
In the different windows of our years

Marry Me and Love Me Again

Copyright 1995 Francis E. Delaney   P-9523-MR

YOU KNOW, WHAT LIFE IS

In life's special world

What is life

When it is different

Than what it should be

With the feelings God gives you

When you can understand

Those who live in life's special world

You know what life is

And you can handle it

So in all of your caring moments

When you hear the flower cry

You're the answer to their shortest prayer

Someone loves me, Someone cares

Copyright 1995 Francis E. Delaney   P-9524-SA Sister Angela

NASHVILLE, CLOSER TO THE TOP

Nashville, and the things you do
Loving me and Nashville too
I had a secretary
More damn jobs than I cared to do

I took jobs I didn't want to do
I climbed the corporate ladder
Like any other fool
I got closer to the top
Loving you and Nashville too

Nashville, I got closer to the top
Loving you and Nashville too
I had a secretary
And she fell in love with me

Then, when I didn't know what to do
I put my arms around you
And fell in love with you
Nashville and the things you do
Loving me and Nashville too

Copyright 1995 Francis E. Delaney   S-9525-MM

I DON'T HAVE TO DREAM ANYMORE

I've seen life from all the corners of its love
I used to dream about all the things that will be
Now I find that life is fine
I look at life and I see mine
I Don't Have To Dream Anymore   P-9526-MR

ARE YOU ALRIGHT

How many times has somebody asked you
Are You Alright
How many times have you asked them
Too many   P-9528-MR

SOUNDS

Some people can not hear
They do not look around
Their world has only one sound
They find life and love
In the Sound of Love

Copyright 1995 Francis E. Delaney   P-9529-HS

SO FAR AWAY

Let me hear your thunder
And feel the heat of your day
For when the sun comes around
And the moon goes down
We'll be loving
So close, Yet, So Far Away

Like thunder in a rainstorm
And the heat of its day
Moonbeams in starlight
Lighting cutting through
So close, yet, So Far Away

Like the winds of the tall trees
The fragrance of the rose
Winter changes to rain
Summer's coming on
So close, Yet, So Far Away

I feel the fragrance of the rose
As the wind of the tall tree touches me
I watch your winter change to rain
And feel your summer coming on
So close, yet, So Far Away

You're so close, yet, So Far Away
We're so close, yet, So Far Away

Copyright 1995 Francis E. Delaney   S-9527-MR

YOU'RE ALWAYS THERE

Yesterday I saw a rainbow
And you were there
Holding on to it
With all your loving care
You're Always There

Today I saw a butterfly
And you were there
Holding on to it
With all your loving care
You're Always There

I remember yesterday
And the love I lost that day
You were there
Holding on to yesterday
You're Always There

What will tomorrow be
Tomorrow is today
A quiet night, a busy day
A rainbow butterfly
You'll Always be There

Copyright 1995 Francis E. Delaney   S-9530-DM

FALLING IN LOVE WITH TROUBLE

How do you describe your feelings inside
When your Falling In Love With Trouble

How do you decide what you should do
When you answer this
Your Falling In Love With trouble

I listen to my heart. It's feeling for yours
You listen to my heart and it's reaching for mine

How do we describe our feelings inside
And the answer is
Falling In Love With trouble   S-9531-MR

SUMMER THEME

Instrumental —Title for music only

Copyright 1995 Francis E. Delaney   S-9533-MR

CHRISTMAS IN SPACE

Santa went from star to star
Visiting the planets near and far
Then his reindeer climbed the chimneys of the stars
To the planet of dreams, Christmas in Space at Blinkys Place

Christmas in Space is where it starts
With all the children nobody wants
They took with them what was theirs on earth
A little glass of water and a little dirt
A bird, an animal, a flower and a tree and Blinky
And they gave life to their planet of dreams
Beyond the chimneys of the stars and the internet screen
So far away only love can see, Christmas In Space at Blinkys Place

So take a look at your Christmas sweetheart
If you can see, a little glass of water and a little dirt
A bird, an animal, a flower and a tree and Blinky
Then you got Christmas right here on earth
Christmas in Space at Blinkys Place, Is at your place

The nicest place you can be, where life slows down to let you see
Just how very nice things can be
Where the flowers meet the trees, the butterflies and reindeer fly free
Where love becomes what life should be
Christmas in Space at Blinkys Place
With all its families

Copyright 1995 Francis E. Delaney   S-9534-MR

IN THE WINTER OF MY LOVE

In The Winter of My Love summer's coming on

I walk the lonesome road
In this world turning cold
Till I seen your eyes that said, Hello
And your walk that told me not to go

I walk this lonesome
In my world full of, No's
Your soft and lovely form keeps me warm
Summer sun upon a winter storm

As the winter of my life begins to show
I hear your thunder and feel the heat of your day
For, In The Winter of My Life, summer's coming on

If I never love your baby things
With wedding rings and all those things
There will be no more tears from these eyes
For, In The Winter of My Love, summer's coming on

I walk the lonesome road
In my world turning cold
I watch your winter change to rain
And feel your summer coming on

As the summer of your love begins to glow
I hear your thunder and feel the heat of your day
For, In The Winter of My Love, Summer is turning on
You're turning On

Copyright 1995 Francis E. Delaney   S-9532-MR

WATER AND DIRT

God covered the earth with Water and Dirt
Gave it sight with the sun in the sky
Colored its nose with the fragrance of a rose
Let it hear the animals and birds in the miracle of birth
Gave it a taste of food from Water and Dirt
And a touch of heaven right here on earth
The miracle of His birth

Now, He looks at His masterful work and He sees
The miracle of Life washed away in Ware and Dirt
And the haze of the sky, reflects the rose that is scotched
From the wars that have discolored His earth
He sees the animals and birds that have left His earth
He holds His children who have died from eating the water and dirt
He sees you and me and He cries
For we don't try to keep the earth alive, with the miracle of birth

Now, He watches the beginning of the end of His earth
For each little baby aborted before birth
Takes with him what was his on earth
There's not much that we can say
But there is a world we can save
We can give birth to that little baby
For he is the miracle of life
She is the earth

Copyright 1995 Francis E. Delaney   S-9535-MR

GREEN TO BLUE

I place my love
In the care of Mary
And watch it turn from green to blue
From the eyes of Maureen who loved me
To the eyes of Mary that do

I place my heart
In the heart of Mary
And listen to its loving beat
From the heart that loved me
To the heart that does

I believe in miracles
For my love is now
In the care of the love that loved me
And in the heart of the one who does
For only she will know

The miracles of Green to Blue

Copyright 1995 Francis E. Delaney   P-9536-MR

SOMETHING ABOUT ME

There's Something About Me
In every thing I see that likes me
The birds and the bees, flowers on the trees
The stars and the moon and all the things they see

There's something About Me
In every thing I do that likes me
Working and playing, walking and talking
Something About Me likes me

There's Something About Me
In everyone I love, who loves me
Mother and father, sister and brother
Grandpa and Grandma and all the others

When I find the one who loves me
There's Something About Me
In the one who loves me
It's Something About Me that likes me

Copyright 1995 Francis E. Delaney   P-9537-ER

MINI SKIRTS AND WHITE LEVIS

I have seen many pretty things
Bumble bees in sunshine trees
Lollipops and tinsel string
In Mini Skirts and White Levis

You are all of life's pretty things
Your love is life's tender dream
All the things I visualized
In Mini Skirts and White Levis

Your beauty is in laughter's tears
When your walking in my eyes
A pleasure beyond love shy
In Mini Skirts and White levis

You're life's elegant times
My succulent wines
All the things I realize
In Mini Skirts and White Levis

Copyright 1995 Francis E. Delaney   S-9538-MR

EMPTY BUBBLES

Sitting at the country bar
Countless endless bubbles
Leave yet another scare
On this heart, full of empty tears
The loves that didn't last

As the empty bubbles disappear
The memory of your love reappears
In a little empty glass sitting on the bar
Full of Empty Bubbles

Sitting at the country bar
Her tears in a glass of wine
Her love has left her sitting in the past
In the glass full of empty bubbles

She drinks from the empty glass
All her loves in that glass
Disappear into the past
She is free at last

No more Empty Bubbles
No more looking back

Copyright 1995 Francis E. Delaney   P-9539-JC

TOO MUCH, FOR ONE NIGHT

I often wondered
What a woman's life is like
How many times does someone ask them

I'm sitting in this restaurant
Watching this waitress
Four different guys asking her

They didn't know, I knew you
So, I asked you too
What else could I do

She looked at me and said
Too Much, For One Night

I still wonder
What a woman's life is really like   P-9540-MR

BEAUTY OF A ROSE

When you begin to know
Someone sleeping in your mind
You see the Beauty of a Rose
Awaken in the Sun

Copyright 1995 Francis E. Delaney   P-9541-MR

SUN AND RAIN

The flowers and the trees
Need the love of the sun and the rain
Thier love is all they need

The birds and the bees
Need the love of the flowers and the trees
Their love is all they need

The moon and the stars
Need the love of their God
To hold them in place for all to see

A man and a woman
The love of their God
Holds them in place
His love is all they need

Copyright 1995 Francis E. Delaney   P-9543-MR

GOTTA GET BACK, To Where We Were Before

I ride the oval road
Every lap the track
I love you more and more
Loving you as I go

Slam it to the floor
And let it roar
Gotta Get Back to where we were before
And love you more

I ride the oval line
Every lap of the track
Faster and faster I go
Loving you as I go

Doesn't matter if I'm first or last
When I cross the finish line
Your loving is on my mind
Loving you more than I did Before

Slam it to the floor
And let it roar
Gotta Get Back to where we were before
One more lap around your track
Loving you as I go

Copyright 1995 Francis E. Delaney   S-9542-MR

WAITER, the

Why would any man want to be a waiter

I asked a Waiter one day

Why are you a Waiter

He said my wife is a waitress

She made more money than me

Now, she's asking me

What do I want to be a Waiter for, and

Why do you make more money than me   P-9544-CR

WHY DID YOU DO THIS TO ME

Why Did You Do This To Me
Tell me, someone else was in love with me

Why didn't you say it was you
Why Did You Do This To Me

Copyright 1995 Francis E. Delaney   P-9546-DK

WONDERFUL WORLD OF WOMEN, the

The Wonderful World of Women
The wonderful world of love
It's the way they look, walk and talk
A little bit of love or a lot
The tenth day of the month, to the last day of the year
Love fed by Gods loveliest gift
The wonderful world of love
The Wonderful World of Women

I can't right the wrongs I wrote
But I can forgive myself for loving you
You turned me on and never turned me off
Free and easy, you kept me home
Pajamas with no strings, a pair of gold rings
That's the way it was in the valley of love
The wonderful world of love
The Wonderful World of Women

God called you when your work was done
I can't keep that hurt from showing
Your love made my heart cry
From the first time we said, Hello
To the last dance in the rain, you gave my life, love
All the songs I've written and sung
To my woman, my audience of one
In The Wonderful World of Women

Maureen, (1942-1993) Thanks for loving me
In your wonderful world of love, The wonderful World Of Women

Copyright 1995 Francis E. Delaney   P-9545-MM

GLASS OF WINE

Do you need another glass of wine
More time, another love or mine

I need another glass of wine
To taste that love one more time

I need more time
To find another love like mine

You need another glass of wine
More time, another love, mine   P-9547-MR

THE WAY HE LOOKS AT YOU

I don't like the way he looks at you
You don't see him look at you
The way I see him look at you
I don't like the way he talks to you
With empty words that fool you
When he looks at you
Ask him why
There's no love in his eyes

Copyright 1995 Francis E. Delaney   P-9549-MR

RING FINGER, LEFT HAND

Don't stand close to a man
Don't hold hands
Unless you want
To do the things you want to do
With the one you want to do them with

Don't ever say I do
Its the wrong thing to do
Unless you want
To do all those things your mother told you not to do
With the one you want to do them with

When you say I do
You have a ring on your finger
Ring finger, left hand
You've been taken and been had
But look at all the things you got
When you get him mad

All the things you never had
All the love
All the kids
You would never have
Without the ring on your
Ring Finger, Left hand

Copyright 1995 Francis E. Delaney   P-9548-DK

MAN AND WOMAN

You Are A woman

I am a man

Give me the women

I'll give you the man

Your are woman

The touch of your hand

The warmth of your love

Loving your man

God made the man

And from the man

God made the woman

Man and Woman

Copyright 1995, Francis E. Delaney   P-9550-MR

STOCKING BOOTS AND TEDDY BEAR SWEATERS

Stocking Boots and Teddy Bear Sweaters
And the things you never say
There's nothing better than your love
In Stocking Boots and Teddy Bear Sweaters

I love, loving you
Love note letters and pillow fight feathers
And I love you, loving me
The way you love, loving me

Texas boots, mini skirts and white levis
And all the things you like to do
There's nothing better than your love
In Stocking Boots and Teddy Bear Sweaters

You love, loving me
Love note dinners in any kind of weather
I love you Loving me
The way you love, loving me

Stocking Boots and Teddy Bear Sweaters
And the things you never say
There's nothing better than loving you
And the things you love to say

I love you, loving me
The way you love me

Copyright 1995 Francis E. Delaney   S-9551-MM

DOES ANYBODY KNOW WHY

Can you tell me, why
It isn't easy
When you first begin to love
Does Anybody Know, Why

When you look through my eyes
At things you thought you would never see
Can you tell me, why
Does Anybody Know, Why

Can you tell me, why
I can see it in your eyes
Despite all the reasons why
Your love is still alive
Does Anybody Know, Why

Can you tell me, why
Should I say Good-by
Despite all the reasons, why
The earth is still alive

Does Anybody Know, Why

Copyright 1995 Francis E. Delaney   P-9552-MR

BOOTS ON THE FLOOR

Shuffle up and turn around, shuffle on down
To the music on the floor, step around

Pick up the pace, turn around, shuffle on down
To the music in your boots on the floor

Hold your partner on your arm, heels up and toes down
Step around to the music on the floor
Pick them up and kick them down
To the rhythm of the music on the floor

Pick them up and kick them down
Pick them up and put them down
To the beat of the music
In your Boots On The Floor

Hold your partner on your arm, boots up and boots down
As you swing around the floor, pick up the pace
Pick them up and put them down
To the rhythm of her music on the floor
Boots On The Floor, Boots On the floor

Pick them up and put them down
Snuggle up and turn around
To the beat of her music on the floor
Hold your partner in your arms
Boots On The Floor

Copyright 1995 Francis E. Delaney   P-9554-MR

MAYBE I WOULD NOT BE HERE TOMORROW

Maybe I Would Not Be Here Tomorrow
So touch me Today
So we know Tomorrow

Maybe I would not be here Tomorrow
So kiss me today
And we'll hope for Tomorrow

I don't know where life will carry me
For today is Tomorrow

Maybe I Would Not Be Here Tomorrow
So love me Today
Remember me Tomorrow

I don't know where life will bury me
So Tomorrow is Today

Maybe I Would Not Be Here Tomorrow
So love me Today
Remember Me Tomorrow

Copyright 1995 Francis E. Delaney   S-9553-MM

THANKS FOR ALL THE ROSES   1996

Thanks For All The Roses
Gods loveliest flowers
In life and in song
The bud of the rose
The petals that fall

Thanks for all the songs
Of all the roses I know
As I write their song
All the feeling, I feel
On the last note that falls

Thanks for all the love
That comes along
In each and every song
The tears that I bring
To the hearts that I have touched

Most of all I thank, Maureen
For the love of this rose, God called home
For all the roses that come along
All their words and all their love
Are in each and every song that I see

All the feeling, I feel
On the last note that falls

Copyright Francis E. Delaney   S-9601-MM

UNTIL YOU SAY I DO

You're the only one
Who can feel your love
In the heart of the heart
That loves you

You can't touch it with your hand
Or taste it with a kiss
Sex is only sex without it
And you never know, who
Until You Say I Do

What ever your status in life may be
Love is the purity of chastity
Everything else is something else
And you never know, who
Until You Say I Do

I never knew why, I never said, I do
Until You Say I Do

You can't touch it with your hand
Or taste it with a kiss
Sex isn't love without love
And you never know, who
Until You Say, I Do

Copyright 1996 Francis E. Delaney   S-9602-MR

XYLAPHONE

Your A Lot Of Woman
A real live love
Your real beauty
Is it's treasures
In the seasons of you

Your a Lot of Woman
In the youth of love
You are all of its zeal
Attractiveness, reveal
The seasons in you

All of these virtues
I find in you
Different sounding notes
My musical XYLOPHONE
The seasons of you

Copyright 1996 Francis E. Delaney   P-9603-MD

LOVE IS GONNA CATCH ME

Love Is Gonna Catch Me
A flower caught the bee
Once it feels its movement
It never wants to leave

Love is Gonna Catch me
A sailboat on the sea
Once you feel its sail
You never want to leave

Love is Gonna catch Me
In the arms of your love
Free from all the things that have to be
Love is going to catch you, loving me

Love is Gonna Catch Me
In the arms of your love
Free from all the loves that left me
Love is Gonna Catch Me. Loving you

Copyright 1996 Francis E. Delaney   S-9604

YOU'RE CAUGHT IN MY MIND

I love you always
For You're Caught In My Mind
My heart is loving
Loving your love

I love you always
My always is forever
Bright as the sun
Light as the moon

I love you always
Your heart holding mine
In the windows of your mind
You're caught In My Mind
I love you always
In the blood streams of my mind

You're caught In My Mind
Your love is always on time
For you're loving me, in all ways

Your always Caught In My Mind

Copyright 1996 Francis E. Delaney   S-9605-MR

OUT OF MY MIND

Mariola, marry me, love me, Out Of My Mind
Your real live love holding me
And I'll love you out of your mind
My real live love holding you for the first time
Out of My Mind in real live time

Rosiola, marry me, love me Out Of My Mind
Your real live love touching me
And I'll love you out of your mind
My real live love touching you for the first time
In real live time, Out of My Mind

Kiss me with your real live love
Loving me out of your mind, in live time
My real live love kissing you for the first time
Out of my Mind, in real live time

Mary, marry me, love me
My real live loving you for the first time
In my lifetime, Out Of My Mind, in real live time
Loving you for the first time
In real live time, Out Of My Mind

Copyright 1996 Francis E. Delaney   P-9606-MR

REAL LIFE'S LOVE

Sometimes you dream and wish
And wish it wasn't a dream
You realize it wasn't a dream
It was Real Life's Love

When that love has passed away
You sit and dream and wish
You realize it's not a dream
It's a real live wish
For a real life to love

Have I found a love to love in real life
Or is it just a dream of a wish
To find another love of mine

Sometimes when you don't understand
That there may be only one love for you
And the past, present and the future
Is a life long love

Real Life's Love

Copyright 1996 Francis E. Delaney   P-9607-MM

TWO HEARTS

Two Hearts

Running out of time

As they unwind to the end of time

They will always remember the wine

Your years touching mine

Two hearts

Kissing for the

Last time

Copyright 1996 Francis E. Delaney   P-9608-MM

WHAT WOULD YOU DO

What Would You Do
If I kissed you

What would you say
If I asked you

What would you do
If I Don't   P-9609-MR

ONE HEART

This heart of mine
Is running out of time

As it unwinds to the end of time
Will it find another heart like mine

I don't remember a time
I can't remember the heart that loved mine

A heart that ran out of time
It's tears touching mine

One heart kissing mine
For the last time

Copyright 1996 Francis E. Delaney   P-9611-MM

MARIOLA BLUES

No one knows you
Better than me
Your feelings running free

No one loves you more
By special request
You were born for me

I see you in my mind
Tasting the sweet wine
Warm beautiful feelings
On the window sills of your mind

The Mariola Blues, I wish were mine

No one knows me
Better than you
My feelings running free
On the window sills of my mind

Mariola Blues and mine

Copyright 1996 Francis E. Delaney   P-9612-MR

TURNED ME ON and NEVER TURNED ME OFF

When my heart starts to love
It never turns off
It will never turn you off
You Turned Me On and Never Turned Me Off

I'll kiss you on your talking door
If your heart wants more
I'll never turn you off
You turned me up and never turned me down

I'll kiss you on your hearing door
Ask your heart if it wants more
I'll never turn it off
It Turned Me On and Never Turned Me Off

I loved you with all your love I got
And heavens loving door was never closed
You turned me in and never turned me out
Turned Me On and Never Turned Me Off

I turned you on and you never turned me off

Copyright 1996 Francis E. Delaney   P-9610-MM

CAN'T STOP NOW

Life is the mystery of love
That feeling when you won
Even when you loose
Can't Stop Now
Life is loving you

Listen to your song
Every song is different
Every word is true
Can' Stop Now, loving you

The winds of our emotions
Are ripples upon the oceans
Everything I set in motion
Can't Stop Now

When you loose
Life is known you
When you win
Love, is loving you

Can't Stop Now

Copyright 1996 Francis E. Delaney   S-9613-MR

LAST DANCE IN THE RAIN

In love from the start
Through the joy and the pain
Until death did we part
The Last Dance In the Rain

.

I dance with your tears
Remember the years
The pleasures of loving
The Last Dance in the Rain

I dance and your eyes
Answer the question, why
Our love is still the same
The Last Dance in the Rain

I dance and your arms
Are holding me again
As God takes away your pain
The last Dance in the Rain

Copyright 1996 Francis E. Delaney   S-9614-MM

FIRST DREAM

It wasn't long
After you were gone
I seen you in a dream
First Dream about you

Dressed white with lace
Kneeling in place
It was so real
I thought you were there

In this beautiful building
We used to walk through
Stained glass windows
Statues all around

I was looking for my dog
She was barking at me
I went to pick her up
But she wasn't there

I looked in your eyes
I was going to kiss you
But you were not there
I woke up

Looked for the dog
She was gone
Before the First Dream

Copyright 1996 Francis E. Delaney   P-9615-MM

REMEMBER

A lifetime is the time
You spend together
Measured only in the moments to remember
The years between Oct. and Sept.
All the days with you
I'll Remember
My time in life, loving you

When our eyes touched our hearts
We know from the start
All the words of your heart
Roses in the wine
It happens in time
I'll Remember
My time in life, loving you

A lifetime is the time
We spend together
Measured only in the tears to Remember
The years between May and April
All those days with you
I'll Remember
My time in your life, with you

Copyright 1996 Francis E. Delaney   S-9617-MM

IT HAPPENS, The Other Part Of Love

How much can one heart take
How many tears to shed from my eyes
A love that ran out of time
How many tears must any heart shed
Before it loves again

It Happens, despite ourselves
Another love sitting on the shelf
When it Happens, all the loves
Come together for our last

When your heart is in love
You can see it in your eyes
I see it in yours when yours read mine
It Happens when the heart can't lie
Because the eye cries for its other half of love

The emotions of the past
Try to surpass the task
Love takes a different path
Love moves in and the other part of love
Fills our empty years at last

When you've been alone
And the tears have left your eyes
And you don't think it can happen
It Happens, for the eye can't lie
Because the heart cries for its other half of love

Copyright 1996 Francis E. Delaney   S-9616-MR

I'M NOT GOING TO CRY in my wine

I'm Not Going To Cry in My Wine
The tears in my eyes
Are from your heart to mine
There're all the reasons, why
The music of a xylophone
Is a violin playing in my mind

I listen to your music
Singing in my mind
Each little note a tear drop
From your heart to mine

I'm Not Going To Cry in My Wine
For the love that has left me
Has always been mine
From the first to the last
I have loved you all the time

There's a new love affair
In the hallways of my mind
Playing on the love strings
In your heart and mine

Copyright 1996 Francis E. Delaney   P-9618-MR

SUNDAY MORNING, WEDNESDAY NIGHT

Sunday Morning, Wednesday Night

Sunday Morning bright
Driving down the road
Turn to the right
Breakfast every Sunday Morning

Dinner every Wednesday night   P-9619-MR

WALK IN THE WIND

I can not see the wind

But I feel its force

I can feel your love

And I carry its torch

It's a Walk In The Wind

Copyright 1996 Francis E. Delaney   P-9621-MR

IT WILL BE BETTER IN THE MORNING

It Will Be Better In The Morning
When I am gone and you find this letter
Just another sad love song
Of all the things that went wrong
Your pick-up is gone

When you sober up
You'll find me no more
Just empty bottles on the floor
And I'll find I don't have to sober up no more
For I left my empty bottles
With you, laying on the floor

You say you love me
What good is loving me
If you can't remember when
Or what you done

It Will Be Better In The Morning
When I'm gone and you find this letter
Just another sad love song
Of all the things that went wrong
Your pick-up is gone

Copyright 1996 Francis E. Delaney   S-9620-JC

DOES ANYBODY KNOW, WHAT LOVE IS

Does Anybody Know
What love is
Ask me why, and I'll tell you
Love is love And only God knows why

A spider spins her web
A butterfly is not a fly
A sailboat floats
A rock can't swim
Love is not love
When you know, why

Love is love
When you know
How, when, where and why
Your love is like the spider
The butterfly, a sailboat and a rock
They all know, why

Copyright 1996 Francis E. Delaney   P-9622-MR

CHILDREN OF THE STARS

When The moon is out off sight
It's a beautiful sight
In all of Gods galaxies
Are we the only, Children of the Stars

What is it all out there for
If it isn't for
The children on this star of earth
To meet and greet the Children of the Stars

It will be in our history
In the lifetime of the little ones we see
For the children of this star of earth
Will meet and greet, the Children of the Stars

As I walk on the moon
With a galaxy of beauty
In all of Gods universe
Are we the only, Children on the Stars

As we walk on the stars
In His galaxies of beauty
In all of Gods galaxies
Are we the only. Children on the Stars

Copyright 1996 Francis E. Delaney   S-9623-MR

LOVE STUFFIN

Keep it up, keep it up
There's never enough
Of that wonderful stuff
Love is building up

If your figure is at six o'clock
Or a quarter to three
There's never enough
Of that lovely

Love Stuffin   P-9624-MR

LOVE TODAY

Love Today

Tomorrow may never be

Yesterday

Copyright 1996 Francis E. Delaney   P-9625-MR

LOVE IS PILING UP

When your over weight

What is that stuff

Fat

When Love is Piling Up

And you got enough

Time to say good-bye to the

Fat

Slim down and get trim

If you fall in love

Begin again

Love is Piling Up

What is that stuff, Love

Copyright 1996 Francis E. Delaney   P-9627-MR

I WANT TO LOVE YOU, but you won't stand still

I Want To Love You
But you won't stand still

There's nothing I can do
Till you want me too

First you have stop
And let the world stand still

When your world stops spinning
And love starts winning

Love me or set me free
But, don't stand still

I Want To Love You
But, you won't stand still

Copyright 1996 Francis E. Delaney   P-9626-MR

ONE WHO LOVES MORE

When loves has finally won
It's nice that there was only one
Now there are three
Which one loves me more

When love is all around
The sound of its music
Is the heartbeat of the one
Who needs you more

When love wins again
It will be nice to know
That there is only one
Who loves me more

Someday I'll find the one
Who loves me more
To the words and music
One Who Loves Me More

All the others
I meet in life
Will be the songs
I write about you

The One Who Loves Me More

Copyright 1996 Francis E. Delaney   P-9628-MR

COLOR IN THE RAIN

Colors in The Rain
The birds and the bees
The leaves on the tree
The deep blue sea
The golden sun looking at me

I look in your eyes
See the Colors In The Rain
I touch the color of your hair
Taste the wine on your lips

I hug you every time it rains
And in my hands I hold
All the colors in the rain

The birds and the bees
The leaves on the tree
The deep blue sea
The golden sun warms me

With all your, Colors In The Rain

Copyright 1996 Francis E. Delaney   P-9629-DA

BLUE LAVENDER

On a hillside, flowers all around
Two people on the hill
Watching the clouds go by
In a sky of Lavender Blue

I remember it's true
Two strangers in a room
Feeling a love gone by
In the moods of Blue Lavender

Every time I see a cloud, people on a hill
As the cloud kisses the sky
I feel your love passing by
With the touch of Lavender Blue

On a hillside with you
I remember it's true
Two strangers in a room
Friends now, with the Little Flower

Dressed in Blue Lavender

Copyright 1996 Francis E. Delaney   P-9630-DA

NOT SUPPOSED TO BE IN MY MIND

Your Not Supposed To Be In My Mind

Every time I read some ones mind

There you are

Sitting on the window sill of my mind

Your Not Supposed To Be In My Mind

I have not met you, yet

There you are

Running on the back roads in my mind

Your Not Supposed To Be In My Mind

Until I met you

There you are

In all the things I see near and far

Copyright 1996 Francis E. Delaney   P-9631-FD

MUSIC AND RAINBOWS

What does a rainbow
Have to do with music
It's the colors in the sound
That make the music

Every sound I see
Is a color looking at me
What color do I see
I see colors of love watching me

I see its colors
In the rainbow over me
I hear its sounds
In the colors I see

What does a rainbow
Have to do with you and me
Every time I see a rainbow
You're holding me

Every sound that I hear
Is a color of the rainbow
Touching me

Every color that I see
Is a sound of that rainbow
Loving me

Copyright 1996 Francis E. Delaney   P-9632-MM

I'M NOT GOING TO NASHVILLE ON THURSDAY NIGHT

I'm not going to Nashville on Thursday night
I'm staying at my place on Wednesday night
Gotta find out who loves me
The first one to show, is the first one I will love
The first one to say I do, is the last one I will love
Staying at my place on Wednesday night
Gotta find out if it's all my fault
When I could not say good night to your lovely sight
When I stayed out all night

I'm not going to Nashville on Thursday night
I'm not waiting in line for a piece of your time
It's just not right

Staying in my place on Wednesday night
I'll buy you dinner to hear you say
"It was nice the way it was on Wednesday night
Now I'm in Nashville on Thursday night
You gotta come to Nashville
If you want to take me out
It doesn't bother me if it's all my fault
When my boss and her boyfriend throw you out"

I'm Not Going To Nashville On Thursday Night
I'm not waiting in line for a piece of your time
It's just not right
Unless it's all my Fault, when you stay at night

Copyright 1996 Francis E. Delaney   S-9633-MR

SHE'S JEALOUS

She fell in love with me
In the Autumn of nineteen ninety-three
Her chemistry of love, loving me
She's Jealous, loving me

There's nothing better
Than the love of a woman's jealousy
Making sure, no other woman's love
Will ever satisfy me

She's Jealous loving me
Like no other woman ever loved me
There will never be another love
Like the love of this woman loving me

She's Jealous, loving me
No other woman ever loved me
With the love of the woman who loved me
She's Jealous, loving me

Copyright 1996 Francis E. Delaney   P-9634-MR

SLEEPING IN MY MIND

Sleeping in My Mind, pieces of time
Moments that unwind
In droplets of wine
Tell a story
Of a time and a place
The rose met the wine

Sleeping in my mind
The rose and the wine
A woman and a man
Touching hands in time
As the clock unwinds
Its little hands
Touching yours and mine

Sleeping in My Mind, pieces of time
Moments that unwind
Little hands in time
Holding yours and mine
Ticking backward into time
When your heart met mine
Their eyes looking at mine

Sleeping in My Mind

Copyright 1996 Francis E. Delaney   P-9635-MR

IF SHE WAS MINE

IF She Was Mine
I wouldn't have the time
To dream   P-9638-MR

SWEET DREAMS

Life would be good to me
If you were mine
Sweet Dreams, dreaming with me

Be My Sweet dreams
As our love comes alive
Keep me in love with you

Sweet dreams be mine
Your love will keep me sweet
For you were mine for a time

Sweet Dreams of mine
Your love, loved mine
For a yesterday of your time

Copyright 1996 Francis E. Delaney   P-9636-MR

IT'S UP TO YOU, WHAT YOU WANT

It's Up To You What You Want
That over there or this here
It's this or that
And that's that

I want this here
But I can't have it
I'm going after that over there
It's Up To You, What You Want

If you want that over there
Or this here
It's a glass of water
After the wine

Before they catch up with me
It's this or that
And that's that

Copyright Francis E. Delaney   P-9637-MR

LITTLE NASHVILLE

There's a country place
Once you have been there
You'll fall in love with it
Little Nashville is the nicest place
You would like to be

Their love is tender
Their love is sweet
Their music is country
Their looks are great
Every waitress in this place
Has a pretty face

It's love is tender
It's love is sweet
It's music is country
It's food is a treat
Little Nashville is the place to eat

Come to Little Nashville and you will see
Just how nice things can be
Everybody is waiting for the day
To see, Little Nashville
Playing in this place

Copyright 1996 Francis E. Delaney   P-9639-MR

OVER SPILT LOVE

When love spills over
It's just another day
In the life of love

Like a glass of milk, spilt over
You clean up the mess
And get a new glass

You don't cry
Over spilt milk
So don't cry
Over Split Love

When love comes again
Remember it's in a crystal glass
Love is a hard task
The top of the class

If you lose again
You have lost
Over Spilt Love

Copyright 1996 Francis E. Delaney   P-9639.5-MR

CROSSFIRE

Love is the fire in this heart of mine
Crossing the boundaries of your mind
A Crossfire burning between our body, soul and mind
Cross the line and you will find
Your love fire burning in this heart of mine

Love is the fire in your heart of mine
Crossing the boundaries of our mind
A Crossfire burning across our body, soul and mind
Cross the line and you will find
A love burning in your heart and mine

When the fire is burning hard, cross the line
Let the crossfire burn forever and for all to see
Our love is a crossfire burning across the breeze
As our body, soul and mind cross the line

Love is the fire in this heart of mine
Crossing the boundaries of this land
A Crossfire burning across its body, soul and mind
Cross the line and you will find
It's love fire burning in this heart of mine

Copyright 1996 Francis E. Delaney   S-9640-MR

ANOTHER WORLD

It's a different time in a Another World
When the winds of each
Swirl around in space and time
Trying to find Another World of mine

Another World
Where time and space stand still
And the silence of its wind
Become a another never ending love affair

Unlike my world of today
Now, it's just a guess
As to where and when
Love affairs begin and end

As another love of mine
Makes the world stand still
As her space and time
Fill Another World of Mine

Another World
Where time and space are one
And the feelings of our love
Become another never ending love affair

Another time in Another World

Copyright 1996 Francis E. Delaney   S-9641-FD

I THINK OF YOU

I Think of You
When you think of me
And I Know
Your twenties came and gone

I Think of You
When you think of me
And I knew
Your something thirty-song

Every morning of every day
When I Think of You
You made the forties
Before God called you home

When you made fifty-two
We knew it was a miracle
All those years that weren't supposed to be
Happened to you and me

Copyright 1996 Francis E. Delaney   P-9642-MM

RAINY NIGHT IN WARSAW

Rainy Night in Warsaw
Reminds me of the days
When Warsaw wasn't free
Some one else was looking
In your blue, blue eyes looking at me

Riding through the streets of Warsaw
With this stranger asking me
About your friend I never meet
And you were the only one free

On that Rainy Night in Warsaw
I could see that this stranger to me
Wanted to take your blue, blue eyes away from me

Rainy Night in Warsaw reminds me of the days
When Warsaw wasn't free
And someone else was in love
With your blue, blue eyes

On that Rainy Night in Warsaw
I could see that this stranger to me
Wanted to take your blue, blue eyes away from me

Copyright 1996 Francis E. Delaney   S-9643-MR

ANOTHER WORLD

words & music
Francis E. Delaney

VERSE 1: It's a dif-ferent time in an-oth-er world
When the winds of each swirl a-round in space and time
Trying to find an-oth-er world of mine

CHORUS 1: An-oth-er world, where time and space stand still
CHORUS 2: An-oth-er world, where time and space are one
And the si-lence of its wind be-come an-oth-er
And the feel-ings for our love be-come an-oth-er
nev-er end-ing love af-fair
nev-er end-ing love af-fair

VERSE 2: Un-like my world of to-day, now it's just a
VERSE 3: As an-oth-er love of mine makes the wind stand
guess As to where and when love af-
still As her space and time fill an-
fairs be-gin and end.
oth-er world of mine.

Copyright © 1996 Francis E. Delaney
P.O. Box 932 Frankfort, IL 60423

Nap-9641-MR-Ky
All rights reserved

87

FARTHER THAN I CAN SEE

Sometimes I look
Farther Than I Can See

I look across the century
And can't believe what I can See

I leave this verse empty
For I will be there

And I will look
Farther than I Can See

Will the World be there

Copyright 1996 Francis E. Delaney   P-9644-FD

ME AND YOU

I walk to the end of this century

And I see, It's still Me And You

When you passed away at fifty-two

You became cancer free

To walk this world with me

To do the things we couldn't do

See the things we couldn't see

Will it always be, Me And You

Or is there someone out there

That isn't afraid of you

Will someone take your place

And become a part of, Me And You

Copyright 1996 Francis E. Delaney   P-9645-MM

WHICH WAY IS LONELY

When we are here together
Every thing is money
Nothing seems to matter
When someone else is lonely

Which Way Is Lonely
Lonely is the way you are
When someone else
Is in your heart
Walking in your mind

Which way is love
It's in your heart
When your heart is walking
Hand in hand with mine

Which Way Is Lonely
It's the way to love

Copyright 1996 Francis E. Delaney   P-9646-DT

IT'S JUST THE WAY I AM

The thought of loving you
Makes my life worth living too
So when I do the things I do
It's Just the Way I Am

I am just an ordinary man
Looking for an ordinary woman
Someone who will take my life
And make the things I do

The things she wants to do
It's Just the Way I Am
I am a man
With the thought of loving you

Copyright 1996 Francis E. Delaney   P-9647-MR

HOW MANY TIMES HAVE YOU SAID, NO

How Many Times Have You Said, No
Let me count them so you know
You never said, No
It wasn't in your heart or soul
It was only your lips that told me, No   P-9648-MR

HAPP'NING

It's Happ'ning the thought of loving you
Make life worth living, the way that I am

It's Happ'ning, too true to be true
You're something wonderful Happ'ning to me

You're a summer breeze
In a winter dream loving me
You're an Autumn leaf
Leaving the tree

It's Happ'ning, to us
Every morning of every day. We love us

Copyright 1996 Francis E. Delaney   S-9649-MR

HURTING TEARS

You put the tears back in my eyes
The hurt back in my soul
My love back in my heart
Now, there's nothing to do, but missing you

The tears of love that loved you
Are now the tears that fall upon my hurting heart
As my lonely soul remembers
Your love from the start

Hurting Tears
Slowly empty the years you filled with love
Now, my love fills your empty heart
Waiting for your love to start

The tears of love that loved me
Are now the tears that fall upon your hurting heart
As your Hurting tears remember
My love from the start

The tears of love that loved me
Are now the tears that fall upon our hurting hearts
As our Hurting Tears remember
Our love through the years

Copyright 1996 Francis E. Delaney   S-9650-MR

YOU STILL LOOK AT ME

When I wonder, what love is all about
All I have to do is look around
With all your gentlemen friends in town

Your boy friend I have never met
A mystery to all, at six foot three
Even thought your long time friend is jealous of me
You Still Look At Me

The gentle man from down the street walking flat on his feet
He's head over heels in love with you
He doesn't like the other three of us
What he doesn't see, You Still Look At Me

You Still Look at Me, looking at you
I wonder what they see
When they look at you, looking at me

The gentleman from out of town
Fastest talker and the richer than all
Because of the way he looks at you
I can see, your just another trophy in another town

He's not at all like the other three
For he can see, You Still look At Me
Looking at you

Copyright 1996 Francis E. Delaney   P-9651-MR

VAGES BLUES

All the places I have been
Here you can find both
Just another day at work for all the folks
Who make Las Vegas work

A gambling town for love or money
Your a gambling fool
When you win or lose
The Las Vegas Blues

The chances of winning both are slim
But when it comes to love or money you can't have both
His money can buy your love
His love will give you The Las Vegas Blues

The chances of winning both are slim
But when it comes to love and win you can have both
I got no money to buy your love
I just got what you gave me, your love

The Las Vegas Blues

Copyright 1996 Francis E. Delaney   P-9652-BR

WARSAW BLUES

Wednesday night in Vegas
Isn't easy thinking of you
Reminds me of the days
When you weren't free
Someone else like me
Had the Warsaw Blues   P-9653-MR

ALL THE DIFFERENT FACES

Every time I find myself alone
I see All The Different Faces

When there was only one
Life was young and love was one

Now All The Different Faces
Are just another face

When there was only one
Life was good and love was won

Copyright 1996 Francis E. Delaney   P-9655-MM

SONG BETWEEN THE MOUNTAINS

Every time you love me, I hear your heart
Song Between The Mountains
All the things I love are in it
Up, close and personal when I am loving you

Every time I love you, you hear my heart
Song Between The Mountains
All the love you want is with it
Up, close and personal when you are loving me

The chill is off the flower
In minute specks of dew
The blossoms of your heart
In the Song Between The Mountains

Your heart loving mine, loving yours
Your love, loving me, loving yours

Every time I look at you, I see your heart
The way it looks at me
All the love we need is with it
Up Close and personal our Song Between The Mountains

Copyright 1996 Francis E. Delaney   S-9657-MM

IS IT OVER

Just tell me. Is It Over
And I will go away

To places I have never been
To love affairs you kept away

Is It Over, when life goes on
Someone else takes your place

Is It Over, when a life time
In a short time is a love forever

Is It Over, when the way it was
Will be forever

Is It Over, when your new love
Remembers me forever   P-9654-MR

I FORGIVE MYSELF FOR LOVING YOU

I Forgive Myself For Loving You
I want to thank you for your heart
The way it looks at me
Up, close and personal
When you are waiting on me

Copyright 1996 Francis E. Delaney   P-9656-MR

LIGHTS OF NEVADA

The look in your eye
Is a diamond in the sky
A mirror of the stars in my eyes
The Lights of Nevada, roaming the night
Flashing lights, flickering stars dance in my mind
To the beat of the music I see
In the Lights Of Nevada, loving the night   P-9658-SR

COUNTRY MUSIC

It was a country show
For the young and the old

Maybe it will be the only one
There may be no more

There ain't nobody
Walking out there any more

Only time will remember you, me and
The Legends of Country Music

Copyright 1996 Francis E. Delaney   P-9659-BR

SUN BURN

Took a walk in the desert
Temperature, one hundred fourteen
Sun burning on the desert
Sun Burn in my heart
For a heart that stopped   Nap-9660-MM

BOTTLE OF HONEY, we are still together

You wonder why love is the way it is.
Some people stay together
Some go their separate ways

We are still together
Holding on to each other
Through good times and bad

We are still together despite it all
All the men that wanted you
All the women wanting me

Our love is forever, for it's made from love
Like a Bottle Of Honey
We are still together

Copyright 1996 Francis E. Delaney   P-9663-MM

ALLY MAY, I may never see you again

I may never see you again
But, then I may
You never can tell
When love comes to stay
Ally May

We may never meet again
Like the Legends of Country Music
And the Beverly Hill Billy's
I'll see you again. Ally May

Your picture is talking to me
For on the screen or in person
You are as natural as can be

Your in a picture with me
So, no one can say
I never met, Ally May

Copyright 1996 Francis E. Delaney   P-9661-DD-AM

PAIR OF WHITE LEVIS

Sitting by a slot machine
A Pair of White Levis

I asked her
What she would like to do

She said, Nothing with you
I don't want to lose to you, too

She put a quarter in the slot
Got four hundred quarters in the pot

She turned around and said
What would you like to do

I said, I thought you were someone else
I don't want to lose to you, too

Copyright 1996 Francis E. Delaney   P-9662-SR

SUMMER CAT

Amongst the cotton tail
And the tumble weed
There's a cactus desert flower
I call Summer Cat

I'm like the tumble weed
Running on the sand with the desert wind
Caught in the arms of a cactus flower
Are you Summer Cat

Like the Summer Cat flower
Your beauty is unique, one of a kind
A snowflake on the desert
A flower in the sand
Are you Summer Cat

In the sea of sand
The summer cat flower is like
A sailboat on the sea, alone but not alone
For in the land and on the sea
Is the love of both
The flower and the boat

You and me in words that float to the
Music of the flower in the sand, Summer Cat

Copyright Francis E. Delaney   P-9664-MR

DON'T EVER LET ME LOOSE AGAIN

When you find that love that found you
And you know there's no one else
Don't ever let it look for love again
Don't ever let it loose again

Don't Ever Let Me Loose Again
For with out your love to hold me
It isn't easy to walk away
When someone else wants to play

She had different ways
In all the things one would say
In all the ways she cared
And when she loved me

She said,
"Don't Ever Let Me Loose Again"

Now, I'm looking for that love
I may never find again
But if I do, I will say
Don't Ever Let Me Loose Again

Copyright 1996 Francis E. Delaney   P-9665-MM

TOO MUCH HEARTACHE

Too Much Heartache in this heart of mine
Time to turn it around and let it love again
And as its tears unwind
They fall to love, one more time

Too Much Heartache in this life of mine
Time to turn it around and let it love again
And as its tears re-wind
They climb to love one more time

Too Much Heartache
In too many tears
Now it's time for too much love
In too few years

I don't want to be anybody's heartache
So when I love you and I am gone
Let your tears climb, to love one more time

Too Much Heartache in this love of mine
Time to turn it around and let love, love again
And as its love re-winds
Will someone find it in time

Too Much Heartache in two many years
Now it's time for too much love in too few years

Copyright 1996 Francis E. Delaney   S-9666-BR

OUT OF MONEY, FULL OF DREAMS

Out of Money, Full Of Dreams
We are in love
Out of money
You're my dreams

Now we know, Why
The words and music sing
For the love of both
Was in the heart of you and me   P-9667-MM

NOW, I KNOW WHY

As the days and nights go by
The music of the stars begins
Which one will the Grammy sing
As the sun and the moon pass by
The music of our years is here
As the days and the months become years
You're the music in the song
Which words will the Grammy sing to your music
Now, I Know Why

Copyright 1996 Francis E. Delaney   P-9668-FD

ROLL OF THE DICE

Roll the dice on the boat of Chance
Play blackjack once or twice

The slot machines may pay you back
It's the Roll of The Dice

Roll the dice in the game of life
Have heartache once or twice

Saying I do, may pay you back
It's the Roll of the Dice

When you have a love that last
No questions asked

Roll the dice in the game of love
It may last

It's the Roll of The Dice

Copyright 1996 Francis E. Delaney   P-9669-MR

FOLDED ARMS

Folded hands point to heaven
Folded Arms hold me
In heaven, the big sky   P-9670-SR

IF I HEAR FROM YOU

Time to never see you again
As you get on the plane
Time for me to forget
Unless, I Hear From You   P-9671-SR

SUSAN, Indian Sue

Straw hat, Indian dressed
Black hair braided on back
Black eyes in light blue
Saying Good-bye
To my last look at you

Copyright 1996 Francis E. Delaney   P-9672-SR

CHECK OUT, Your Boots

Check out time has come and gone
Your boots and mine
Walking to the time
When your world met mine   P-1973-SR

YOU'RE SPECIAL, ANYWAY

Where ever you go, what ever you do
I'll Always remember the day it was you

The look your eye as it looked in mine
The softness of your love touching my mind

You're Special, Anyway I look at it
Walking and talking you still got the touch

I'll always remember you that day
In a moment of love

You made my day, when you said
"You're Special Any Way"

Copyright 1996 Francis E. Delaney   P-9675-NO

LOVE'S A PRETTY RIDE

Across the oceans of blue sky
In the valley of the clouds
Mountains touch the sky
As I look into your eyes
I see the sunset, across the southwest sky

In the valley of the clouds
I see my world running by
As the sun sets in your eyes
Will I catch up with it
Or will it pass me by

Across the oceans of blue sky
In the valley of the clouds
Mountains kiss the sky
And with Nikki by my side
Love's A Pretty Ride

I can see it in my eyes
I can feel it passing by
Like looking down between the clouds
My world's up-side down, Nikki by my side
Love's A Pretty Ride, through the Southwest Skies

Copyright 1996 Francis E. Delaney   P-9676-NO

DON'T SMILE AT ME

When your heart is in love
It's a song in your mind
A smile in time
So, Don't Smile At Me

Standing in space on a flight with you
Every time you smile
I'm loving you
Standing in space, no where to fall

Your smile is like the sun
Warms the earth below me
Your beauty is in the sunset
Holding me, Don't Smile At Me

There's only a few smiles
In this world that I see
Don't Smile at me
For I can see, you

Copyright 1996 Francis E. Delaney   P-9674-NO

GOT A LITTLE COOL

On the flight from Vegas to Chicago
It Got a Little Cool

Isn't it the little moves
That put you in the grove

All I did was ask, can I move
For I seemed to be in the way

Well the flight attendant said, No
There isn't any other seat for you to go

Sitting on an aisle seat
She kept running to me

Tried to keep out of her way
Got to close to the woman next to me

Flight attendant said to me
It's a little cool isn't it

Between two beautiful women
It Got A Little Cool

Copyright 1996 Francis E. Delaney   P-9677-NO

SUDDENLY IT'S SUMMER

Maybe it was just the feeling
In the cool of the flight
A love affair begins
As the flight of 889 ends

Coming into Chicago
The sun setting in the west
She says to me, don't go away
I got to return to Vegas on this plane

Suddenly It's Summer
In the coolness of the night
We landed in Chicago
She flies back to Vegas

In the lives of two people
It will always be summer
Maybe it was just the mystic
In the magic of flight 889

Copyright 1996 Francis E. Delaney   P-9678-NO

BLACK WATER

When the water is hot
What do you do
Have another cup of coffee
Black Water

It's one of the oldest medicines of time
It's life is centuries old
It's good for the young and old
It's not the coffee, it's the hot water   P-9679-NO

EVERY LITTLE LOVE

Looking down at the clouds passing by
Reminds me of every little move
That passed me by   P-9680-NO

YOU LOOKED BUT I WAS GONE

Didn't want to say good-bye to someone I didn't know
As the passengers boarded your plane, I was watching you

Didn't want you to see, your rainbow in my eyes
Standing alone, You Looked but I Was Gone you closed the door
I Looked and you were gone

Copyright 1996 Francis E. Delaney   P-9682-NO

YOU STILL GOT THE TOUCH

It isn't often when you see
A flight attendant waiting on me
Who is as old as me
She Still Got The Touch

All the smiles and all the walk
All the fears and all the talk
In all the ways you do
You Still Got the Touch

Your smile takes my heart
And your walk touches mine
Your talk makes me feel
Tears that can't cry

I look in your eyes
Their sun, sets in the sky
In all the ways I see you
You Still Got The Touch

Copyright 1996 Francis E. Delaney   P-9681-NO

YOU LEFT ME CHICAGO

You Left Me Chicago
At Midway airport
Waiting for the bus
To take me to my car

Now I sit here and write
Why didn't I
Take the rest of the ride
And return to love

I guess I'll never know
Why I didn't buy
A ticket to your love
For the rest of the ride

You left me in Chicago
I let you go on the plane
Someday we may meet again
For the rest of the ride

Every time I look
Southwest in the sky
Your smile touches mine
As we walk across the sky

Copyright 1996 Francis E. Delaney   P-9683-NO

CAN'T GET AT IT, RIGHT NOW

Had a chance to get at it
Everything got in the way
No time, no place
And some one else's pretty face
Can't Get At It Right Now   P-9684-NO

LOOKING AT YOU, LOOKING AT ME

You Look at Me
I look at you
Although you're gone
I still see you

I find someone new
I see you
Looking at me
Looking at you

Someday I'll find her
When your not looking any more

I will be looking at her
She will be looking at me

Copyright 1996 Francis E. Delaney   P-9685-MM

TEARS YOU LEFT BEHIND

You may never know
How many tears
You leave

You say Good-bye
Never see the tears
You leave

When good-bye is forever
You will never know
The Tears You Left Behind   P-9686-BR

KATI

Sitting at this country bar
Thinking of the way it was
And the way it might have been
Thanks for all your help

Life goes on
It's still the same
The lights are dim
Your eyes are bright

Kati passed away that night

Copyright 1996-Francis E. Delaney   P-9687-KW

MAYBE IT WAS JUST ME

Maybe it Was Just Me
But how can that be
When nothing goes right
When it goes wrong

Isn't it always some one else fault
Think about it for awhile
If it wasn't you
Maybe It Was Just Me   P-9688-NO

IT WAS A COUNTRY RIDE

It Was a Country Ride
Nikki left on a plane

Kati left me at the bar
It was the country in them

The lights are dim
It's dark in here

The sun is bright in the sky

Copyright 1996 Francis E. Delaney   P-9689-NO

KEEP IN TOUCH

Friends Forever

Keep In Touch

Like the sky above

And the earth below

No walls to hold us

No strings attached

No one to own us

No promises of love

Like the sky above

And the earth below

Friends forever

Keep In Touch

Copyright 1996 Francis E. Delaney   P-9690-MR

BE WITH ME

I understand the reasons
You will always Be With Me

On the day I asked you for a date
I didn't know you
You didn't know me
I understood why you didn't show

The second time I asked you
You got to know me
I got to know you
I understood, why

The last time I asked you
I seen you there
I passed by, left you sitting there
I didn't understand why I didn't show

When you told me
I understood, why
You will always
BE WITH ME

Copyright 1996 Francis E. Delaney   P-9691-MH61

EASY IN AND EASY OUT

You think you know
All the answers
And find you don't

Travel here and there
This town, that city
What is the difference
When your not there

Easy In and Easy Out
Each love affair
Comes and goes
Time travels on

When that time stops
You look around
See what you found
She's my way

Easy in and Easy Out
This love affair
Came to stay
Left in a different way

Copyright 1996 Francis E. Delaney   P-9692-MR

SAGINAW BAY

I found my love on Saginaw Bay
On that day, the boat gave away
And the bay tried to take my life away
I found my love on Saginaw Bay
As my strength gave away
I said the prayer of Saginaw Bay
To love my wife and kids one more day

And I thanked the Lord for my mother
Who taught me not to be afraid
Of the waves of Saginaw Bay
She saved my life that day

I found my love on Saginaw Bay
On that day I was saved
I got more love than I gave
And I knew I couldn't walk away
From the love I found on Saginaw Bay

I found my love on Saginaw Bay
When my love goes astray
I say the prayer of Saginaw Bay
To love my wife and kids another day
And I thank the Lord for my mother
Who taught me how to say the prayer
On the waves of Saginaw Bay
She saved my love that day

Copyright 1996 Francis E. Delaney   S-9693-DK

THE WAY YOU LOOK AT ME

Texas boots in mini shirts and white levis
And the Way You Look At Me
Telephone ringing and the pager singing
Fancy boots, ladies suits and cross your heart
The Way You Look At Me

Birthday suits in baby boots and high heel shoes
And The Way They Look At Me
Telephone ringing and the pager singing
Stockings boots, stirrup pants and just my size
The Way you Look At Me

I Look at you and you look at me
I see life and I see love in The Way You Look At Me

Dinner's on the table in doggie bags
Pumpkin in the window children in our bedroom
Telephone ringing, the baby's singing The Way You look At Me

Diapers a due, only Mama or Papa can do
Then it's time for a feeding or two only Mama can do

Dinner's on the table in love letters
Pillow in the window, music in the bedroom
Telephone ringing, the baby's crying The Way You Look At Me

Telephone is quiet the pager is off
Baby's sleeping and the cat is out, Now Mama's singing
The Way You Look At me

Copyright 1996 Francis E. Delaney   S-9694-MR

I WALKED THE STREETS OF NASHVILLE

I Walked The streets Of Nashville
On the internet highway
And I feel a love that walked these streets before
When She's Country was just the girl next door

When country music was a fiddle and a banjo
And bluegrass music played on the floor
Her love was young and far away
And She's Country was just the girl next door

I Walked The Streets Of Nashville
On the Tennessee Highway
For I felt her love that walked the streets before
Playing on the streets of Nashville, where she played before

When Country music was a banjo and a fiddle
And Bluegrass music played on the floor

I can say I Love You
By playing your song once more
For She's Country is much more
She's the grandmother of your song
A banjo and a fiddle and the girl next door

Copyright 1996 Francis E. Delaney   S-9698-DM

HURT

Pulled a Hamstring
That Hurt
Will It Ever go away   P-9695-FD

SHADOW OF A LOVE

No matter what you do
It seems to follow you
All the years you love
In the Shadow Of A Love   P-9696-MR

NO MORE BIRTHDAYS

Days come and go from rain to snow
From the words to the music
There's someone else
I will get to know
Someone who will know me
Someone I don't know

Copyright 1996 Francis E. Delaney   P-9697-FD

GETTING BETTER

The hurt is Getting Better
The hamstring is singing again
There's a hurt that doesn't want to go away
The silhouette of your love follows me today.   P-9699-MR

EVERYTHING IS ALL YOUR FAULT

Everything Is All Your Fault
When I look back in time
Every time I sit at Table twenty-seven
Every thing is all your fault   P-96100-MD

PRETTY AND BEAUTIFUL

Some days your pretty
Some days your beautiful
Your Pretty and Beautiful   P-96101-LT

ALL THE WAYS I LOVE YOU

Got a birthday card from you
Forgot to send one to you
You don't know, you don't understand
All The Ways I Love You

Copyright 1996 Francis E. Delaney   P-96102-DK

UNLESS I KNOW

All the things you say and do
All that you don't
Are all the things I say and do
And all the things I don't
Unless I know, it's there   P-96103-MD

BRANDY

Come with me on my ocean of poetry
My poems will always be
Poetry in motion with Brandy

And on this boat of poetry
We will cross the oceans of eternity
Where you will always be, Brandy

Brandy, walk beside this ocean with me
Hear the words it says to me
Its waves, moments of poetry

Gentle but strong
Weak but fearless
The waters of the world
Poetry and Brandy

Copyright 1996 Francis E. Delaney   P-96104-BP

CARING

Thanks for Caring
Sharon   P-96105-ST

LONG WAY HOME

With tears on your cheeks
You leave to go home

You may never return
To the tears you left behind

Either way you go
It's a Long Way Home

Home is where you were born
Life is where you love

Wherever you are
It's a Long Way Home

When there's no love at home
It's a Long Way Home

Copyright 1996 Francis E. Delaney   P-96106-MR

QUIET

Why so Quiet
For So Long
No way to Ask
When your coming back

What ever the reason
No one will ask
Why so Quiet
When you come back   P-96107-DK

VALENTINE

I don't suppose
You will be my Valentine
Sometimes you can't say it with a card
But you will always be my Valentine

Someday I'll put
All my little stories in a book
Sometimes you can say it with a book
You will always be my Valentine

Copyright 1996 Francis E. Delaney   P-96109-DK

FRIENDS ARE BLUE

When love has turned
Its back on you
And you don't know
What to do

When they say Good-by
Don't let them see your tears
Someone new will come along
And ask you are you blue

When your more than friends
You don't cry when you say good-by
Another world has left you in the Blue
Friends Are Blue

If you want to feel good
Smile on both sides of your life
For everybody loves you
When everybody tries

When they can't have you
Friends Are Blue

Copyright 1996 Francis E. Delaney   P-96110-KD

I WANNA FEEL GOOD AGAIN

I Wanna Feel Good Again
The trills and chills of loving again
Knowing I'll never feel down again
I Wanna Feel Good Again

Your love is unique and your heart is gold
I'll be loving you growing old
The smile on both sides of our face will be in love again
Full of the devil and feeling good again

I Wanna Feel Good Again
Live as life can be
Full of the devil and feeling love again
I Wanna Feel Good Again

Your love is unique and your heart is gold
I'll be loving you growing old
The smile that didn't want to smile is smiling again
Full of love and feeling good again

Known that no one will know my love again
Full of the devil and loving you again

Copyright 1996 Francis E. Delaney   S-96111-KD

REINDEERS CAN'T DANCE

Reindeers are animals that can't dance
In the movies they are prancing
They move about gaily and proudly
Having pride they are arrogant and magnificent
In the world of animals they are very fine
They are splendor, gorgeous and supreme   P-96112-AP

WHEN A WOMAN LOOKS AT A MAN

When a Woman Looks At a Man
She sees all that he understands
He can or he can't
She will or she won't
She does or she don't
For in that second or two
A man is shook and took
What does it mean and what does it say
When a Woman Looks At a Man

Copyright 1996 Francis E. Delaney   P-96114-MR

HAVE YOU A RING ON YOUR HAND

You Have Ring On Your Hand
A love in your heart
But the look in your eye
Asking why, will forever be in mine
In another world of time

I see the ring on your hand
And your looking back
For the ring on my hand
Ring finger left hand, is holding your heart
In another world of time

As time goes by
I wonder Why
Your eyes tell mine
You Have a Ring On Your Hand

The look in your eyes When you say Good-by
The tone of your talk
The way you walk
Tells me your in love
With the ring on your hand

You Have a Ring On Your hand
Ring finger, left hand

Copyright 1996 Francis E. Delaney   S-96113-MD

NOW, IT'S TIME FOR ME TO LEAVE

Now It's Time For Me To Leave
Another love affair of mine
And like the ones before
You walk softly in my heart
Blame it all on me
All that you did not do or say

Now It's Time For Me To Leave
For a love has come your way
Unlike the ones before
He walks gently in your life
Blame it all on me
All that I did not say or do

When it's time to leave
A love that will never be
It will always be
Looking for someone to love

So when it's time to leave
Go away, for there will be another day
When you will find someone else
Walking in your mind, and softly in your heart
Just say, its time for me to stay

Copyright 1996 Francis E. Delaney   P-96115-MR

NO MORE OF EVERYTHING

You don't know
What you had
Until it's not there

You gave my life, love
All that, and you loved me too

Your love made my heart cry
Last dance in the rain
Hour glass, no more sand

Life was a song
In melodies of love

My dream came true loving you
Can't keep the hurt from showing
Now what do, I do

Roses in bloom, in a picture on the wall
No More of Everything

Copyright 1996 Francis E. Delaney   P-96116-MM

DARK EYES

When I awake
I find the sun shinning
It lights a dark room

When I find you
I'll find me again
I know what heaven is
Dark Eyes in a dark room

You will make every dream
I ever had, come true
You will make them real
You'll give them life

My love will be in time
With your music in my mind

When I find you
You will find me
Your the light in my room
Dark Eyes in a dark room

Copyright 1996 Francis E. Delaney   P-96117-FD

WALKING SOFTLY IN MY HEART

There's gotta be a better way
For your feeling will always be with me
Walking Softly in My Heart

A feeling that will be
Forever with me

Every time a new love starts
Your love slowly walks away
Making room for some one new to stay

I don't ever want to forget you
So your love has gotta stay
Walking Softly in my heart

As another year comes to its end
Another love comes my way
Will you stay when she is
Walking Softly In My Heart

Copyright 1996 Francis E. Delaney   P-96118-MM

NEW YEAR, NEW LOVE   1997

It's a new year
And a new love
When the old love is renewed
Or a new love begins
It's a new love affair

It's time once again
To take your love
Make it what you want it to be
And if it lasts another year
It will be a new love affair

Make every year a new love affair
Old love or new
Your love will always be
Year after year will it be renewed
New Year, New Love

Copyright 1997 Francis E. Delaney   P-9701-KD

COOKIE'S SONG

When I first met Keri
Everyone called her Cookie
Never asked her, why
Perhaps that's, why
She asked me to tell her story

It was the first time
Anyone asked to write her song
And when she said
"I wanna feel good again"
That was COOKIE'S SONG   P-9702-KD

HAVE YOU GOT A DATE

Once upon a time
Someone asked me
Have You Got a Date

Didn't know what to say
Or how to say it
Never asked her for a date

Should have

Copyright 1997 Francis E. Delaney   P-9704-MR

I AM BLESSED

I Am Blessed with what I've got
Even though I haven't got a lot

I am Blessed with the children I've got
With the look in their eye
When they began to walk
When they started to talk
When they went to school

I Am Blessed with the children they got
I look in their eyes
Watch them walk
Listen to them talk
They go to school

When I hold them in my arms
I got all that I want
I got my children
I got my grandchildren
I got a lot

I AM BLESSED

Copyright 1997 Francis E. Delaney   P-9703-EL

TEACH ME TO LOVE

As I walk through life
Teach me to care
For all the people in my life
Teach me to know
The meaning of right

As I walk teach me to talk
To say the things I should say
To write the words that I hear
Teach me to know
The meaning of life

TEACH ME TO LOVE
All that you give me
Not, all that I want
All that you gave
I love all that I got

When you said
"I love you
Teach Me to Love"
I Got all that I want
The meaning of love

Copyright 1997 Francis E. Delaney   P-9705-MM

STOP PICKING ON ME

Stop Picking on me
Unless you're gonna be
The best that you can be
You can't play with me

I'm not just another guitar
So if I'm not a part of your heart
You can't play me
STOP PICKING ON ME   P-9706-CJ

SINCE YOU LOVED ME

When you loved me
Everything was beautiful
When you passed away
The sad beauty of that day
The music you left me
The words that I say
SINCE YOU LEFT ME

Copyright 1997 Francis E. Delaney   P-9710-MM

BLACK WATER LILLY

Black Water Lilly
In the middle of a pond
White water lilies all around
Sun shining on the pond
Butterfly lands without a sound

Black Water Lilly
In a vase on the wall
Golden frame all around
Picture of love, I knew
Shadow in the night without a sound

Black Water Lilly
In high heel shoes
Wine cup and lady bank roses
Peeking through lattice wood work
Of a black lace dress

Black Water Lilly
Loving the sun
Picture on the wall
Flower in the water
Love in my heart

Copyright Francis E. Delaney   P-9707-MM

SEASONS

As my eyes search the prairie
I feel the summer in the spring
And I'm waiting for the snow
To bring me winter once again

When these seasons pass
I'll be waiting for the fall
When all the green is gone
I'll be waiting for your call

When spring comes again
And the rain begins to fall
I'll send you a rainbow
It's the brightest one of all

And if you remember summer
When we met and fell in love
You'll see my picture in the rainbow
Signed with all my love

Wait for the rainbow
With all the seasons gone
And listen for the wind
It will carry me along

And if you remember summer
When we met and fell in love
You'll see my picture in the rainbow
Signed with all my love, to you my special friend, SEASONS

Copyright 1997 Bernice Rickey, F.E. Delaney   S-9708-BR

FIRESIDE AT NASHVILLE NORTH

Sitting by the fireside
Silhouette in my eyes
Your shadow from fire
Holding on to me

On a cold winter night
The lights were out
The fireplace burning
The feeling in my heart

This place was closing
It would be no more
No more of the music
The Country in your heart

I'll never forget
The last time you were there
Kissed him, danced with him
Said, Good-bye to him and to me
And--Nashville North

Copyright 1997 Francis E. Delaney   P-9709-NN

THINGS YOU NEVER SAY

In the wonder of the world around me
The beauty of its day
I hear in its midnight light
The Things You Never Say

In the miracle of the world I see
The twinkle in your eyes
The stardust with its twinkle, mingle with
The Things You Never Say

In the mysteries of the universe
It's oceans of stars
A love affair of its endless beginning
Your feelings
In the Things You Never say   P-9711-MR

HAD NO IDEA

From Country club
To the Honky Tonk bars
I looked around
And I have found
Wedding rings sitting alone
Waiting for someone
HAD NO IDEA, You were there

Copyright 1997 Francis E. Delaney   P-9713-ER

BEST THING I HAVE EVER DONE

The Best Thing I Have Ever Done
Was loving you the way it was
If you were here today, I'd love you today
It would be the best thing I would ever do

The Best Thing I have Ever Done
Can never be re-done
If your the one who loves me now
I can leave the love that left me
And give you all the love you need
It would be the best thing I will ever do

Can I leave the love that left me
And give you all the love you need
If your the one who loves me now. I can love again
It will be the best thing I'll ever do

The best thing I will ever do will never be un-done
If your the one who loves me now
You can leave the love that left you
And give me all the love you need
It will be the best thing you will ever do

I can leave the love that left me
And give you all the love you need
If your the one who loves me now
We can love it again
It will be the best thing we have ever done

Copyright 1997 Francis E. Delaney   S-9712-FD

THROUGH A LOOKING GLASS

When you hear a spider
And feel a bird
You touch a butterfly
And see its music in words

When you feel
Some ones feelings
You hear, touch and see them
Through a Looking Glass

You hear a spider
As it spins its web
Touch a bird
As it feeds by hand

You can listen to the music
Of a butterfly
You can see the words
Through a Looking Glass

When I look at you
I can see and hear
Your words and music
Through your looking glass

Copyright 1997 Francis E. Delaney   P-9714-MD

MAN IN ME (the)

I rode the open road
Tasted its dusty glow for the Man In Me
Seen the world from the darkest side of the road
Made of steel and bone
Fine tuned, motorcycle man

Two years in a full body cast with no chance
Your looking at a miracle
When your listening to me
Made of steel and bone
Fine tuned Motorcycle man

With her music in my hands
And a woman who understands
That loving a man made of steel and bone
Is loving a fine tuned man
The Man In Me the motorcycle man

With the will God gives you
It's a miracle what the human body can do
With a guitar in my hands and a woman who understands
The Man In Me, just how far the motorcycle man can go
Riding down the country road

Walking and singing the songs of the motorcycle man

Copyright 1997 Francis E. Delaney   S-9715-CZ.

NEVER DONE THIS BEFORE

Floating in a space
Tied to a cord
And in a sack
Never Done This before

What was that
I'm out of the sack
Slapped on the back and crying
Never Done This Before

What was that
It's out of a sack
With another one waiting to be tapped
Never done this before

What was that
Mama put it in a sack
First time I smelled that
Never done that before

Ever since I was born
Everything I ever did
I never done it before
I NEVER DONE THIS BEFORE

Copyright 1997 Francis E. Delaney   P-9716-GM

WHICH WAY WILL YOUR BOOTS BE WALKING WHEN I LEAVE

Which Way Will Your Boots Be walking When I Leave
Will they be walking away or walking with me

The band is playing, your music is on the floor
My eyes are looking at you
My boots ain't on the floor but my heart is dancing with you

The rhythm of its beat a fireside dancing
To the rhythm and the beat of your country ride
The music in your boots on the floor

I love walking and I love talking
And I love looking at you
I love loving you, love riding
To the beat of Nashville North with you

Country sliding to the rhythm of your Country love
A driving dance to a country legend
And we're going to play it again

The band is playing, your music is on the floor
Your eyes are looking in mine
My boots on the floor and my heart is dancing with you

The rhythm of its beat, the barmaids dancing
To the rhythm and the beat of Nashville North
The music in their boots on the floor
Which Way Will Your Boots Be Walking When I Leave
Will they be walking away or walking with me

Copyright 1997 Francis E. Delaney   S-9717-MR

ANGELS IN THE NIGHT

No More being blue
Not known what to do
When my Angels In The Night
Are sleeping tight
I think of you

For when I asked you, are you blue
Now I know what I want to do
If your in love with me, I love you too
And if Angels In The Night
Know it too, It's true

I had no idea it was true
Now, in my dreams
I'm holding you
With my Angels In The Night

Even though you're nowhere near
I can feel you here
Like my Angels In The night
Your always in my sight

As I listen to my song
I feel Good Again
Sleeping tight
My ANGELS IN THE NIGHT

Copyright 1997 Francis E. Delaney   P-9718-KD

GARDEN OF ROSES

Roses in the garden
Thorns on the bush
Blossoms in beauty
My Garden of Roses

Among the roses are,
Rustic dog tail curl
Regency blue bells
Lady bell roses

Cotton wood seeds
Buttercup flowers
Eggplant blossoms
Florida moss

Pink Vanda orchid in crystal
A flower forever
Blue Jeans on you
In my Garden of Flowers

Copyright 1997 Francis E. Delaney   P-9719-MR

TINY TEAR DROPS

Tiny Tear Drops
Little bubbles in the wine
Lost in my mind
Bursting in time

I hold on to your tears
In my glass of wine
In each little bubbles
There's a tear drop of mine

As time goes on
There's more bubbles in the wine
Lost in my mind, I find mine
And tell myself it's time

Time to find
One more love
One more time
One more wine

Tiny Tear Drops
In my mind

Copyright 1997 Francis E. Delaney P-9720-MM

GENTLE

Be Gentle on my body
And I'll love till the end of time

Be Gentle on my hills of love
And the valley of the little ones
And we'll play our song
On Gods instruments of love
As we sit beside the sea shores
At the foot of rainbow hill at the end of time

Be Gentle on my body, gentle on my soul
Gentle as a rainbow as it lays upon the sky
Gentle as a sea wave as it draws upon the shore
And I'll be Gentle on your body
As the rainbow hugs the sky, and the waves stroke the shores
Till the end of time

Be Gentle on my body and gentle on my soul
And we will love each other at the end of time
For when we find the end of the rainbow
The waves will have washed away the shores
And we will play our love song
On Gods instruments of love
As we lay beneath the sea shores
At the foot of rainbow hill at the end of time

Copyright 1997 Francis E. Delaney (68) S-9722-LL

WOODLAWN TAPER

The Woodlawn Taper is a rolling along
Singing his song, Mama Ain't Bad
The electric cop pulls him over to buy him one more
The Woodlawn Taper is doing his job
Checking the bars to see if his men are on the job

Bobby Tommy and Gregory sitting at the bar
Watching T. P. Psycho walking the line
As California Dave and the Woodlawn Taper
Tap dance to the Woodlawn taper song

Tall Tom above it
All watching T.V. sitting at the bar

The family Carr, walking to the bar
Because Dick won't tell them where he parked is car
The Rock and the Gear and the Wedge
Wiggle with Margie's Little bit wiggle
Dancing on the floor

Tall Tom Above it all
Watching Margie's little bit of wiggle
Walking toward the bar
Till the Woodlawn Tapers Last Call

(cont)

(cont)

Scotty's turned Country teaching the dance
To Big Boat Bob and Little Wolf
And the rest of Tall Toms boys
At Bruce's line dance class
Five-o-one at the Woodlawn saloon

Tall Tom Above it all
Squeezing Margie's little bit of wiggle
Sitting on the bar
Till the Woodlawn Tappers last call

T.P. Psycho has crossed the line
With the writer of this song
As the steel and wire band
Put the wiggle in the boots on the floor across the land

Tall Tom above it all, kissing Margie
Till the Woodlawn Tapers last call

No more alcohol
Tall Tom drank it all
What's this? Little bit of wiggle
And whose, Mama Ain't Bad

Copyright 1997 Francis E. Delaney S-9721-TW

DIDN'T I TELL YOU NO MORE

Well I was writing these poems
As fast as I can
They along one by one
And when she said
Didn't I Tell You No More
I had to write this one

Well I keep on writing one by one
Sooner or later I would write the right one
Little did I know it wasn't about Nashville and me
Well I should have taken your advice, when you said
Didn't I Tell You No More

Well I thought I'd write a little story
About a grandmother and her family I met
Her son's boat broke in half in a storm on the lake
Separated and getting divorced, he almost lost his life
Nothing seem to matter till I wrote their story
Three years after, they're still together today

His mother and me went separate ways
But we still listen to that little story
The song of Saginaw Bay that I write
When Nashville told me
Didn't I Tell You No More

Copyright 1997 Francis E. Delaney   P-9723-MR

NOTHING, BUT LOVE

You never gave me nothing
But, Baby you got my love
If your love is Nothing But Love
Baby, Baby, Baby you got my love

All the things we never did
Will be the things we do
All those things are only worth something
If your love is Nothing But Love

You got my love in the evening
In all the things we do
Till the moon sets in the sunrise
Baby, Baby, Baby, you got my love

You got my love in the morning
When I awake to see, Nothing But Love
All the beauty you give to me
Baby, Baby, Baby, what you gonna do

Copyright 1997 Francis E. Delaney   P-9724-DK

COLORADO BLUES

Met this lady in Las Vasgas last year
Reminded me of someone I knew
Said her name was Sue
She was beautiful too

I asked her where she came from
She was a full blooded Indian
Lived in Keota, in the Pawnee National Grasslands
Where the grass is as green as the sky is blue

Black hair braided, as long as her back
Her skin golden as a sun set
Her eyes were black set in light blue
Colorado Blues

We both left Las Vegas, same day different plane
I looked in the eyes of this beautiful Sue
You remind me of some one I used to know
Moe, looked exactly like you

She gave me her picture
Her eyes black set in light blue
Colorado Blues

Copyright 1997 Francis E. Delaney   P-9725-SR

MOMORY OF YOU IS ALL I NEED

The Memory of You is All I Need
The memory of the dreams
I had for you and me
Are now dreams of the love you left me

All the things we said and done
All the help we gave to everyone
All those things we never did
Are all that I will do

All the songs I write today
Will be the songs of Tomorrow and Today
The songs of Yesterday are gone
Take them with you, sing your songs

Now I write the first of seven c-d
About the people I met and will meet
As I write the first one listen to them too
When I finish the last one
You can listen to hers too

The Memory of You Is All I need

Copyright 1997 Francis E. Delaney   P-9726-MM

BOOTS ON THE FLOOR

Boots On The Floor
Boots On The Floor

Left foot, right
Right foot, left
Turn Around

Hold your partner in your arms
Heels up and heels down
As you dance around the floor
Swing her around, spin her around
To the rhythm of her boots on the floor

Left foot, right
Right foot, Left
To the beat of her music
In your boots of the floor

Slap your boots and turn around
Boots on The Floor

Copyright 1997 Francis E. Delaney   S-9727-MR

PERFUME WINE

When I'm blue I think of you
Your love is first in line
Resting in the perfume
In my little bottle of wine

Love and wine, mysteries of time
The scent of each is in my mind
All the love I ever need is mine
In your little bottle of perfume wine

As the perfume in my mind
Taste the succulent wine
Your soft and gentle scent
In my little bottle of wine

The star never shines in the sunshine
The rose never blooms in the moon-shine
Their love, there wine forever mine
In my little bottle of wine

Your love resting in the perfume
In a little bottle of Zinfandel wine

Copyright 1997 Francis E. Delaney   S-9728-MD

LOVE IS TELLING SOME ONE, NO

When a love affair ends
You find another friend
It's a part of life
Love is Telling Some One, No

Control your emotions
Don't let them know and
You will always be in control
Of any situation you know

The emotions of love
Run, high and low
Say, Yes and No

Be in control
You will always know
The reason why, love is life's love
Love Is Telling Some One, No

Copyright 1997 Francis E. Delaney   P-9729-KD

FOREVER LAST

Have you ever wondered why
Some things seem to last
All the things you remember
Forever Last

There's a first time for everything
Most of the time they don't last
They pass through your mind
Lost in time

All the things you can't remember
Are forever free from your mind
The things you remember
The love and the pain in life

FOREVER LAST

Copyright 1997 Francis E. Delaney   P-4730-KD

SUN DOWN

You write a new chapter
In the melody of love

Riding west on Illinois thirty
At Illinois Route forty five
I seen a rainbow in the sky

It was like a balloon
And as big as the sky
All its colors in my eyes

First time I seen a round rainbow
Sunshine in its colors
Hanging in the sunset
Riding west on Illinois thirty

Sun Down
Illinois Thirty at Route 45

Once I saw a round ball of lightning
It was big and it was blue
Dancing in the sunset
In my rear view mirror

Sun Down
On 151 street at Route 43

Copyright 1997 Francis E. Delaney   P-9731-MM

THE LAST ONE

You can see the universe
Looking at the stars you see
You can count them one by one
But you'll never count the last one

You look at the oceans
How many fish in the sea
You can count them one by one
But you'll never count the last one

A diamond is a star in the sun
Sparking all its beauty into one
And if it's asking are you blue
You count the last one

How many diamonds in the sun
You can count them one by one
And when you count the last one
The last One is the one you love

Copyright 1997 Francis E. Delaney   P-9732-MR

FIDDLERS WALTZ

Every flower has a star when it closes for the day
It's on a leaf among the flowers
That are blooming in the breeze
In the waltz of the violin, The Fiddlers Waltz

When you see a fallen leaf, watch a flower grow again
You'll see its love never goes away
It just closes for the day
In the waltz of the violin, The Fiddlers Waltz

A leaf falls from a tree, flower closes for the day
The leaf is free from its tree
The flower blooms again for all to see
In the waltz of the violin, The Fiddlers Waltz

When you look in the universe and see a star that only you can see
Are you the flower that closes for the day
And is loved by the star only you can see
In the waltz of the violin, The Fiddlers Waltz

When I look in the universe and see a star only I can see
Am I the flower that closes for the day
And is loved by the star only I can see
In the waltz of the violin, the Fiddlers Waltz

In the Fiddlers waltz, the fiddler is loving me

Copyright 1997 Francis E. Delaney   S-9733-DK

LOOK INTO THE SUN

When your love has left you
Nothing is the same
The sun is not as warm
The wind is tame
The rain isn't wet anymore
The sun has gone down

I look into your eyes
The sun becomes warm
The wind is strong
The rain is wet again
Tears of love
Look Into The Sun

Hold on to my tears
The rest of my years
I'll love you
Like the sun loves the rain
Laying on a rainbow
All the colors of its love

The loves of the past
Remind me of the eyes I see
The wind and the rain
My heart in a storm
I look in your eyes
I Look Into The Sun

Copyright 1997 Francis E. Delaney   P-9734-MD

PONY TAIL ROCK

If it's the shape you like to know
Tell her once and let her know
And if she doesn't say, No
You got yourself a rock and roll country show

When it's walking slow, it's country heart and soul
The Grand Ole Opry show
When it's walking fast, it's a driving rock and roll
Beatles and Rolling Stones

Which way does the pony tail walk
Is it country or rock and roll
Dance to the country rock
Is it rock and roll, is it a country show

Swing, sway and rock away to a new kind of day
When you awake and find that pony tail is looking at you

If it's the shape you want to love
Ask her once and let her know
And if she doesn't say, No
You got yourself a rock and roll country show

Swing, sway and rock away to a new kind of day
When you awake and find her pony tail is loving you

To her country rock and roll
The country rock, the Pony Tail Rock

Copyright 1997 Francis E. Delaney   S-9735-LT

PUT YOUR BOOTS ON, DAD

Country woman needs a country man
Country kids need a country Dad
Put Your Boots On, Dad
Dance to the music
In your boots on the floor

Put Your Boots On, Dad
You can always hunt or catch a fish
You can watch a rerun of a game
But, how many times
Can you let her charms in different arms

Put Your Boots On, Dad
Your country woman
Needs a country man

When she's dancing with someone else
He knows she's a country woman
Without a country man
And the beauty of her charms
Dance to the music in his boots on the floor

So, Put Your Boots On, Dad
Hold your woman in your arms
Dance with the music of her charms
To the music in your boots on the floor

Copyright 1997 Francis E. Delaney   P-9737-KJ

TOUCH OF LOVE

What's the magic of this place
Is it the mystic of loves taste
Or the memory of loves past
Is it just a dream or a touch of love
That will forever last

Now, it's time for me to do
The things I have to do
So the memory of my love
Will forever be a touch of love
In the lives of those who knew me

Is there time for me to be
The man all my loves made me
Will the touch of their love, touch everyone
How many times will love touch me
How many times will it be number one

How many of their songs, will be #1

Copyright 1997 Francis E. Delaney   P-9736-MD

TENNESSEE

I can see the beauty of Tennessee
Gentle slopes of the valleys, narrow winding roads
The old country home, blossoms on the tree
I'll always remember Tennessee

I can touch the feeling of Tennessee
For I can feel her music, the beat of her heart
The old country home, Nashville, Tennessee
I'll always remember Tennessee

Just a touch of Tennessee is all I need
Everything I see touches me
The heart of Tennessee is a part of me
I'll always remember Tennessee

When I look in the eyes of Tennessee
I can see that I have touched the heart of Tennessee
She's in love with me
I'll always remember Tennessee

Just the sight of Tennessee is all I need
Everything I see touches me
The heart of Tennessee is a part of me
I'll always remember Tennessee

I fell in love with Tennessee

Copyright 1997 Francis E. Delaney   S-9738-MD

UNIVERSAL LANGUAGE OF LOVE

Universal Language
Is the language of love
Everyone understands it
Everyone knows
The signs of the language of love

The sign of the eyes that look
The sign of the heart that feels
The sign of the things we hear
The sign of the touch of love
The Universal language of love

From coast to coast
From sea to sea
We watch in wonder
All the things we see
Universal language of love

Copyright 1997 Francis E. Delaney   P-9739-MD

WAITING FOR SOMEONE TO LOVE

Waiting for someone to start
To unlock the love in my heart
Waiting For Someone To Love

The love strings in my heart
Playing in the hallways of your mind
Waiting For Someone To Love

Waiting for someone to know
The feeling of the love in my heart

Waiting for someone to care
Knowing when we are there

Love's in our heart
In the music of love

Waiting For Someone To Love

Copyright Francis E. Delaney   P-9740-MM

WALK ACROSS THE WORLD

If I had the time
The things I like to do
If I know I could do them with you
I'd Walk Across The World to love you

If I had the time to see
All I would like to see
If I see me in love with you
If your world was mine
I'd Walk Across The World to love you

I'd Walk Across The World
Loving you in all the ways
You were meant to be
I'd love you around the world
As I walk Across The World

I do all the things I do
See all those things with you
I'd go around the world loving you
As I Walk Across The World
Loving you

Copyright 1997 Francis E. Delaney   S-9741-MD

TILL IT'S GONE

You never know, what you got
Till It's Gone
And you remember the way it was
And ask yourself, what went wrong

Another time, another place
A different face
And you remember the way it was
And ask yourself, what went wrong

You never know what you got
Till It's Gone
A love affair still there of a life you shared
Now it's Gone, what went wrong

When life deals you a losing hand
Close the curtain, leave the show
Say good-bye it's time to go
You never know, what you got

TILL IT'S GONE

Copyright 1997 Francis E. Delaney   S-9742-FP

LOVES ARROW

I didn't know Loves Arrow
Hurt so bad, cut so deep
That my heart doesn't know
How long my eyes have cried
With no one to wipe them dry

I didn't know a love so strong
That it would last so long
Keep my heart full of song
It would be hard to find
Another love as strong

I didn't know Loves Arrow
Hurt so deep, pain so long
And it would be hard to find
A love who would believe

Each love affair begins and ends nowhere
A heart without a song
A love without love
No Hurt, no wound, no tears
No love, would believe

That Loves arrow
Cut so deep, hurt so long
My heart doesn't know
How long my eyes will cry
Waiting for someone to wipe them dry

Copyright 1997 Francis E. Delaney   S-9743-FD

THE WAY YOU WEAR YOUR HAIR

I look across the room
Walk backwards through its years
I remember how, when and where
A moment that we shared
Changed, The Way You Wear Your Hair

You look across the room
Walk beside the moon
You remember the way it was
A time, a place that never was
Changed, The way You Wear Your Hair

Every time that I am there
Moments that we share
In this place and everywhere
I remember the day
You changed, The way Your Wear Your hair

A love affair that is always there
In The Way Your Wear Your Hair

Copyright 1997 Francis E. Delaney   S-9744-MD

HOW LONELY WE ARE

If I knew I could
Do the things I should
If I knew you would
Do the things you could
We'd never be, How Lonely We Are

It is time to find
No more lonely times
Take this heart of mine
And as its love starts
You'll never be, how lonely you are

Let your heart ask your mind
To let you love
This heart of mine
And we'll never be How Lonely We Are

The look in our eyes
When we say good-bye
The tone of our talk
The way we walk
They're telling us How Lonely We Are

Let your heart ask your mind
To let you love
This heart of mine
And you'll never be
How Lonely We Are

Copyright 1997 Francis E. Delaney   S-9745-DT

CAN YOU SEE, WHAT I CAN HEAR

Can You See, What I Can Hear
A voice on the wind when you are near
What color is the wind
The wind has no color it can not be seen
It is soft, it is warm, it's gentle, it is strong
The voice of a song singing on the wind

Can You See, What I Hear
The voice of a storm, thunder in the wind
What color is thunder
Thunder has no color it can not be seen

Can You See, What I Hear
A voice on the wind singing I love you
What color is love, love has no color
It can not be seen
It's the roll of the dice, snake eyes looking twice
It is wise, it is shy looking in your eyes

Love is soft, it is warm, it is right or it is wrong
Feelings that are strong, tender in a storm
It is good, it is sad, it's feelings for a love
You can see and hear in the touch of tears

All things we can not see
Yet, love draws there picture
In the voice of its song
Singing on the wind, Can You See, What I Hear

Copyright 1997 Francis E. Delaney   S-9746-LD

WINDOWS OF CHRISTMAS

The Windows of Christmas light my shades tonight
With the sights and sounds of a country Christmas night
In a Santa Claus suit and a long white beard
A built-in pillow front and rear
His smile is bright, his eyes the Windows of Christmas
That light my shades tonight

The dog is a-barking, the cat's in the bird cage
The kids are in bed. The turkey is asleep
The tree is aglow and I am too
I'm gonna go crazy tonight
I'm gonna to love my Santa tonight

If you never love anyone, you gotta love Santa Claus
If it all didn't happen, I would have never met you
This pretty place, your Windows of Christmas shining bright
In the eyes of the children on a country Christmas day

The cat's in the dog house, the dog is a barking
The kids are awake. The turkey dressed
The oven is a—Go—and I am too
I'm gonna go crazy tonight
I'm gonna love my Santa tonight

He's the Window of Christmas
That lights our shades at night
With the sights and sounds of a country Christmas night
If you never loved anyone you gotta love Santa Claus

Copyright 1997 Francis E. Delaney   S-9747-MG

SHE'S NOT YOURS, SHE'S MINE

When you leave her alone too long
Someone else will sing your song
She's Not Yours, She's Mine

When she talks about you
There's no spark in her life
No pep in her step
Her eyes don't smile
You left her alone too long

When I sing your song to her
She's Not Yours, She's Mine

I'm the spark in her life
The pep in her step
The smile in her eyes
She's fallen in love with me

There's nothing you can do
You left her alone too long
When I sing her song
She's Not Yours, She's Mine

Copyright 1997 Francis E. Delaney   P-9748-LT

LINDA JO   1998

Linda Jo, Linda Jo
The look that took a second or two
Is a look that will last forever
What does it mean and what does it say

Linda Jo, Linda Jo
I'd hold you in my arms
And every time you say, Look at me
Our love would be like it never was
More than it ever was, Linda Jo

Linda Jo, Linda Jo
The dance that took a minute or two
Is a dance that will last forever
What did it mean and what did it say
Of a love that can only be, Linda Jo

Linda Jo, Linda Jo
When your charms are in someone else's arms
I'd find the time to keep them mine
No one else would be closer than me to, Linda Jo

Linda Jo, Linda Jo
The look that took a second or two
Is a look that lasts forever
What does it mean and what do you say
Of a love that can only be, Linda Jo

Linda Jo, Linda Jo, When I look at you, Look at me

Copyright 1998 Francis E. Delaney   S-9801-LT

LOADS OF LOVE

I was riding my sixteen wheel truck
Stopped for an angel on the road
She sat next to me
I asked her where she came from
And this is what she said

I came from heaven
But I went through hell to get there
My love is like a load of post holes
An empty truck looking for a load of love

When you ask, I'll love you
Like I'd never love again
Keep your wheels spinning
Hauling loads of love

It's time I put my love
In the arms of the man I love

When he's in my arms
He will be in heaven
He went through hell to get there
Hauling LOADS OF LOVE

Copyright 1998 Francis E. Delaney   P-9802-MD

CHERRY BLUE

When I seen you in Cherry Blue
It was the first time
You were the way you are
As we danced to the swing of things
I placed my love in care of you

Why did you leave, you knew it was true
Where did you go, I looked for you
Your glass was empty
My love was full and in care of you

The cherry red wine in the glass was mine
Placed in care of you
My heart is blue
Love changed it from cherry red to Cherry Blue

Why did you leave, you knew it was true
Where did you go, I looked for you
Your glass was empty
My love was full and in care of you

The cherry red wine in the glass is mine
Placed in care of you
Our hearts are blue
Love changed them from cherry red to Cherry Blue

Love changed, from cherry red
To CHERRY BLUE

Copyright 1998 Francis E. Delaney   S-9803-KD

WALKING BOTTLE (motorcycle man)

I used to be as bad as bad could be
Before a broken back, the life it took from me
Now I'm on my feet again, motorcycle man loves again

I'll never be as bad as bad can be or as drunk as I used to be
Motorcycle man is in love with the woman
Who found the lover in the man I used to be

My love won't stop till my heart stops
And the Walking Bottle walks no more

Now I drink from the Walking Bottle
For the pleasure of the woman loving me
For the pain goes away as I love
The woman who found the lover and the man in me

My love won't stop till my heart stops
And the Walking Bottle walks no more

I used to be as drunk as drunk could be
From that broken back and the years it took from me
Now I'm on my feet again drinking from that bottle again

I drink from the walking bottle
For the pleasure of the woman loving me
For the pain goes away as I love
The woman who found the lover and the man in me

My love won't stop till my heart stops
And the Motorcycle man loves no more

Copyright 1998 Francis E. Delaney   S-9804-CZ.

TEACHERS LADY

Lady dances with her teacher
And she knows what she wants
Doesn't matter what people say
For she believes in what she has

Look at life a special way
When you love dance
You know no one loves you more
For you believe in what you have

When you believe in what you have
You look at life a special way
All that matters is another day
When you believe in what you have

The lights are bright it's clear in here
I look at you it's hazy dim
For the tear in your eye clouds mine
When you believe in what you have

All that matters is another day
I look at you it's hazy dim
The tear in your eye clouds mine
She knows what she has

The waltz of the Teachers Lady

Copyright 1998 Francis E. Delaney   S-9805-CZ

IF THERE WAS ANOTHER YOU

If There Was Another You

I think of all the love I've had

And all that love

Was the best I ever had

But when you look my way

I see all the love I never had

If There Was Another You

I'd have all the love I never had

Now I roll out my mind

In this little ink upon this line

What would I do

With another you

Copyright 1998 Francis E. Delaney   P-9806-MD

HILLS OF COLLEEN

Of all the counties in dear old Ireland
There's one county that isn't there
The county of Colleen seven emeralds
And a diamond on the Hills of Colleen

You can see what I feel when your love is near
It is perfectly clear with the fire of the sun
Your eyes touch my heart with a spark of love

The spark is there in your eyes of love
With the fire of the sun
What have I done your love has begun
A fire in my heart from a spark of love

Spark of love, fire of life, I know when it's there
For I see and hear the beat of my heart
The fire in my heart from a spark of your love

The spark is there in your eyes that shine
With the fire of the sun
What have I done, my love has begun
A fire in your heart from a spark of my love

Seven emeralds and a diamond
On the HILLS OF COLLEEN

Copyright 1998 Francis E. Delaney   S-9807-CO

ONE TIME

One time I went fishing
With a stick and a string
Thought I could catch anything

One time I went hunting
With a cap pistol for a gun
Thought I could hunt anything

One time I went riding
In an old beat up car
Thought I could go anywhere

One time I looked for love
And when I found her
I found, she found me first

That love that found me
Is the love that takes me
Looking for that love again

When I find it
I'll find she found me first

Copyright 1998 Francis E. Delaney   P-9808-MM

I WALKED ON THE STEEL

I Walked On the Steel
High in the sky
In this building going up
It touches the sky

She was a part of this place
Wrote her name on the last steel beam
Picked up by a crane
Lifted to the top of this place

I Walked on the Steel
Her name on it's face
Someday when this place is torn down
This beam will once again lay on the ground

If there's anyone around
They will say
Look at all the names on this beam
Laying on the ground

What story did they tell 100 years ago
Is there anyone left
Who wrote a name on this beam
Is there anyone who remembers

The love of the names on this beam
Laying on the ground

Copyright 1998 Francis E. Delaney   P-9809-MM

LINES OF FORCE

You don't hear much about the Lines of force
There're the lines you can not see
When you call across the street
Watch a picture on TV

There's only so much room for the Lines of Force
There're the lines you can not see
In the internet of space the web that covers the earth
How many Lines of force are left

Too much air in a balloon and it burst
Too much water in a pool and it overflows
Too much power on a circuit and it trips
Too much pressure in a heart and it will die

You don't hear much about the lines of force
There're the lines you can not see
Like the big bang that made the universe
Is there a big bang that will take it from us

For when the Lines of Force burst

There will be nothing left

Copyright 1998 Francis E. Delaney   P-9810-FD

PRETTY ALL OVER

You're Pretty All Over
In all the corners of my mind
Rainbow on its window panes
Your smile prints your picture
In the memory of my mind, everywhere pretty

You're Pretty All Over
Wherever you are
Close or far, everywhere pretty
Everywhere is where I want to be

You're Pretty All Over
In all the moments of my time
Pretty pictures in the mirrors of my mind
Everywhere pretty

A thoroughbred on the blue grass of Kentucky
Its pony tail dances to its Tennessee walk
A pony ride on the hills of Kentucky
Maybe I'll be lucky, love Kentucky
Everywhere pretty

You're Pretty All Over
Wherever you are
Everywhere pretty
Everywhere is where I want to be

Copyright 1998 Francis E. Delaney   S-9811-LL

PUTTING THE PICTURES AWAY

I find it's time to leave
All the love I've had
With tears in my eyes
I kiss my love good-bye
Putting The Picture Away

As the years go by
Old memories fade away
In all the tears I cried
Putting away the pictures

You try not to remember yesterday
But, today gets in the way
Tomorrow becomes another day
Putting The Pictures Away

When a new love comes your way
The pictures of that day
Become pictures in a new way
Today, tomorrow and every day
Putting The Pictures Away

Copyright 1998 Francis E. Delaney   P-9812-MM

PRETTY ALL OVER

words & music:
Francis E. Delaney

VERSE 1: You're pretty all over in
VERSE 3: You're pretty all over in

all the corners of my mind Rainbow
all the moments of my time In the

on its window panes As your
memory of my mind Every-

smile prints your picture in the memory of my
where pretty pictures in the mirrors of my

mind Eve - - ry - where pretty
mind Eve - - ry - thing pretty

VERSE 2: You're pretty all

o - - ver, wher - - ev - er you

are Close or far Eve - ry - where

pret - - - ty Eve - ry - where is where I want to

Copyright © 1998 Francis E. Delaney
P.O. Box 932 Frankfort, IL 60423

Lap-9811-LL
All rights reserved

PRETTY ALL OVER

page: 2

be CHORUS: A thor-ough-bred on the Blue-grass of Ken-tuck-y Its po-ny tail danc-ing to the Ten-nes-see Walk A po-ny ride on the hills of Ken-tuck-y May-be I'll be luck-y, love Ken-tuck-y Eve-ry-where pret-ty

VERSE 4: You're pret-ty all o-ver, wher-ev-er you are Close or far Eve-ry-where pret-ty Eve-ry-where is where I want to be

© 1998 **FRANCIS E. DELANEY** all rights reserved.

SOMEONE NEW

When you find yourself in the eyes of Someone New
Just look beyond the things you can see and do
You'll find a world you can't believe, you loving me
The middle of this world burning in this heart of mine

I find myself in the eyes of Someone New
And all the things that be seen I see in you
In the middle of this world
You draw your picture in the eyes of Someone New

And I find myself in the eyes of Someone New
And look beyond the things I can see and do
I find a world I can't believe, you loving me
The middle of this world loving in this heart of mine

I look into the eyes of Someone New
No one's loving you
You'll find me in the middle of this world loving you

The middle of your world loving in this heart of mine
As you look into the eyes of Someone New
No one's loving you
You'll find me in the middle of your world loving you

Copyright 1998 Francis E. Delaney   S-9813-CO.ky

GONNA DO IT RIGHT THIS TIME

Gonna Do it Right This Time
Leave the old world in the past
Don't say her name
Don't mention the fact
Of a love affair that was always there

When someone loves you
You will know
You will feel
You will care
Nobody else will be there

When you find yourself alone
Because God took her home
When it's time to love again
And the new love isn't right
Just mention her name
Bring up the past and it won't last

When you know
When you feel
When you care
Gotta do It Right, This Time
Leave the old in the past
Nobody else will be there

Copyright 1998 Francis E. Delaney   P-9814-CO.

WHY NOT

Do I believe in my wildest dream
The best will be my last love
Who takes my music
To heights I never seen
To the top of the charts
Who will it be
Why Not, you and me

Why not be the best that you can be
Love the one you love
Why Not, love as long as you can
With all the life that you can
And take our music to the top
Who will it be
Why Not, you and me

I believe in my wildest dreams
Impossible as it may seem
One last unbelievable love for me
Why Not, you and me

Copyright 1998 Francis E. Delaney   P-9815-FD

RED RIBBON BLUES

Red Ribbon Hair, Red Ribbon Hair
Red ribbon here and a red ribbon there
It's the answer to how, when and where
I can love your red ribbon hair

Every day we say hello, we'll never say good-bye
For the time table of our love
Is knowing how, when and where
I can love your Red Ribbon Hair

You're Halloween honey, no money can buy
Sweetest treat my eyes will meet
Is when your standing there
Red Ribbon in your hair

Everyday you say hello
Halloween honey no money can buy
I'll never say good-bye
To the sweetest treat my eyes will meet

Red Ribbon Hair, Red Ribbon hair
Red ribbon here, red ribbon there
The time table of our love is when
You take that Red Ribbon from your hair

Red Ribbon here, Red Ribbon there
RED RIBBON everywhere

Copyright 1998 Francis E. Delaney   P-9816-CO.

DON'T GO AWAY

I think of the day
I may leave
The only words I can say
Don't Go Away

You touch my heart
You walk in my mind
When you love someone
You love me

Don't let someone steal your love
Just to throw it away
If you can't make it
The love affair will never play

With the love I found
Think of that day
Love me all the way

DON'T GO AWAY

Copyright 1998 Francis E. Delaney   P-9822-LL

ELLIE LORAINNE

As I look back at the good and the bad times
The people I met, in all the places I've been
All tried to change me with feelings of love
Except you, Ellie Lorainne

I'll always remember the time and the place
You made my day when you said
Would you like to dance
My name is Ellie Lorainne

Now I look back at the good and the bad times
The people I met in all the places I've been
All changed me with feelings of love
Especially you, Ellie Lorainne

Your special anyway I look at it
Walking and talking and dancing with love
You're a fine glass of Champagne, Ellie Lorainne

Where ever you go, what ever you do
I'll always remember the day it was you
When the look in your eye caught mine

Your special anyway I look at you
Walking and talking and dancing in love
Your a fine glass of Champagne
ELLIE LORAINNE

Copyright 1998 Francis E. Delaney   S-9822-EL

NEON WINE

The things that love has done
And all that it can do
I find there's nothing
That can't be done

Like the star in the sky
It's brightness in your eyes
Will forever sparkle
In your little bottle of Neon Wine

When I look in your eyes
I find all that shine in mine
For your little bottle of wine
Is full of all that sparkles

In my little glass of NEON WINE

Copyright 1998 Francis E. Delaney   P-9823-MD

THINK OF ANYTHING, THINK OF ME

Think of Anything, Think of Me
My name is Judy
And when they asked me
What did I say, what did I do

When you loose at the game of love
Never seem to win
All I could say
When they asked me

Think of anything and you think of me
For all that you can think of, I have done
But I still look for that someone
Who will find loving me

Is all the love I took but never gave
Saved it for the days
When they would say
Think of anything and you think of me

Think of Anything
Think of Me

Copyright 1998 Francis E. Delaney   P-9824-JF

OTHER SIDE OF THE ROAD

How many times have you read the sign
The Other Side Of the road
Everybody has been on both sides
The good and the bad, happy and sad

We travel the road from side to side
Sometimes we don't know, why
It's hard to decide
What is right for some
Is wrong for others

Both sides of the road have many streets
Each with it's own name and place
What ever your address may be
There's always a sign
On the Other Side of the Road

If we walk a straight line
Down the middle of the road
What does the sign say
If you know where you're going
"Go straight ahead"

Copyright 1998 Francis E. Delaney   P-9817-CO.

FEEL ME DIFFERENT

God covered the earth with water and dirt
Sprinkled it with laughter and tears
On mountains of hopes and fears
All the feelings I have felt, and all that I ever will
You Feel Me Different, you're all the feelings I ever felt
And all that I never will, till you Feel Me Different

God colored the earth with flowers and trees
Gave food from water and dirt
To the animals and me, with feelings of love
All that God has ever done and all that He ever will do
You Feel Me Different, you're all the things I'll ever do
And all that I never will, till you Feel Me Different

All that I ever was and all that I will ever be
You Feel Me Different, for you're all that I'll ever be
And all that I never will, till you Feel Me Different

God made the earth and all that you see
Gave it to the birds and the bees, you and me
All that God has ever done and all that He will ever do
You Feel Me Different, with the music in your words

All that I ever was and all that I will ever be
You Feel me different, For your all that I'll ever be
And all that I never will, till You Feel Me Different

Copyright 1998 Francis E. Delaney   S-9818-CO.KY

TEXAS DOUBLE-TWO

Last time I saw the Texas Double-Two
The floor was crowded and the music was loud
There, in the middle of the crowd
Was Jenny dancing the Texas Double-Two

That might sound strange to you
But, Jenny was the one I knew
A waitress from Chicago
Dancing the Texas Double-Two

Sitting at the airport waiting for the plane
Young lady passes by and says Hello
My friend says, where do you know her from
I said, never seen her before, just a friendly, Hello

When I looked up again
Jenny was coming down the corridor
She said, Hello Frank, How is everything
I said fine. She said, See you in Chicago

I won't mention my friends name
She may read this someday
And remember what she said

"I suppose you don't know her either
She called you Frank in Chicago"

Copyright 1998 Francis E. Delaney   P-9819-JW

CORNER OF YOUR EYE

I can see it in your eye
Feel it in mine
It's the tear that never shows
In The Corner of Your Eye

When I think of all the loves
Your best I never had
When you look my way
Love is in the Corner of Your eye

I can hear it in your voice
Feel it in mine
As your beauty says good-bye
From the Corner of Your eye

What you feel in your heart
Comes from your eyes
If you see it in mine
Your love is in all the corners of my mind

When I think of all the loves I've had
You're the best I never had
When you look my way
Love is in the Corner of Your eye

I can see it in yours
You can see it in mine

Copyright 1998 Francis E. Delaney   S-9820-JT

ECSTASY

Ecstasy, beyond all we can restrain
An uncontrolled emotion
A mystic trance of the mind
A powerful emotional feeling

It is a word that describes love
All of its joy, all of its fear
A rapture into delight
A swoon in the light of the moon

Love is all of this word
Its beyond joy, a immense bliss
It's all we give and all we take
That lifts us out of ourselves

Into one Ecstasy of love
A frenzied of feelings
Its the free will into the mind
Your love and mine

Was love in ECSTASY

Copyright Francis E. Delaney   P-9825-MM

DANCE JUDY, DANCE

Dance Judy, Dance.
Dance with the fiddle and the steel guitar
Keyboards, drums and bass guitar
Dance to the beat of the music of your love
Dance to the music of my band

Think of anything and you think of me
Win or loose, yes or no. You gotta have a little fun
You don't stop dancing in the middle of love

You don't stop dancing in the middle of love
Dance Judy, Dance. Dance with the music of my band
And love to the beat of my guitar

Love Judy, Love.
Love to the fiddle and the steel guitar
Keyboard, drums and lead guitar
Love to the beat of the music of your
Love to the beat of my guitar

You don't stop loving in the middle of love
Love Judy, Love. Dance Judy, Dance
Dance to the music of my band
And love to the beat of my guitar

Dance Judy, Dance. Love Judy, love
Dance to the music of my band
And love to the beat of my Guitar

Copyright 1998 Francis E. Delaney   P-9826-JT

MAKE ME WANT TO STAY

Rain on the window
Sun shining through
Rainbow windowpanes

This pain of love doesn't go away
Makes me want to stay
Take away this pain of love
Make its tears go away

Let me feel the way you love
Make Me, Want To Stay

If I could break away
From a love that doesn't want to leave
This pain of love
Would become your touch of love

Let me feel the way I love
Let me, Make You Want To Stay

Rain on the window
Moon shining through
Moon-bow windowpanes
MAKE ME WANT TO STAY

Copyright 1998 Francis E. Delaney   P-9827-MD

WHAT A PLACE

Everybody has a place
It has a special face
Times to remember
All the places and faces
That have entered this place

The years come and go
Like the faces I used to know
The voices I used to hear
They are all here in this place
Listen, and you can hear them say
WHAT A PLACE   P-9828-WI

KELLY GREEN

Watching the clouds go by
The sun returning to my eyes
I turned around and I found
Kelly Green

The clouds covered the sun
And I loved for that moment
In the shadow of the sun
KELLY GREEN

Copyright 1998 Francis E. Delaney   P-9829-KG

THE DEVIL IS IN YOUR EYE

I remember the day we first met
All the guys were lined up
Waiting for you to walk by
When I saw you, I knew why

I had no idea
I would be the guy
Who would ask you, why
Everyone's waiting for you to go by

There I was the next day standing in line
As she waited for the elevator
I asked her for a coffee break
I had no idea she would ask me, why

She asked me, why
I asked her, why

She looked into my eyes and said
Because, The Devil Is In Your Eye

Copyright 1998 Francis E. Delaney   P-9830-MM

WHAT TO DO

What To Do

Do I write about

Arizona or Kentucky

M.V. Arizona, is too fast for me

So I'll write about Kentucky

                P-9831-MV

SHE'S A LOT OF TROUBLE

When Arizona asked me why

I wanted to write about Kentucky

Instead of Arizona

Had to tell her

Arizona, is nothing but trouble

She's a Lot of Trouble

Copyright 1998 Francis E. Delaney   P-9832-MV

ROSES TO WINE

Look across the roses
In the fields of wine
There was a time
All the roses were red
In that moment of time
All the roses were mine   P-9833-MM

BARBIE DOLL

Barbie Doll, Oh Barbie Doll

You'll always be a friend of mine

When I think of you

And all the things I'll ever do

With a pencil and a book

I'll never have another friend

Quite like you

Copyright 1998 Francis E Delaney   P-9834-Malina (age 4)

THREE BOTTLES OF WINE

All the roses that were mine
Have passed into time
A part of history
In this life of mine

Now I look at life
And all that pass by
Each love comes and goes
A part of all that will be

When I find someone
Who has the time
To be a part
Of this life of mine

She's not in my story
Of the Three Bottles of Wine
Gallo Red, Rosey and Zinfandel
A part of history, a part of time

Copyright 1998 Francis E. Delaney   P-9835-FD

GOT IT

You Got It
The charm, looks and attitude
The toughness and the beauty
Of a love I once knew

When you tell me your taken
What else is there to do

In a storm the wind blows
When it's over it's gone
Clouds turn to sun
And you move on

I walk on the beach
On Sunny days
As far as I can see
You GOT IT   Lap-9836-CO.

HEART OF FIRE

Heart of fire
Eyes in love
If that's all you got
That's all I want

Copyright 1998 Francis E. Delaney   P-9839-LL

MAYBE SHE WILL SAY, GOOD-BYE

If she doesn't say, Hello
Maybe She Will Say, Good-Bye
For it's time for me to leave
This love I found
In a world I can't see

If it's time for me to leave
I will always see
The beauty of your picture as it leaves me
I will always hear
The love I was near
In the picture I can hear

The ribbon on a pony tail
Sparking in her eye
The love that was there in a world I could see
Is forever a memory of the love I was near
We didn't say, Hello
For we couldn't say, Good-Bye

Copyright 1998 Francis E. Delaney   P-9837-KY

ZODIAC

All the days are gone
Another year coming to its end
Look back upon this year
All the days are gone
Can you remember one

The days of the Zodiac
Numbered from one to twelve
Imaginary words of things
Deeds we may have done
Paths we may have run
Can you remember one

You wear a sign of the Zodiac
It reminds me of one
The day I was there
When someone said
He's flirting with you

I look at the Zodiac
That is what it told me to do
To fall in love with you

Copyright 1998 Francis E. Delaney   P-9838-KY

LET ME HEAR THAT AGAIN

When you hear a song
Call up the station
And ask them to play it again
No, we can't play that song again

Let Me Hear That Again
Why can't you play my song again

It's not on the play list
It was a requested song
So, you can't hear your song again
You have to make another request

If you want to hear your song
No, no, no, Never, never, never

Let Me Hear That Again

Copyright 1998 Francis E. Delaney   P-9840-MV

PINK ROSE, PINK WINE

In the morning when I see
All the flowers blooming
For the birds and the bees

In the afternoon when I see
The sun going down in the sea
A rose in the wine

Pink Rose, Pink Wine
You remind me of a time
Rose wasn't in the wine
She was there all the time

In the evening when I see
The eyes that seen
The flower and the bee
The sun in the sea

Rosey in the wine

Pink Rose, Pink Wine

Copyright 1998 Francis E. Delaney   P-9841-MR

YOU KEEP TRYING TO TAKE ME OUT

You Keep Trying to Take Me Out
And I don't want to say, No

I just say. You go and have a nice time
Every time I don't want to say, No

You Keep Trying To Take Me Out
Better watch out, before I take you out

Guess I better quit asking to take her out
What will I do if she says, Yes

I'll ask my little statue
Why did she say, Yes

What do I do, Now
Maybe someday I'll know

Why, she said
You Keep Trying To Take Me Out

Copyright 1998 Francis E. Delaney   P-9842-KY

EMPTY BOOTS

Thought I'd give you something to do
Type all the poems before I met you
And all that I write about you

Thanks for typing all these poems
And for all the time it takes
Someday they will be in a book
With the Empty Boots in your car

Still going to ask you
For where ever you are
You will always be in the
Empty Boots in your car

Maybe someday driving to Tennessee
On your drive through Kentucky
Listen to me
The Empty Boots in your car

Copyright 1998 Francis E. Delaney   P-9843-KY

FEELING IN YOU (the)

Alone in memory
Years of love

Tears still cry
Love still tries

I understand your eyes
When they ask, why am I shy

It's the way you are
In the mirror of your mind

It's the way that I see you
In the window of mine

Alone in waiting
Years to love

Tears still cry
Loves still tries

When you're shy
I feel, The Feeling In You

Copyright 1998 Francis E. Delaney   P-9844

MAY YOU ALWAYS BE   1999

May you Always Be my friend
For you will always be mine

Every time I see a cloud passing by
Rain falling, tear drops in my eyes
The cloud will always be a friend of Mine

Every time I see a flower bloom
Rain falling from the cloud
The flower will always be a friend of mine

Every time I see leaves falling from a tree
Rain changing turning to snow
The tree will always be my friend

May you always be
Like the cloud, flower and tree
In every one I see

They will always be my friend
For like the cloud, flower and tree
They will leave

Your memory with me

Copyright 1999 Francis E. Delaney   P-9901-MM

TO KNOW, THAT

To know that
It was all your fault
When I came back
Not known it was you

Writing my tunes
To some one else's blues
Week after week, year after year
Not known it was you

To know that
I didn't know
It was all my fault
Not known it was you

When she left, she said
Tennessee in love with you now
I'm not going back to Nashville
For Tennessee loves me now

Writing my tunes
To some one else's blues
To know, That
It was always you

Copyright 1999 Francis E. Delaney   P-9902-MD

LISA, YOUR MUSIC IS PRETTY TONIGHT

Lisa, Your Music Is pretty tonight
It's all the music and all the words
That describe what you are like
All the color I see in all the sounds I hear
Lisa, Your Music Is Pretty Tonight

Your love is aware that it is there
It's like we knew each other before we met
Like words and music of a song
Once together they belong
To the music of the night

Lisa, Your Music Is Pretty Tonight
You're all the music and all the sounds
That describe what love is like
All the colors I see and all the sounds I hear
Lisa, Your Music Is Pretty tonight

I can hear your music playing at the bar
As I write the words
The bubbles in the wine burst in my mind
To the music of the night

Your love is aware that it is there
It's like we knew each other before we met
Like words and music of a song
Once together they belong
To the Music of the night

LISA, YOUR MUSIC IS PRETTY TONIGHT

Copyright 1999 Francis E. Delaney   S-9903-LL

WILMA JEAN

Wilma Jean was as old
As the country bar that held her name
She was there every day
Till her last day

It was bad, bad news
When Wilma closed the doors
On a century of memories
In these old walls

These walls still stand today
In a nightclub of a different name
Another century of memories
In the new names on the wall

When I pass by these old walls
I'll always remember Wilma Jean
She always got her two dollars
At the front door

Copyright 1999 Francis E. Delaney   P-9904-WJ

LITTLE BIT OF WIGGLE

That little bit of wiggle
Is as old as the hills
From Adams apple to Noahs Ark
God's best piece of art

Take a look at the world today
That Little Bit of Wiggle
Is in every thing He made

There's a Little Bit of Wiggle
In the littlest bug in the tallest tree
All the animals, birds and bees
The flowers and the leaves

That Little Bit of Wiggle
When your walking away
I feel like Adam
Don't know what to do or say

Take a look at yourself today
That Little Bit Of Wiggle
Is in everything we made

Copyright 1999 Francis E. Delaney   P-9905-LL

AM I READY

Am I Ready to say, I do
I don't think so
I don't think your ready
For the love of, I do

Look at all those
That you will have to say
I can't, I don't, I won't
Because I said, I do

Am I Ready for the love of, I do
When I see that love
In you or someone new
I'll be ready to love, I do

Someday you will say, I do
But if I never say, I do
Remember the one who asked you
AM I READY

Copyright 1999 Francis E. Delaney   P-9906-LL

WATERMELON WINE

When it's time to love
Put away the pills
Throw away the doctor bill
Try a little loving and you will find
Nothing's better than a glass of
Watermelon Wine
Keeps your heart ticking, feet kicking
With the love symptoms
Dancing in a little bottle of
WATERMELON WINE   P-9907-MV

THINGS I SHOULD NOT DO

Things I Should Not Do
I should not fall in love with you
My mother told me she would never do
The things I should not do

Never say, Yes
To the things you should not do
Until you say, I do
To the things I Should Not Do

Copyright 1999 Francis E. Delaney   P-9908-LL

TWO THOUSAND YEARS

Through all of the years
Happiness and tears
Walking and talking
Living and loving
Through a small piece of time

How many times have I asked you
How many times will it be
Two thousand times Two Thousand years

All that we lived
All that we loved
In the short time of life
No other lives have been in love
Like yours and mine

To live a life that never ends
To love the one you love
In the life time of your years
How many times have I loved you

Two thousand times TWO THOUSAND YEARS

Copyright 1999 Francis E. Delaney   P-9909-MM

DO YOU KNOW ME

Someone asked, me
Do You Know Me
Someone said, No

You Know.
When you say Hello
But you don't know

Someone asked me
Do You Know Me
Someone said, Yes   P-9910-MH

DON'T LOOK BACK

All the days gong by
Is called the past
All the days coming on
Is called the future

Today, is when the future meets the past
Look into the future
Forget the past
All the days coming on are free at last

Tomorrow is another day
DON'T LOOK BACK

Copyright 1999 Francis E. Delaney   P-9913-MR

IT WILL BE NICER TONIGHT

I know we just met
I can't do it now
I'll play the music tonight
It Will Be Nicer Tonight

You were right
It's nicer tonight
On a lonely night
Your a beautiful sight

Her story was short
Single with kids
Her loves all gone

I said, Did you see that guy
Look at you
When you said
It Will Be Nicer Tonight

Her story is now
Her love is that guy
When he asked her, she said
It Will Be Better Tonight

Copyright 1999 Francis E. Delaney   P-9911-MV

THE EYES OF TENNESSEE

I look into the night
The stars in my eyes
Remind of the sparkle
In a glass of wine

Every time I see a star
No matter where or how far
It reminds me of you
My Little bottle of wine

The star in your eye
The sparkle in the wine
This very nice time
In this place I call mine

The Eyes Of Tennessee
Where she tells me
All the things she can't say
I can read in the Eyes Of Tennessee

Written as a poem
Someday they will be in a book of mine
Some are songs, c-d in time
Little stories from the

EYES OF TENNESSEE

Copyright 1999 Francis E. Delaney   P-9912-MD

MAMA AIN'T BAD

Mama Ain't Bad, Oh Mama Ain't Bad
With a little bit of wiggle, Mama Ain't Bad

Wiggle it right, wiggle it left
Wiggle it here, wiggle it there
With a little bit of wiggle, wiggle what's left

Humm, Mama Ain't Bad, Mama Ain't Bad
With a little bit of wiggle, mama Ain't Bad
Mama Ain't Bad, with a little bit of wiggle
Whose Mama Ain't Bad

Wiggle it right, wiggle it left
Wiggle it in, wiggle it out
With a little bit of wiggle, wiggle a kiss

Humm, Mama Ain't Bad, Mama Ain't Bad
With a little of kissing, Mama Ain't Bad
Mama Ain't Bad, Oh Mama Ain't Bad
With a little bit of kissing
Whse Mama Ain't Bad

If there's someone you like to wiggle with
Change partners if you wish
To kiss the one you wiggle with

Mama Ain't Bad, Oh Mama Ain't Bad
With a little bit of wiggle, kissing Mama Ain't Bad

Copyright 1999 Francis E. Delaney   S-9914-LL

HAND TO HAND

I hold my hands Hand to Hand
And I thank the Lord
He made a woman and a man
And I thank Him
For the woman I met Hand to Hand

With our hearts dancing in love
I'll hold your hands, Hand to Hand
With all the eyes of our love, we understand
He made a woman for a man
This woman for this man

When I love you Hand to Hand
I am yours
Hold my hands with yours, heart to heart
And I love, the love
Of this woman, loving this man

A never ending love affair
That began when all the eyes of love
Touched HAND TO HAND

Copyright 1999 Francis E. Delaney   S-9915-MV

LIFE'S A LONG SONG

Love me never
Or now and forever
And we'll never grow old
For in the eye of the heart
Love never grows old

The eye of the flesh and
The eye of the mind grow old
The eye of the heart
Is here, now and forever

It takes a long time to find love
It takes a lifetime to grow old
In the eyes of the heart, flesh and mind
Love is a long song

Love me now
Again and forever
We'll always be young
For in the eye of the heart

LIFE'S A LONG SONG

Copyright 1999 Francis E. Delaney   P-9917-LL

I'LL KEEP ASKING FOR YOU

I'll Keep Asking For You
As long as I can see

The stars in the oceans
Diamonds in the sea

I'll Keep Asking For You
When you say, Yes

All the stars that are in the oceans
Are blue diamonds in the snow

For every, No
There is a, Yes

A love beyond the dreams
For you and me

Your eyes
Oceans in blue
Stars and Diamonds in the sun

I'LL KEEP ASKING FOR YOU

Copyright 1999 Francis E. Delaney   P-9918-LL

NEVER IS, NOW

Before you're born

You're younger than life

And when you appear

With a breath and a tear

To See and hear

Life and love are dear

Never Is Now

You are, here   P-9916-MV

ALL THE THINGS THAT I SEE

All the things

That I see

I see, in me

Copyright 1999 Francis E. Delaney   P-9919-FD

I'LL PRETEND IT'S YOU

When I'm eye to eye with someone new
I think of you
All the days with you
The things I've said and never could do
I'll Pretend It's You

All those feelings will always be true
In the arms that love
Your eyes looking through
The eyes of someone new
I'll Pretend It's You

When I'm loving with someone new
I'll be loving you
And as she falls in love with me
I'll do the thing I couldn't do
I'll Pretend It's You

All your feelings will always be
In the arms that love me
Your eyes looking through
The eyes of someone new
I'LL PRETEND IT'S YOU

Copyright 1999 Francis E. Delaney   S-9920-LL

TENNESSEE WINE

A flower awakens each day
It's star shines in the sunshine
When it rains, its rainbow is mine
In a little glass of Tennessee Wine

The sun awakens each day, and on its way
It goes from east to west
From the eagles highest nest
To the grapes of wine, to warm this heart of mine
In little glass of Tennessee Wine

The eagle flies through the tunnel of my mind
To the melody of the rhapsody of time
Love dancing in the hallways of my mind
Tennessee Wine

When the moon is in the wine
Days I have nothing to say
I sit beside the moon
Watch your movements in the room

The moon awakens each night and on its way
It goes from east to west
Moon light, lights up my night
With the words I write
With a little glass of Tennessee Wine

The sun opens the day, the moon wakes-up the night
To the melodies of love, in the mystery of the wine
In my little glass of TENNESSEE WINE

Copyright 1999 Francis E. Delaney   P-99921-MD

YOU HAVE WHAT I LOVE

You Have What I Love
What do you have
You, have you

I want all that you have been
All that you will be
I want you as you are
No changes, please

I want all your tears
Through all the years
They are all the love you gave
And all that you will give

What do you have
You have what I love
You have you
And I love you

What ever you have done
What ever you will do

In life and in love
Your pretty and your fun
You, have you
YOU HAVE WHAT I LOVE, YOU

Copyright 1999 Francis E. Delaney   P-9922-LL

LOVE DOESN'T CARE

What is the matter with them
Their wives are beautiful
Their wives are true
They are sad and lonely
Don't know what to do

If the one you love doesn't care
Never seems to be there
But he is somewhere
I gotta get this job done
I'll be home late
Don't Wait

Love Doesn't Care
You go here and there by yourself
Because your love doesn't care
You dance with everyone
Except the one you love
Love Doesn't Care

Love Doesn't Care
When you have become
Just another love affair
Life isn't fair
When love isn't there
LOVE DOESN'T CARE

Copyright 199 Francis E. Delaney   P-9923-KD

TELL, NO ONE

Someone told me a story

Said to, tell no one

This is a story

I can't.

Tell no One

Yes, it's about that

No, it's not about me

Everybody has a story

They can't

Tell, No One

So Don't tell this story

To, No One

Copyright 1999 Francis E. Delaney   P-9925-?

NEVER FELT LIKE THIS

Never Felt Like This
Never knew love could reach
Heights I never knew
Wish it would last
As long as the one before

My second love lasted as long
Seems like yesterday
When she passed away
Now both my loves
Look for a new love for me

Never Felt Like This before
Is there someone there
Do I want to love one more
Can I love someone else
As much as I loved before

How will I know
I'll love one more
When she tells me
Ours will last
As long as the ones before
NEVER FELT LIKE THIS BEFORE

Copyright 1999 Francis E. Delaney   P-9926-MM

NEVER BEEN THIS WAY

Never Been This Way
Never walked the streets for love before
As I walk the streets I never walked before
I find love in every door

I can't be so wrong when your so right
I can't feel so strong if it were wrong
You can't keep saying no, when you know its true
You can't wash away love in a glass of hard wine

Let it out of the bottle pour a glass for me
Let your love be mine and Let it be me

Never Been This Way
Never washed away love before
As I walk the streets I never walked before
I look for your love in every door
Hoping to find it just once more

Let it out of the bottle, pour a glass for me
Let your love be mine, and let it be me

Never Been This Way
Never walked the streets in love before
As we walked the streets we never walked before
We find love stronger than before
Hoping to love, love just once more

Copyright 1999 Francis E. Delaney   S-9927-MV

THAT'S ALL YOUR GOING TO HEAR

No, No, No

Never, Never, Never

THAT'S ALL

YOUR EVER GOING TO HEAR   P-9928-MV

ME

Who is Me

Me is you when you read this

You are not Me

If you were, you wouldn't read this

About me, would you

Copyright 1997 Francis E. Delaney   P-9929-ME

WABASH AVENUE SWING

Seems like a long time ago
When I seen you walking down the street
But it was only yesterday
When I stopped to watch
The Wabash Avenue Swing

The afternoon sun peeking through
The el-tracks on a Downtown Chicago street
To warm the beauty of this woman
Walking down the street
On a Wabash Avenue Swing

Her sun colored hair riding on the wind
In time with her high heel shoes
Walking down a windy city street
To warm this heart of mine
Sun shining on her Wabash Avenue Swing

When I stopped to watch it
All the traffic stopped
To watch that Wabash Avenue Swing
It was like the day we met
When all work stopped

That's the only work I did
As I walked around the floor
Just to get a peek
At her Wabash Avenue Swing

Copyright 1999 Francis E. Delaney   P-9930-MV

I STILL LOOK AT YOU

The love I have known
All that I have loved
They walk softly in my heart
And gentle on my mind

The things I've said and done
And all I never did
If there was another you
I'd walk across the world to love you

Each and every time
You walk across my mind
In a land I never knew
You're beautiful to love

Do you want a little bottle of wine
And when you pour it in this little glass of mine
You ride the rivers of my mind
Through my eyes of time
To this heart of mine

Copyright 1999 Francis E. Delaney   P-9931-MD

DANCING IN THE DOG HOUSE

I don't ever want to leave you
I don't ever want to say good-bye
I just want to love and dance with you
Dancing in The Dog House, busting wood and loving you

To the two-step to the double-two
The cha-cha, waltz and polka too
And when your feeling blue
I'll rock and roll to the disco too
With a step or two of the jazz with you
I don't ever want to leave
Dancing In The Dog House, busting wood and loving you

When I slow dance with you
The bust is close and the goose is too
I'm dancing in the dog house with you
Love dancing and kissing you
I want to be first in line
In or out of the dog house
Busting wood and loving you

Boot scooting boogie, electric slide
Watermelon crawl, and wiggle dance
With you under the mistletoe
I'll samba and tango with you
Twist and snake the Bossa Nova with you
I don' ever want to leave
Dancing In the Dog House, busting wood and loving you

Copyright 1999 Francis E. Delaney   S-9932-LL

HONKY TONK WALTZ

If we make it through the cheating years
We'll make it all the way
Love that is there will always be
Come and dance with me
Love is where it's at

One, two, three, four, five, six
One, two, three, four, five, six
One, two, three, four, five, six
To the beat of the Honky Tonk Waltz

We can search the world over
In all it's honky tonks
From sea to sea, when you return
Come and love with me
Home is where it's at

Life is short, memories are long
For our two cheating hearts are still in love
With the waltz of the honky tonk years
Love is where it's at
Home is where it is

One, two, three, four, five, six
To the beat of the HONKY TONK WALTZ

Copyright 1999 Francis E. Delaney   S-9933-MV

ACROSS THE CENTURY

The end of a century
Is coming to time
As I look across the century 2000
I see a different world

When the next century
Comes to its end
Will anybody be here
To look, Across the Century 3000

I will not be here
You will not be here
Will the children of our children be here
To look, Across the century 4000

When two thousand years pass
Will our world be all the stars we see
Are we really
The children of the stars

As we look, ACROSS THE CENTURY

Copyright 1999 Francis e. Delaney   P-9934-FD

BAND OF GOLD

How can I explain, this feeling in my brain
Your love rushing through its veins
To fill this heart of mine

You feel what I think, felt what I thought
Someone I ordered finally came
To start it again

I wanna give you everything
I wanna give you my name
The music in the band
The band of love in this Band of Gold

With this Band of Gold, I give you this great love
You give to me to give to you
For the rest of your life the music in the band

You feel what I think, felt what I thought
Someone I ordered finally came
I wanna give you my name

With this Band of Gold, I give you this great love
You give to me, I give to you
All the love that I can for the rest of my life

I give to you give to me
All the love that we can for the rest of our life
The music in the band, The BAND OF GOLD

Copyright 1999 Francis E. Delaney   P-9935-LL

HOW WILL I KNOW

Everybody thinks they were, but they weren't
One day she called him Daddy, and I had to ask him, why
Her father died when she was fourteen, never knew her mother
One day she called me daddy, and I did the best that I could do

I answered all her questions
And when I didn't know the answer, I asked her what she would do
She said, Daddy, How Will I Know, what my love can do

Love has many different meanings
Your love is everything that's good
And when you finally find the one you love
It will be the strongest attraction that you will ever know

She got caught up in the game of love
Thought she was a gift to the world
She loved and loved and when she finally won
She didn't know the answer
She asked me, Daddy   what would you do

Love isn't easy to find, sometimes it takes long time
To find someone who is with you all the time
I had to tell her that the guy she fell in love with
Was calling her, his weekend honeymoon
He has five kids and they have a mother

She said Daddy, I have one more question.
How Will I know, if I'm the only one.
You will know before it starts, that it isn't right

Copyright 1999 Francis E. Delaney   P-9936-JW

MUSIC IN THE BAND

She was just another woman
With a band of gold on her hand
But there was something different
About this woman and this band

When she hugged and kissed me
She told me that I would understand
And every time she walks gently in my mind
The Music in the band begins to play

She was just another woman
When she told I would understand
The music in the band
Was a hug and a kiss from the one you loved

Now several years have passed
I listen to all the music in the band
And I understand, that in every woman
There is music in the band

Is she just another woman
No band of gold on her hand
I listen to her music and she understands
When she hears her MUSIC IN THE BAND

Copyright 1999 Francis E. Delaney   P-9937-DA-LL

HILLS OF KENTUCKY

Take a ride down U.S. sixty-five
When you come to Kentucky
The beauty of the blue grass land
Blue grass music playing
In the Mountains of Kentucky

Take a walk in the trees
Like the thoroughbreds of Kentucky
The trees are lean and green
Standing tall beside the sunshine
On the Mountains of Kentucky

Come travel with me
See the beauty of this land
A flower blowing in the breeze
It's beauty teasing me
On the Hills of Kentucky

Take a ride on the Mountains of Kentucky
A thoroughbred running free
The trees singing with the breeze
Loving Kentucky to the music of the land
The beauty of loving the HILLS Of KENTUCKY

Copyright 1999 Francis E. Delaney   P-9938-KY

IF YOU WERE HERE

If You Were Here
You wouldn't believe your ears
Of all the poems and songs
I have written about you
Only four have been recorded
Since you passed away

There are three hundred new poems
Sixty-eight new recorded songs
About Gods loveliest flowers since you are gone
Three c-d with one more
I guess you don't want anyone to hear
The beautiful music of our years
Maybe I don't want to let go

If You Were Here
And I was there
I guess I wouldn't want anyone to hear
All the beauty of our years
Maybe you don't want to let go
Maybe you want to listen to the flowers I hear

Copyright 1999 Francis E. Delaney   P-9939-MM

WHAT A CAR

It's an old car
Wrinkled and weathered by time
Leaning to the left
It has a dull shine

Like your old car
Wrinkled and weathered by time
Leaning to the right
Old eyes shine bright

Look in the old car
Memories of years
Still in there, in place
With that old car taste

Look in my old eyes
Memories of years
Still in there, in place
Your pretty face

Copyright 1999 Francis E. Delaney   P-9940-LL

WHY CAN'T I FALL IN LOVE WITH YOU

When I'm out with the moon, I count its endless stars
All the love I shared when it was there
All the years and all the tears
That made it all worth being there

Why Can't I Fall In Love With You, Why can't it be you
Why can't I break through
These doors of a love that was always true
Why Can't I Fall In Love With You

The sun is warm once more, your love touches me
I can count the stars, I see
Touch every leaf on a tree
Why Can't I Fall In Love With You

Why can't I love, when I want too
Why can't you be you

Why Can't I Fall In Love with You
Why can't it be me So I can walk through
The doors of a love that will always be true
Why Can't I Fall In Love With You

Why can't I love you when I want too
Why can't it be you

Why Can't I Fall In Love With You

Copyright 1999 Francis E. Delaney   P-9941-DL

YOU, ME, NASHVILLE AND TENNESSEE

When you walk my way
The fiddle and lead guitar
Begin to play
Your eyes touch mine

In the eyes of Tennessee
The steel guitar begins to play
When you walk away
The keyboards, drums and bass guitar
Begin to play

When I see and hear the music
Of the Steel and Wire Band
I can feel the touch of a special love
Between You, Me, Nashville and Tennessee

It's the fiddle and first guitar
Playing with the steel guitar
Keyboards, drums and bass guitar
The music in the band

YOU, ME, NASHVILLE AND TENNESSEE

Copyright 1999 Francis E. Delaney   P-9942-LL

PARKING LOT .

The Parking Lot is empty

She don't park there anymore

We used to talk now and then

On the back Parking Lot

When she got her promotion

She moved up to the front Parking Lot   P-9943-LL

NEVER FORGOTTEN

There are some things you never forget

Like the day we met and the day you left

The good and the bad

Are NEVER FORGOTTEN

Copyright 1999 Francis E. Delaney   P-9945-MR

SUNDAY MORNING BLUES

Breakfast in a little cafe
Blond hair, blue eyes
And the sadness of the blues
Sunday Morning Blues
Waiting on me

I asked her why so sad
Married and divorced from a cop
Thinks he still lives there
He watches me everywhere

I don't know why, I was special in her eyes
Maybe it was my blond hair, blue eyes
And the sadness of my Sunday Morning Blues

Last time I saw her, said she was going to leave
I don't want you to get hurt
My "X" detective dressed in blue
My Sunday Morning Blues is watching you

I walked over to her "X"
Maybe it's time for me to leave
So, I'm going to leave you
My blond hair, blue eyes and the sadness of the blues
My SUNDAY MORNING BLUES

Copyright 1999 Francis E. Delaney   P-9944-CO

ACROSS THE TABLE

Everyday you were there
Suddenly your gone
No more of everything
Across The Table

I lost everything
When I lost you
You were I needed
Sitting Across the table

Now I found some one new
Will the miracle of love
Touch me again
Across the table

I found all I need
When I found you
Will your love look at me
Across the table

Everyday you are there
You're all I need
More of everything
Sitting ACROSS THE TABLE

Copyright 1999 Francis E. Delaney   P-9946-MM

ONLY HAVE ONE (you)

Some days you sit around
And the world isn't there
You wonder where it went
And Why

The world that you knew
Is now a world that is new
Still the days come and go
Like the days of old

The people are the same
With different names
Life comes and goes
The new world becomes old

Nothing has changed
For life is still life
Love is still love and
YOU ONLY HAVE ONE

Copyright 1999 Francis E. Delaney   P-9947-MV

BEYOND THE SUN

No touch, ever felt
No words, ever said
No look, ever saw
No song, ever sung
The meaning of the feeling
In my body, soul and mind
Your love, Beyond The Sun

You put love on top of the chimneys of the stars
A height no other love has reached
Thirty billion light years Beyond The Sun

No picture ever showed
The beauty of your soul
No poem ever told
The story of our love
The mystic of the magic in your eyes
That takes my love beyond the sun

Only one story ever told
Surpasses the story of our love
The story of Christmas, a Little Infant
Who made the chimneys of the stars
And the meaning of the feeling
In my body, Soul and mind
Your love, BEYOND THE SUN

Copyright 1999 Francis E. Delaney   P-9948LL

PRETTY, SHORT AND PETITE

Where ever I go
The show is the same
Your on my mind
And in the show
I find you everywhere I go
Pretty, Short and Petite

I go beyond the things I see
What's the meaning of being
It's just a place to be
Another night to see
Everything I want to see
Pretty, Short and Petite

I go beyond the things I dream
To that place for us to share
Where no one will care
I love your image in the dream
You're everywhere I want to be
Every thing I want to see
PRETTY, SHORT AND PETITE

Copyright 1999 Francis E. Delaney   P- 9950-LL

CATHLEEN

You don't often get to see
Some thing you though you would never see

I knew that of the things I could do
This is the one I waited to see

Thought I'd never get you married
Thought you would never find the right guy

A baby in her mothers arm
Waving at me

Mama looking across the room
Mama waves too

The right guy wants to know
Why baby Cathleen waved too

Copyright 1999 Francis E. Delaney   P-9949-MR

SOMEONE

Somewhere out there
There's Someone who cares
For all that I see

For the flowers and the trees
The birds and the bees
The air and the sea
The animals, fish and the flee

Someday there will be
Someone who cares
For all that I see, will be

Like the flower and the tree
The bird and the bee
The air and the sea
The animals, fish and the flee

Someone out there
There's Someone
Who cares

Copyright 1999 Francis E. Delaney   P-9951-FD

LADY BUG

Why do butterflies fly
Every which way and why
I'm flying in the sky
Falling in love

Why do lightning bugs glow
Does anybody know
Are lady bugs, ladies
Every which way and why

What will you say
When I ask you
Will the answer be, no
Or does everybody know

Lady bugs love
When lightning bugs glow

The butterfly lands
On the flowers it loves
The lighting bug glows
Looking for love

When the lady bug glows
Every which way and why
Everybody knows
The lady bug is a lady

When the butterfly, flies
The LADY BUG sleeps

Copyright 1999 Francis E. Delaney   P-9952-LL

WHEN I WAS YOUR AGE

When I Was Your Age
I was looking for you
And I fell in love with someone, like you
A dream I thought I'd never see
Until I seen you

When I Was Your Age
I was loving like you
Loving someone like me
Now, I'm falling in love with you
Falling in love with me

Love has no age
It's as old as love
And as young as the one you love
When I Was Your Age
You were younger than love

When I love you
People will ask me
What is it like
When you love me

When you love
I'm loving you
WHEN I WAS YOUR AGE

Copyright 1999 Francis E. Delaney   S-9953-LL

FOR YOU, I WILL DO IT

All that I have done
Was it for you
All that I will ever do
Will I do it for you

As I fall in love
Will the beauty of your love
Love my love
For You, I Will Do It

Now, I look beyond my dreams
I can see
All that I may ever be
Will it be you

For You, I Will Do It
And as they pass from me to you
Make them beautiful and true
So they will always be
In the loving arms that loved me

All that I will ever do
Will I do it for you

FOR YOU, I WILL DO IT

Copyright 1999 Francis E. Delaney   P-9954-LL

BEAUTIFUL KENTUCKY

Leaving Tennessee
Driving through Kentucky
Stopped for a cup of coffee
At a Crackle barrel store

She asked me where I was from
I'm going back to Illinois
But, I'm falling in love with Kentucky
And I just might want to say

The smile on her face is all over this place
Where ever I look, I see a pretty face

Every picture in my eyes
Of this beautiful place
Is a picture I'll put
With a memory in my mind

Of a thoroughbred walking
Looking in my eyes
The time and the place
I fall in love with Kentucky

When I leave Kentucky
I don't know where I will go
I'll put away the pictures
On the back roads of my mind

To remind me where I fell in love
With Beautiful Kentucky

Copyright 1999 Francis E. Delaney   S-9955-LL

THE LAST DAY OF THE MILLENNIUM

The things you said and done
Are the songs I wrote and sung
Our laughter and tears, hopes and fears
We'll always remember
On the Last Day of The Millennium

May the new year be as lovely as the old
Laughter and tears
Are moments of gold
On the last day of the year

May the new year
Bring love to the young and old
Their hopes and fears
In moments to hold
On the last day of the year

May the new year be as the old
None have been cold
For what you say and do
Is the song I'll write about you
When you are there

On the last day of every year

Copyright 1999 Francis E. Delaney   P-9956-LL

RED RIBBONS BLUES

I got the Red Ribbon Blues
Falling in love with you
All the roses are gone
Last one I saw was you

Roses are red, violets are blue
Ribbons come in these colors too
Red birds are red, blue birds are blue
Robbins are singing the blues

I got the Red Ribbon Blues
Falling in love with you
All the roses are yours
Last one I saw was you

When it changes from red to blue
All the red ribbons are yours
And if we say, I do
All the blue ones are mine

I got the Red Ribbons
Falling in love with you
If you got them too
It's time to say, I do

Copyright 1999 Francis E. Delaney   S-9957-LL

URSULA

Ursula, do you remember, you were there
At the end of a long love affair
Began in love and left in love
The beat of her heart, it will always be there
In my little glass of Gallo wine

Ursula, do you remember, you were there
For a new love affair
It began with love and left with love
The rose in the wine, it will always be there
In my little glass of Rosy wine

Ursula, do you remember, you were there
For a very special love affair
Rare, beautiful star in the wine
The look in her eye, it will always be there
In my little glass of Zinfandel wine

Ursula, do you remember
Who's in the glass of Rhine wine
When you see her, you have seen them all
The heart of my love, her rose, her star
In my little glass of Rhine wine

Ursula, you got it all
When I look at you, I see them all
The Gallo red wine, the Rosy, the Zinfandel and the Rhine
The heart, the rose the star of my love
Lisa, in my little glass of Rhine wine

Copyright 1999 Francis E. Delaney   S-9924-UR

BLINKY, THE BLUE NOSE SPACE DEER   2000

Out of the Chesterfield Galaxy of beauty
Came a little blue nose and a big white tail
And Santa called her
Blinky, my blue nose snow deer

Now when Santa went down the last chimney in Frankfort town
She pranced around with her boots in the air
Dancing with Santa reindeer
To her music in the night

Winking and blinking at Santa's reindeer
Every time she winked they blinked
As Santa's reindeer danced
To there music in the night

Blinky, pranced here and there
Her boots high in the air
Wondering how, when and where
Santa will take her out

Make her a part of the holiday treat
For children on this earth, on planets near and far
From earths ring of gold to the chimneys of the stars
The chimneys of the children of the stars

Copyright 2000 Francis E. Delaney   S-0001-LL 1958

SOMETHING DIFFERENT ABOUT YOU

All the words that describe
The words I love you
All the feelings I have felt
Before I met you
There's Something Different About You

All those feelings and all those words
That have come before you
Are the feelings I felt
From the first day I met you
I knew, there was Something Different About You

The first time I fell in love
She married someone special because you were there
The second time we never said I do because you were there
Now, I'm in love with you and I'll say, I do
If you are there, there's Something Different About You

If I keep trying to take you out
I'm going to find out
That Nashville and Tennessee was not a dream
For the music in the band is in the band of gold
On your hand and mine in Nashville, Tennessee

There's Something Different About You

Copyright 2000 Francis E. Delaney   P-0002-KY

YOU KNOW I'M GOING TO ASK YOU

You know I'm Going to Ask You
To walk with me to the end of time

I want to see you more
Talk more then once a week

Your spirit has touched me
In ways I never thought could be

You Know I'm Going To Ask You
To marry me

No one has to know the answer
Only you and I know

Everybody wants to know
If you know

I'm going to ask you

Copyright 2000 Francis E. Delaney   P-0003-KY

YOUR LOVE

My days are so full
There running into my nights
I'm walking in my sleep
Talking in my dreams

Spending the days and the nights with you
Walking, talking and loving
In another world with you

For all that was a dream
Is alive, walking and talking
When I awake, will it be a dream
Or will I find your love with mine

All that I love is all that I need
To make me what I want to be, Your Love

To spend the days and the nights with you
Walking and talking and loving
In another world with you

All that I love is all that I need
To make me what I want to be
All that I need is, Your Love

When I awake will I find my dream
You, Your Love and me
Under the Christmas Tree

Copyright 2000 Francis E. Delaney   P-0004-LL

KEEP ME WITH YOU

When you don't want to go
I like the way you say, No
It makes me just a little blue
Keep Me With You

Everywhere I go
I meet someone like you
I tell myself, No
To Keep Me With You

How many times can I tell myself, No
How many days and nights must I go
Before someone takes me from you
Keep Me With You

Every time you can't go
I keep asking myself, why
I find the answer in your eyes
Keep Me With You

Every time you don't go
I keep asking myself, why
I find the answer in your heart
KEEP ME WITH YOU

Copyright 2000 Francis E. Delaney   P-0005-LL co

LOOSING YOU

Is this feeling, the way you feel
When love begins to make you blue
Am I Loosing You

Is it time for me to leave
And journey on my way
To find that special love
A new born son

Am I Loosing You
Or will our love never end
When you return, to love

Only time will tell
When love is born again

Has my journey come to its end
Have I found the love I never knew
Am I Loosing You

It will never end
When I am born again

AM I LOOSING YOU

Copyright 2000 Francis E. Delaney   P-0006-LL

BECAUSE I SAID, YES

It is just a word
Why do people say, Yes
Are you happy, Yes, are you sad, Yes
Why are you both, happy and sad

BECAUSE WE SAID, YES

Copyright 2000 Francis E. Delaney   P-0007-MM

DON'T SIT DOWN

When love blooms
Don't play opossum
What is meant to be, will be
Don't Sit Down

The sun watches the moon go down
The flower blossoms honey for the bee
The opossum hangs from a tree
It was meant to be

Stars shine in the night
Sparkle in your eyes
And light the waters of the seas
It was meant to be

The universe is Gods playground
It's all that we can't imagine
Love is a little bit like that
It was meant to be

Copyright 2000 Francis E. Delaney   P-0008-MA

HAS IT JUST BEGUN

I look through the year
All that I have lived
I watch, in wonder of all that I did
Thought there was no more to do
Till I met you

I walk through the raindrops
Falling from above
Frozen tears on my face
Love standing still
Walking through life I couldn't
Till I seen you

Every day wanting you
Every way your precious love a special gift
Will I knew you
Is it over or Has It Just Begun

I walk through the raindrops
Falling from the trees
Real tears on my face
Love's first taste, love's last taste
I Thought I saw and felt it all
Is it over or

HAS IT JUST BEGUN

Copyright 2000 Francis E. Delaney   P-0009-KY co

CHRISTMAS IN SPACE, at 2000 Blinky Place

Santa went from star to star
Visiting the planets near and far
His reindeer climbed the chimneys of the stars
To their planet of dreams
For their Christmas In Space at 2000 Blinky place

Christmas in Space is where it stars
With all the children nobody wants
They took with them what was theirs on earth
Love, a little glass of water and a little dirt
A bird, an animal, a flower and a tree and Blinky

They gave life to the planet of dreams
From the internet screen to the chimneys of the stars

So take a look at your Christmas sweetheart
If you can see
Love, a little glass of water and a little dirt
A bird, an animal, a flower and a tree and Blinky
You got Christmas at your place
Two thousand Blinky Place

The nicest place you like to be
Where life slows down to let you see
Just how very nice things can be

CHRISTMAS IN SPACE, this earth with all its families
At 2000 Blinky Place, Your Place (our place)

Copyright 2000 Francis E. Delaney   S-0010-LL

YOU AND ME

All that we never could be, we are
Out of money, full of dreams
Dreams that make us richer
Then any job could be
Dreams that make us a part of each other
In a world we never could see
You and Me

A world where You and Me
Become all that life can be
For we found a way to fall in love
In a way we never dreamed
To be the best that we can be
You and Me

Sometimes you feel you don't know what to do
When all, your dreams are painted blue
Hold each other in love
Be the best that you can be
And the rest of life will be
A painted picture of
You and Me

Now, I wonder as my mind wanders
About the source of all my dreams
Does it seem, could it be, we're in love
It's not a dream
You and Me

Copyright 2000 Francis E. Delaney   P-0011-B&C

FIRST TIME (the)

I want to hold you, the First Time
Feel my heart, tell my soul
To love you, the First Time

I want to kiss you the First Time
Feel your melody teasing me
To love you, the First Time

I want to love you the first time
Love you till the last time I love you

You turned me on and never turned me off
Again and again, every time
In love from the First Time
Till the last time I love You

When I leave, I'll wipe away my tears
For I'll be there, The First Time
You love again

You turned me on and never turned me off
Again and again, every time
Loving you from the First Time
Till the last time I loved you

Copyright 2000 Francis E. Delaney   P-0012-MM

MY NAME IS MARY

Sitting by the fireplace on a quiet Christmas Eve
The Melody of Mary lingers on in me
Christmas is what Christmas is
The melody of Mary

When she held me in her arms and said My Name is Mary
The melody of Mary in every kiss
With love first taste, she looked into my eyes and said
"My Name Is Mary"

I realize no man alive has been loved as much as I
A different time, a different place and a different Mary

Will I ever hold those words in my arms again
Will I ever feel the melody of "My Name Is Mary"
Will I ever be loved like that again
Every time I say, thanks for loving me"
I'll remember every day

As you hold me in your arms and say, "My Name Is Mary"
The melody of Mary in every kiss
With loves first taste I'll look into your eyes and say
I realize no man alive has been loved as much as I
A different time, a different place and a different Mary

With loves first taste
She looked into to my eyes and said
My Name Isn't Mary, It's Maureen

Copyright 2000 Francis E. Delaney   P-0013-MH-MM 63

KEEP ME WITH YOU

words & music
Francis E. Delaney

VERSE 1: When you don't want to go
VERSE 2: Eve-ry-time you can't go

like the way you say no It
keep ask-ing my-self why

makes me just a lit-tle blue
find the an-swer in your eyes Where you

Keep me with you
keep me with you

Eve-ry-where I go I meet some-one like you I

tell my-self no To keep me with you

CHORUS: How man-y times can I tell my-self no How man-y

days and nights must I go Be-fore some-one takes

me from you Keep me with you

#LAP-0005-LL   © 2000 FRANCIS E. DELANEY all rights reserved.   RL
P.O. Box 932 Frankfort, IL 60423

CHRISTMAS IN SPACE
AT BLINKY'S PLACE

BLINKY
"Christmas In Space"

Blinky RECORDS

Copyright 1970 Francis E. Delaney
P.O. Box 932 Frankfort, IL 60423

Map-6907-MH-57
All rights reserved

SLAM IT TO THE FLOOR Nascar song

Slam it to the Floor
Gotta get back to where we were before
Gonna love you once more

Every lap of the track
I love you more and more
Loving you as I go
As I go Loving you on the Nascar road

Slam it to the floor
Gotta get back to where we were before

Every lap of the track faster and faster I go
Loving you as I go
Racing to the top of the charts

Doesn't matter if I'm first or last
When I cross that finish line
Your loving is on my mind
Loving you more than I did before

Slam it to the floor. Let it roar
Gonna tell everyone once more
Gotta get back to where we were before
Gonna love you once more

One more lap around the track
Loving you as I go
Slam it to the floor for one more
Loving you before I go

Copyright 2000 Francis E. Delaney   P-0014-LL

FEELING (the)

I got that feeling
First time I saw you
If you got it too
Love's Feeling me, Feeling you

Is it just another love affair
That comes and goes nowhere
A feeling that is here but not there
Or is it love

I got that Feeling
Last time I saw you
If you got it too
Love's Feeling you, Feeling me

I look and I feel, my feelings
I ask myself, do you feel it too

That feeling, that doesn't go away
For I'm in love with you

"I see your eyes, your heart and soul loving me"
But most of all I feel your FEELINGS loving me"

Copyright 2000 Francis E. Delaney   P-0015-LL

SONG OF CHRISTMAS

When Mama Kisses Santa Clause
And Daddy says 'Let's Roll"
Color your world, color it free
You gotta love it to be free

Color your Christmas tree
Color it Free
With the colors of your country

The children of this world
Will color it free
Their sons and their daughters
Will keep it free

Now it's up to you and me
To look across the graves of all the centuries
They fought to keep this world free
For you and me

Will it be here tomorrow
Or will it just be history

Color your Christmas Tree
Color it free
With the colors of Your Country

Copyright 2000 Francis E. Delaney   P-0016-FD

LOUISIANA HONEYMOON

Press the petal to the floor
Slam it to the floor
Gotta get back to Louisiana
And love you once more
One more Louisiana Honeymoon

Mardi-Gar dancing to the jazz of its rhythm and blues
Louisiana loving me on a Louisiana Honeymoon

Press the petal to the floor
Slam it to the floor
It's Mardi-Gar time in Louisiana
It's time for one more
One more Louisiana Honeymoon

Louisiana loving to the jazz of her rhythm and blues
Mississippi doing the Louisiana slam with the Gulf of Mexico
Louisiana loving me, to a Louisiana Honeymoon

Press the petal to the metal
Slam it to the floor
It's Christmas Time in Louisiana
A Christmas Honeymoon
One more Louisiana Honeymoon

Christmas singing to the beat of your rhythm and blues
Mississippi dancing the mistletoe wiggle with the Gulf of Mexico
Louisiana loving me, on our Louisiana Honeymoon

Louisiana loving to the beat of her rhythm and blues
Louisiana dancing the Louisiana Slam with the gulf of Mexico
Louisiana Loving me, on our Louisiana Honeymoon

Copyright 2000 Francis E. Delaney   S-0017-LL

EYES OF AN EAGLE

An eagle drifts on the wind
Lands with the touch of a feather
As its wings close for the night
Its eyes look into the night
For the eyes of an eagle
To land for the night

You're an eagle high on the wind
I see your highs and your lows
But only you know
Where the eyes of a eagle
Will land for the night

An eagle riding on the wind
Bold and as proud as she can be
Her beauty describes all that I see
And when she looks at me
I see the Eyes of an Eagle
In the eyes of Eve

Copyright 2000 Francis E. Delaney   P-0018-MD

DO YOU LOVE ME NOW

Sometimes it takes awhile
Sometimes it don't
I look back at all the years
Remember the times
Do You Love Me, Now

I love you now as I did before
I love you all the time
I loved you first and I love you now
And I'll love you till the end of time

It isn't easy to find another love
I look back at all the years since you're gone
I loved you first and I love you now
Now, I'll love the one who loves me now

I'll love her
When she loves me
I'll love her first

Now, I love you
For teaching me, how

DO YOU LOVE ME, NOW

Copyright 2000 Francis E. Delaney   P-0019-MH

I LOVE, ALL OF YOU

God made you
God made me
What He gave to you
He gives to me
In words that rhyme
I Love, All of You

The heart that holds me in your arms
Your eyes tell me why
They talk to me
I hear all that they say
My love tells you why
I Love, All of You

The way that you are
Is all that I see
All that you have
Is all that you give
To all you love

I LOVE, ALL OF YOU

Copyright 2000 Francis E. Delaney   P-0020-LL

WE'LL ALL BE TOGETHER

When someone close and dear
Pass through the window of their years
Tomorrow is Today
Today is moving on to the things that must be done

You have to be, who you are
Do what has to be done
Remember the love one and the ones you love now
We'll All Be Together, when our work is done

We'll All Be Together, memories old and new
All the things we say and do, said and done
All the love we share the bad breaks, and heartaches
We'll All Be Together, when our work is done

Our work is done
When we found a way to love everyone
in all the things we say and do
With all the ones we love

With someone close and someone dear
You have to be who you are
Tomorrow is today, Today is moving on
When Tomorrow is no more
WE'LL ALL BE TOGETHER

Copyright 2000 Francis E. Delaney   P-0021-NW

IT ISN'T THERE (When Your Not Here)

I walk through life
It's joy and pain
The bad breaks and the heartache of loves game
If it isn't in your heart.
It Isn't There

Is there anyone who can handle
The rumors of loves game
The same old things you hear them say
When they were the rumor of loves game

When your not there, It Isn't There
Someone else tries to erase your name
The joy, the pain the bad breaks and heartaches
It isn't here, when your not here

You walk through life
Its joy and pain, bad breaks and heartaches
Of loves game
It isn't in your heart, It's not here
IT ISN'T THERE, when your not there

Copyright 2000 Francis E. Delaney   P-0022-LL

DO SOMETHING

I got a lot of living
And a lot of loving to do
Do Something, If I can do it with you

I got a new way of living
And a new way of loving
Do Something, if you can do it with me

Quit your running and start becoming
The lovely woman you are

You got a new way of walking
And a new way of talking
A new way of living
And a new way of loving

A lot of living
And a lot of loving to do
Do Something, if I can do it with you
For I got a new way of loving you

A cup of coffee in the morning breeze
A glass of wine, dinner in time
The color of your eyes
When you let me try
To, DO SOMETHING

Copyright 2000 Francis E. Delaney   P-0023-MM 1971

IT'S NEVER FOREVER ANYMORE

I remember Grandma
When women were women
Grandpa loved her for a half century
When love was love and men were men

I remember Mama
Tough as any woman could be
She loved Papa for half a century
A century of love has passed away

I remember my love
True as any woman could be
Loved her for a half, of a half a century
A half a century of love has passed away

It Isn't Forever Anymore
When there's only a few years more
So, I'll love you for a half of a half of a century

Someday I will find the other half
If she's the other half of my century of love
She will know me, she will love me and when God calls me
A century of love will have passed away

IT ISN'T FOREVER ANYMORE

Copyright 2000 Francis E. Delaney   P-0024-MV

RUSTY ROSE

Rusty Rose, falls asleep in the evening sun
The shades of night hide its lovely sight

From my roving eyes, moments of time
Pictures in my mind, blooming in time

P-0025-LL

IF I DIDN'T KNOW YOU

If I Didn't Know You

I would not see you

In all that I see

If I Didn't Know You

It was time for me to leave

Copyright 2000 Francis E. Delaney   P-0026-LL

CHRISTMAS TREE

Look at me

The Christmas Tree

Look what all the people do to me

Cut me from the ground

Drag me around

Dress me funny

Throw me away

Doesn't bother me

When I wear the Star of Christmas

I will always be the Christmas Tree

Copyright 2000 Francis E. Delaney   P-0027-LL

FRED (the Cat)

When I look at you
She belongs to me
Like it was yesterday
I still feel the way I felt that day

Fred, I wish I was you
When she holds you close and tight
Calls you Francis instead of Fred
Fred, I wish I was you

You do the looking, you do the holding
You do the talking and the kissing for me
I'll do the loving
When she wants me

I don't need no more heartache
No more tears
I'm not asking for no more, No's
I'm telling you Fred, I wish I was you

In the arms of someone who loves you
Fred, she held me to close
Please get out of my way
We'll always be friends

I need your love too
So I can love her
When she wants me too

Copyright 2000 Francis E. Delaney   P-0028-FV

LIKE IT WAS YESTERDAY

My heart is Like It Was Yesterday
It's feelings, feeling me, feeling you
Feelings that won't go away
Grow stronger each day

My eyes are Like It Was Yesterday
The beauty I saw when I first saw you
Pictures that don't go away
Become more alive each day

Our love is Like It Was Yesterday
For everyday has a yesterday
Love is just a day away
Like It Was Yesterday

If we love, it will be you and me
Like It Was Yesterday
For if you felt me like I felt you
Then you know me and I know you

And everyday
Will be a day
Like It Was Yesterday

Copyright 2000 Francis E. Delaney   P-0029-MV

ALWAYS BE FRIENDS

Five circles in the sky
Friend of all the flags that fly
Like the sky above and the earth below
No walls to hold them, no strings attached

We will Always Be Friends
And if it happens, and love comes
A friend in love is a friend in need
Of all the things that love can be
For all that it never was, it is

The flags and circles on parade
All the things we say and do
When the torch is lit the game begins
All the love we win, we never loose
We Will, Always Be Friends

We will, Always Be Friends
And when it happens, love comes along
For friends in need are friends in love
Of all the things that love can be
Your all that love can always be

Love can, Always Be Friends

Copyright 2000 Francis E. Delaney   p-0030-MV

FOR THE FIRST TIME

I feel my heart tell my soul
To love you, For The First Time
I feel your melody teasing me

I want to love you For The First Time
Till the last time, again and again
Every time in love from the first

If your only a trophy
At the head of some ones bed
Pull the plug, walk out the door, wipe away your tears
And let me love you For The First Time

If your playing around with
With someone else's love
Turn on the light, show him the door, wipe away your tears
And let me love you For the First Time

Copyright 2000 Francis E. Delaney   P-0031-MV

THE LIPS I DIDN'T KISS

Do you remember the times
When you wished you did
Well I remember
The Lips I Didn't Kiss

I still wonder to this very day
It's like walking in a dark room
Looking for something you missed
The Lips I Didn't Kiss

I still walk along the street
Hoping to meet that dream I met
Still holding hands and hoping to kiss
The Lips I Didn't Kiss

I remember the look in yours eyes
The day you called me back
Something that was there, wasn't there
With no light in the dark room

I couldn't find
The Lips I Didn't Kiss

Copyright 2000 Francis E. Delaney   P-0032-MV

YOU HELD ME TO CLOSE

You held me to close
What else is there to say
I didn't stay   Lap-0033-MV

_____

BURGER SONG (WENDYS)

I wish I was a burger in a bag of WENDYS burgers
Singing WENDYS burger song, WENDYS burgers ain't bad

Feel there rhythm in your fingers
As you hold them in your hands
Taste the melody of there lover
As they kiss your lips ride your hips
Through the love land of Wendy's song
Daddy's burgers ain't bad, WENDYS ain't bad

I wish I was a burger in a little box of WENDYS burgers
Dancing to the Burger Song
WENDYS burgers ain't bad

Feel the rhythm of my fingers
As I hold you in my hands
Taste the melody of your love
As you kiss my lips, ride my hips
Through the love land of WENDYS song

WENDYS burgers ain't bad
WENDYS ain't bad

Copyright 2000 Francis E. Delaney   P-0034-LL

WHO WILL SHE BE

When my love passed away
She told me
Someone would come along
She will know

She will know you
Like you knew me
When you met me

You looked at me
I watched you
Before we knew
We knew

Everything is hear
No need to fear
Mama loves you too
Daddy drinks beer

You will know her
When you meet her
She will know
You met her

You both will have to say
What do I say to my friend

Copyright 2000 Francis E. Delaney   P-0035-MM

RED TO BLUE

Roses are red
Violets are blue
Ribbons come in those colors

Red birds are red
Blue birds are blue
Ribbons change from Red to Blue

I'll ask you to say, I do
When I see a red ribbon
They are all yours

If you say, I do
I'll see the blue ribbon
They are all mine

When the ribbons are tied
Red to Blue
All the ribbons are ours

Copyright 2000 Francis E. Delaney　　　P-0036-KY

THANKS, FOR BEING YOU

Thanks, For Being You
Loving me the way that you do
Eyes that touch me
Feel me with feelings

Your feelings touch me
Mine touch you
Our heart knew

With words that tell me
In ways only you can say
Thanks for caring
The way that you do

My heart feels every movement of yours
Ours eyes hear every word our eyes say
Loving me in all the ways I love you
THANKS, FOR BEING YOU

Copyright 2000 Francis E. Delaney　　　P-0037-KY

SOMEONE IS STILL THERE

When your heart is telling you
Someone Is Still There

Memories of a time become alive
My heart tells me someone's there

I can see it in your eyes
Someone Is Still There

Feelings in your heart and mine
Your tears crying in mine

Memories of a love lost in time
Standing still in the mirrors of our mind

Through all the loves of time
In your heart and mine

Someone Is Still There

Copyright 2000 Francis E. Delaney　　　P-0038-MV

IT"S ALL YOURS

If you don't want me, It's All Yours
All the tears, all the laughs
If they didn't mean nothing
Nothing is yours, It's All Yours　　　P-0039-DK

PUT THE BLAME ON ME

Put The Blame On Me
For it's all my fault
I'm' the one who wants to love you

Put The Blame On Me
I can take the heat
For the things I've said and done

Is mine the love you love
If you love me
Put your love on me
Love, like you never loved before

PUT THE BLAME ON ME

Copyright 2000 Francis E. Delaney　　　S-0040-LL

FOR A LONG TIME

What ever way love comes to an end
You try your best to beat the trend
You look for that special love again
And you find, no more For a Long Time

The days and the nights pass by
The weeks and the months
Become the years going by
For A Long Time

Now that love has come to its end
It's time to love a special love again
No more empty years
No more, For a Long Time

I looked here and there since I found you
No more tears or empty years, For a Long Time

The days and the nights pass by
The weeks and the months
Special years gone by will last
In love For a Long Time

Copyright 2000 Francis E. Delaney   P-0041-LL

DON'T DO THIS TO ME NOW

Don't Do This To Me Now
I need your help
The job is only half done
It's got to be all the way
Or it will never be done

Don't Do This To Me Now
Don't leave until it's done
Unless you found someone new
Then it's time for me to find the time
To get the job done

I'll look around until I find
Someone who has the time
Someday we'll get the job done
And you can read all the lines
Since the job was only half done

She will say, don't quit now
Don't leave until it's done
It's got to be all the way
Or it will never be done
DON'T LEAVE ME NOW

Copyright 2000 Francis E. Delaney   P-0042-LL

CALL ME FOR LOVE

When your too busy to do anything
Everything is getting in the way of love
Home is where it's at
Call me home
Call me to love

When we got it all together
Love is where it's at
It is a call to love
Call me at home

When your bicycle ride is over
And the light of your life
Is turned off, by the tears in your eyes
Call me at home

Call me, wipe away the tears
I never loved before
If you want to be loved
Call me to love you

CALL ME FOR LOVE

Copyright 2000 Francis E. Delaney   P-0043-MV

TRY, YES

What you gonna do
When you know it's true
That all those no, no, no's
And never, never, never
Is a love affair that will last forever

Let me kiss you on your talking door
Ask you if you want more
As I whisper in your hearing door
How, when and where
Can I ask you to, Try Yes

Let me love you
Ask me if I want some more
As you whisper in my hearing door
How, when and where
Can I ask you to try more

What's we gonna do
When we know it's true
All those Yes, Yes, Yes
And more, more, mores
Are no more

Copyright 2000 Francis E. Delaney   P-0044-MV

IT'S NEVER GONNA HAPPEN

You can dream about it
You can say a prayer for it
You can try for it
Love is all those things

Never say
It's Never Gonna Happen
Or you will find yourself saying
It has

When you're into a love
You thought never would happen
The love of your past comes alive, says
It's Never Gonna Happen

It isn't gonna happen
Till someone comes along
To take your life to new love
IT'S NEVER GONNA HAPPEN

Copyright 2000 Francis E. Delaney   P-0045-MV

EYES OF LIFE

In the Eyes Of Life
You can hear

All that is not said
See all that is

Hear a bird
You can't see

The wind
That can't be seen

Look into the sea
How many fish can you see

Look into the eyes of love
What can you see

You see the Eyes Of Life
When life loves you

You see all that can be seen
Feel what you see

For all that can't see
Love is the EYES OF LIFE

Copyright 2000 Francis E. Delaney   P-0046-RD

TEMPTATIONS TO LOVE

I used to wonder
How many tears one could cry
As time goes by, I find
Tears are as endless as time

I look at life
All that I have done
I watch in wonderland
All the things I have seen

I used to worry
How many years went by
Till I found
Your tears are endless as mine

Now I look beyond my tears
As your temptation to love
Wipes away my years

Years of tears brought us near
May the Temptations to Love
Last as long as our years

When life leaves
Tears are as endless as time
Their love is forever in our mind

Where we find, what life is
TEMPTATIONS TO LOVE

Copyright 2000 Francis E. Delaney   P-0047-MO

AT THE END OF LOVE

I have known sadness
In the mist of love
I have known happiness
That's the way it was

It was really love
That's the way was
That's the way it is
At The End Of Love

If you haven't felt sad
At The End Of Love
Then it was just a touch
Of the game that people play

It wasn't love
Just loves game
That's the way it was
At The End Of Love

Just a game

Copyright 2000 Francis E. Delaney   P-0048

LONG DISTANCE DRIVER

Long Distance Driver
Big cat on the road
Running too fast
In a hurry to get home

Gotta slow down
There's a bicycle in the road
Tires are off the road
Trailer hit the bicycle

Long Distance Driver is off the road
Trying to stop before the next road
Doesn't know the trailers load
Is on top of the bicycle

Gotta slow down
There's a bicycle in the road
Long Distance Driver is off the road
The boy on the bicycle says, Hello

Long Distance Driver and the boy
Look back at the crash
Both running to fast
In a hurry to get home

Copyright 2000, Francis E. Delaney   P-0049-LE

ALONE WITH ME

Have you ever wondered, why
There's a rainbow in the sky

Have you ever looked in eyes
See that rainbow in the sky

Walk Alone With Me
From one end to the other

Watch the sun color the rain
Touch the rain in all its colors

Why is a rainbow below the clouds
Is the rainbow a cloud

When you see a rainbow
Take another look

If it's in the shape of a cloud
It's over the one you love

See a rainbow in the sky
In the tears that cloud my eyes

ALONE WITH ME

Copyright 2000 Francis E. Delaney   P-0050-LL

HAVE I EVER SAID, NO

Your eyes tell me, yes
Your lips tell me, no
But, your heart never has
That's why it's saying
Have I ever said, no

I hear my heart
Talking to yours
My eyes listen
To every movement of yours
Have I ever said, no

Both of our hearts
Knew at the start
Only our heart
Can tear us apart

Your eyes tell me, yes
Your lips tell me, no
My heart lets me know
Your heart never said, no

HAVE I EVER SAID, NO

Copyright 2000 Francis E. Delaney   P-0051-MV

LESS THAN ME

Have you ever heard the music
Of a spider spinning its web
Or listened to the melody of a butterfly
If you haven't, then you have heard
Less Than Me

Have you ever seen the beauty
Of something you have never seen
Its melody in your mind
If you haven't, then you have seen
Less Than Me

Have you ever had a dream
Of a love you have never seen
Where you can see and feel the dream
If you haven't, then you have felt
Less Than Me

If you never been loved by a dream
Then you never been loved like me
Or the woman loving me
Then you have had
LESS THAN ME

Copyright 2000 Francis E. Delaney   Lap-0052-FD

REAL TIME

Take a time out, look around
All the beautiful things you see
Look at all you have never seen

All the days of your life
And all the things in life
Are lost in time
If you never knew
REAL TIME   P-0053-MM

WONDERFUL WORLD OF WOMEM

In all the songs and stories that have been written

Are all the dreams, all the schemes

Bad breaks and heartaches

All of these come true

In the Wonderful world of a woman

The beauty of her love in the heart of a man

In the Wonderful World of Women

Copyright 2000 Francis E. Delaney   P-0054-DK

WHAT DO I SAY TO MY FRIEND

What do I say to my friend
How can I ask you to be mine

When I know someone else
Is taken your time

What do you say to your friend
When I ask you to be mine

When he holds you
Your holding me

When he touches you
Your touching me

When he kisses you
Your kissing me

And when he wants to love you
What do you say to your friend

I know someone is taken your time

Thanks for being a part of my life
Thanks for being my friend

Copyright 2000, Francis E. Delaney   P-0055-MV

LOVE IS JUST LOVE

When love is to shy
It blocks all that love is
You miss all the things you should see
All that you should hear
And all the love that is yours

When love becomes warm
Listen to all that you see
See all that you hear
When Love Is Just Love
It blocks out all that never was

In all that we see and do
You are just, you
I am just, me
Love Is Just Love

When Love is Just Love
It lets in all that love is
We see all the things we should see
Hear all that we should hear
And give all the love that we can give

Copyright 2000 Francis E. Delaney   P-0056-LL

LOOKING AT LOVE

We don't have to say a word.
We don't have to look
We hear every word.
We feel every look

Every hour of every day.
Your walking in my mind
And I ask myself
Should I ask for love

Looking at love
Is all I can do
For in every look
I'm asking for you

With all of the feelings a man can have
Will I be, all that you need,
Or just another man

I want to give you all that you give to me
All the love in every smile I see
When I'm LOOKING AT YOU

Copyright 2000 Francis E. Delaney   P-0057-LL

YOU HAVE ALWAYS BEEN THERE

You don't want to hear my story
But you have always been there
In Oklahoma, in Texas, Nashville and Tennessee
In Kentucky, in Arizona, Louisiana and me

What else is there to say
What else is there to do
When it's all been said and done
It's all been said and done with you

You're a part of my heart
You color all that I see
With every sound I hear
In every beat of my heart

You can and hear our story
Its laughter and its tears
From Oklahoma, to Texas, to Nashville and Tennessee
From Kentucky, to Arizona, Louisiana and me

You're a part of my heart
You color all that I see
With every sound I hear
In every beat of your heart

YOU HAVE ALWAYS BEEN THERE

Copyright 2000 Francis E. Delaney   S-0058-LL

BILL

Hilary over the hill

Sitting on the windowsill

Over on the hill

She's writing a bill

No ex-president can run again

Bill sitting in Harlem

Thinking of running again

Wouldn't it be something

Watching Bill

Hilary in the senate

Watching the president

Signing her bill

No ex-president can run again

Copyright 2000 Francis E. Delaney   P-0059-BC

REST OF THE WAY

Falling in love with you, is a love I never knew
The spirit of your love touched me
Take me, The rest Of The Way

All the things I've had, and all that I never had
Now fill my body, soul and mind
Take me, The rest Of The way

Love is a butterfly waltzing in the sky
Love is a flower watching it fly
They touch and take love The Rest Of The Way
Touch me, the rest Of The Way

Tears of love touch our hearts
Take our love to the first day
As the smile that brought you my way
Takes me, The Rest Of The Way

When my story comes to its end
Wipe away my tears
All I want to hear is the music of our years
As my love takes you The Rest Of The Way

Tears of love touch our heart
Take our love to the last day
When your smile that brought me your way
Takes me, The Rest Of The Way

When our story comes to its end
Take my tears with you
Take me, the REST OF THE WAY

Copyright 2000 Francis E. Delaney   S-0060-LL

WHEN THE LIGHT GOES OUT

When The Light Goes Out
The glow is gone
The switch is off
The door is closed

Is it over or has it just begun

Turn off love
If it's not right
For some where in your heart
Is a love that is right

It's the teardrop in your eye
From the spark in your heart
That turns on love
That is right

Turn off the light
If it's over
If it's just begun
Turn on love

Is it over or has it just begun

When The Light Goes Out
The glow is gone
The switch is off
The door is closed

Is it over or has it just begun

Copyright 2000 Francis E. Delaney   P-0061-MV

STAY OUT OF MY MIND   2001

When you see a person you don't know
You see them in the tunnel of your eye
Walking into your mind

Stay Out Of My Mind
Don't look, don't peek if your not mine
I don't want you to see
I'm, loving you in my mind

If I ask you to come along with me
There's no way you will
Become a part of my time
Stay Out Of My Mind

If you keep getting in the way of my eyes
You're walking into my mind
Don't let me know
Tell yourself, No

When you come out of my mind
You're a part of real time
Don't let me know
Let yourself, Go

Stay Out of My Mind
So I can hear you say
" Hello" and "Good-Bye'
"Yes" and "No"

And never know, "Why"
Stay Out Of My Mind

Copyright 2001 Francis E. Delaney   P-0101-MA

COUNTRY IN YOUR EYES

Watch a flower grow
A bud will blossom
Its beauty is sweet
Country in your eyes

Love in the kitchen
Butterflies in the field
The birds and the bees
Play in the flowers and the trees

The love that's in your heart
Awakens in me
All the ways that you are
Country in my heart

The tears in your eyes
Open your heart wide
From the mountains to the seas
Country in Your Eyes

Across this land of yours and mine
There's a flag that fly
Red, White and Blue
It Colors

The Country In Your Eyes

Copyright 2001 Francis E. Delaney   P-0102-LL

JUST ME

Make it all worth living
Give life, a love
Give it all
That never was

You are you
You don't change
You're not someone
You never were

I am, Just Me
I am a Man
You are a woman
You are just you

I am a man
In the wonderful world
Of a woman

In that wonderful world of love
You are just you
I am, JUST ME

Copyright 2001 Francis E. Delaney   p-0103-LL

IS THERE MORE OF YOU FOR ME TO LOVE

You came into my life when I needed you
You make me smile and make me laugh
Make my love more than it ever was
Is There More Of You For Me To Love

Have I loved you as far as you can go
Is it time for me to leave, to walk away from love
Is There More Of You For Me To Love

More of the words you say and the words you don't
More of the things you do and the things you won't
More of the love you gave and the love you give
Is There More Of You For Me To Love

I came into your life when you needed me
I make you smile and make you laugh
Take your love to where it never was
Is There More Of You For Me To Love

Have I loved you as far as I can go
Is it time for you to love, all the feelings of my love
Is there more of me for you to love
Is it time for me to be all that you can make me
Is it time for me to love all the feelings of your love

You came into my life when I needed you
You make me happy and make me sad
Take my love to heights it never was
Is There More Of You For Me To Love

Have I loved you as far as I can go
Is it time for me to leave, walk away from love
Is there More Of You For Me To Love

Copyright 2001 Francis E. Delaney   S-0104-LL

ARE YOU THE REASON WHY

words & music:
Francis E. Delaney

I look a-cross the years Lis-ten to words I no long-er hear

Mem-o-ries in tears, a can of beer

Are you the rea-son why

I would nev-er feel this way If I nev-er met you

VERSE 2:
Would have nev-er touched my dream Or a bot-tle of Jim Beam

BRIDGE: Some peo-ple live a life-time Things nev-er

change Some live their lives In a bot-tle of

wine Then there is me I found life's beau-ty

CHORUS:
In a real live dream I found you,

© 2001 FRANCIS E. DELANEY all rights reserved.
P.O. Box 932 Frankfort, IL 60423

#LAP-1006-LL

RL

A LITTLE BIT MORE THAN LOVE .

I look into your eyes
Watch them laugh and watch them cry
Watch them touch my heart
And wonder why the feelings inside
Are a Little Bit More than love

You look into my eyes
Watch them laugh and watch them cry
Watch them touch your heart
And wonder why the teardrops inside
Are a Little Bit More Than Love

It's a Little Bit More Than love
A pleasure to describe the feeling inside
You're a Little Bit More
Your the feeling inside

Look into your eyes the feeling inside
Make them smile, make them laugh
When your eyes touch mine
Our hearts wonder why
It's a Little Bit More than Love

It's a little bit more
A pleasure to describe the feeling inside
You're a Little Bit More Than Love
You're the feeling inside

Your a little bit more.

Copyright 2001 Francis E. Delaney   P-0105-LL

ARE YOU THE REASON, WHY

I look across the years
Listen to words I no Longer hear
Memories in tears, a can of beer
Are You The Reason, why

I would never feel this way
If I never met you
Would have never touched my dream
Or a bottle of Jim Beam

Some people live a lifetime
Things never change
Some live their life
In a bottle of Jim Beam

Then there is me
I found life's beauty
I found you
My real live dream

Then there is you the reason to be
All that I see in my real live dream
I'm still alive
Are You The Reason, why

There's is still me
I found life's story in other peoples dreams
In a can of beer. a glass of wine
And a bottle of Jim Beam

ARE YOU THE REASON, WHY

Copyright 2001 Francis E. Delaney   S-0106-LL

THE FEELING INSIDE

I look into your eyes
Watch them laugh and watch them cry
Watch them touch my heart and wonder, why
The Feeling Inside
Is a little bit more than love

You look into my eyes
Watch them laugh and watch them cry
Watch them touch your heart and wonder, why
The tear-drops inside
Are a little bit more then love

It's a little bit more than love
A pleasure to describe the feeling inside
You're a little bit more than love
Your The Feeling inside

Look into your eyes the feeling inside
I make them smile and I make them talk
When your eyes touch mine
Our hearts are in time
It's a little bit more than love

It's a Little bit more than love
A treasure, a keepsake, the feelings inside
You're a little bit more than love
You're THE FEELING INSIDE

Copyright 2001 Francis E. Delaney   S-0107-LL

NOW, YOUR ACTING LIKE A WOMAN

Now, Your Acting Like A Woman
What happened to the way you were
A flower full in bloom
A rose bud in the breeze, determined to be
In all the ways a woman can be

The rose bud has bloomed
To the beauty I see

Protected by nature in all of her ways
A woman is a flower in bloom

Honey for the bee
A treat for the birds
Gods lovely creature
And in the eyes of this man
A blossom to bloom

Now, Your Acting Like A Woman
What happened to the way your were

A flower in bloom

A woman in love

Copyright 2001 Francis E. Delaney   P-0108-LL

WATER AND DIRT

God colored the earth with Water and Dirt
Gave it sight with the sun in the sky
Colored its nose with the fragrance of a rose
Let it hear with the animals and birds with the miracle of birth
Gave it a taste of food from Water and Dirt
And a touch of heaven right here on earth
With the miracle of His birth

Now, He looks at His masterful work and He sees the miracle of life
Washed away in Water and Dirt
The haze in the sky reflects
The rose, that is scorched from the wars that have discolored His earth
And as the animals and birds leave His earth
He sees you and me, we don't try to keep His masterpiece alive
In the miracle of birth

Now, He watches the beginning of the end of His earth
For each little baby that is aborted before birth
Takes with him what is his on earth, a little Water and Dirt
A little light from the sun in the sky
A rose, an animal and a bird and a taste of food
And the touch of heaven right here on earth
The miracle of birth

There is not much that we can say, but there's world can do
We can give birth to that little baby, he is the miracle of life
She is the earth, made of Water and Dirt
To give birth to His universe

Perhaps someday the Bill of Rights will say
Once conceived you have the right to breath

Copyright 2001, Francis E. Delaney   P-0109-MM

ALL THAT TOUCHES ME

As our world becomes one
All that I see and hear touches me

Your, All That Touches Me

Your love touches all the senses of life
See, hear, taste, touch and smell

Every beat of your heart
Takes me through its fields

Your, All That Touches Me

Every beat of my heart
Tells me all my senses know

Your, All That Touches Me

In all that I see

All that I hear

All that I taste

All that I touch

All that I smell

All That Touches Me, In the words that I write

Copyright 2001 Francis E. Delaney   P-0110-LL

EMOTIONS OF LOVE

Emotions of Love

Roll out of your eyes

To warm this heart of mine

Feelings of a love

That stand still in time

I look in your eyes

I see mine

Your heart holding mine

Emotions of a time in our mind

Your love loving mine

Emotions of Love

Copyright 2001, Francis E. Delaney   P-0111-MM

LETTERS IN LOVE

The words you found
In your Letters In Love
Are the words I found
When you turn around
And see the sights and quiet sounds
Of a love affair without bounds
Letters In Love

The words I found
In your Letters In Love
Are the words I find
When I turn around
And see the sights and quiet sounds
Of a love that has passed on
Letters In Love

In this world of today
I turn around and see
The internet in the universe
What does it see
That we can not
Sights and sounds
Without bounds

Letters In Love

Copyright 2001 Francis E. Delaney   P-0112-FD

NEXT TO YOU

When I'm Next to you
Your smile makes life a pretty place to be
The shadow of your silhouette
Touches me in all of loves ways

I look around and see no sound
But in my heart I know
Love is a quiet place to be

You look around and see no one
Every time it happens
Me, Next to you

Dose not, matter where you are
It's a pleasant place to be
All of life's beauty
Next to me

If my life touches you
Yours touched mine
If it all didn't happen
We would have met

Me, Next to You

Copyright 2001 Francis E. Delaney   P-0113-LL

WHEN NO, MEANS YES

When No, Means Yes
No is easy to say
It's a way to escape
To where you have been
Where no one will ask
For a Yes or a No

I can ask you to say Yes
You can always tell yourself, No
For when love is love, you know
It's not yes or No
When No Means Yes
It's Love

It's love, when you know
There's no other way
To describe the feeling inside
When No Means Yes
It's easy to say, Yes
For no one will tell you, No

I'm asking you now
For all that is yours
Is all that I have
And all that I have is you
My miracle of love
When No Means Yes——

You

Copyright 2001 Francis E. Delaney   P-0114-LL

WHEN THE MUSIC PLAYS

When the music plays
Your heart sings a song
I listen to your song
Feel your love
When the Music Plays

Oh, the music played
Through all of the years
It was loud, it was soft
It was happy, it was sad
When the music played

Now the music plays again
It plays loud, it plays soft
It plays happy, it plays sad
It plays. for today and tomorrow

As the music plays
My heart sings a song
Listen to your heart
Feel it's love

When The Music Plays
It's a duet to love
Today and tomorrow

Copyright 2001 Francis E. Delaney   P-0115-LL

I WANTA CHEAT WITH YOU

When you never cheat
It's hard to start
Even though my love has left me

To love some one new
 Is a challenge I never knew

Don't change a thing
For It's still there
It made me aware

I can't cheat on you
Because, I Wanta Cheat With You

Can I cheat with you
Say good-bye to the past

Hello, to the future

If I can have you the way you are
I Wanta Cheat With You

Copyright 2001 Francis E. Delaney   P-0116-LL

YOU

If the love I never knew
Was in all those years
Before I met you
Are You, the love I never knew

Are You, the reason why
A love I never knew
Said, I do, to someone new
Are You, the reason I'm still blue

I want to say Hello, to you
And Good-bye
To all I never knew
Is the love I never knew
You

Are You, the reason why
I never said, I do
All through the years
I didn't know You

Is the love I never knew
In all the years since I meet You
Is the love I never knew
YOU

Copyright 2001 Francis E. Delaney   P-0117-LL

TAKE A WALK AROUND THE MOON WITH ME

On the ride to the moon
I'll ask you to say, I Do
So we can lose the blues

Take a Walk Around The moon With Me
In the light of the moon, I will look at you
On the face of the moon, I will hold you
In a shadow on the moon, I will kiss you
Love's playing on the moon

Take a Walk Around The Moon With me
On the dark side of the moon
I'll ask you, to say I Do
In the cradle of the moon, I'll love you
In the cradle of the moon, we will lose the blues

When the sun covers the moon
An eclipse of love, a solar affair
On the face of the moon

A solar affair, you loving me
On the dark side of the moon
An eclipse of love
On the face of the moon

Take a Walk Around The Moon With Me
We will lose the blues

Copyright 2001 Francis E. Delaney   P-0118-MH 66

WHY

Sit down

Take a look

At all who pass

Through your life

All you know

All you don't know

Ask them all

Why ?

Me

Why

Copyright 2001 Francis E. Delaney   P-0119-LL

JUST LOOKING AT YOU

I live, the impossible dream
I feel the songs feelings
For all that was impossible was possible
Just Looking At You

Now, I feel the song, Feelings
It's the feeling inside
When all that is impossible, is possible
Just Looking At You

Live, the impossible dream
For no one else has ever felt you like me
Feelings that never were are there
When I'm, Just Looking At You

Feelings say, I love you
The impossible dream is possible
For I have fallen in love with you
Just Looking At You

I live, the impossible dream
For you have fallen in love with me
Feelings that never were are here
When I'm, Just Looking At You

Feelings say, I love you
The impossible dream is true
For I have fallen in love
JUST LOOKING AT YOU

Copyright 2001 Francis E. Delaney   S-0120-LL

TENNESSEE SUNSHINE

Riding in the countryside
In the Tennessee Sunshine
Clouds come and go
The sun says, Hello

Driving the streets of Nashville
Walking on the sidewalks of Tennessee
Dinner at the Stockyard Restaurant
Tennessee memories

Hair golden by the sun
Eyes lightened by suntan
Looking from a bronze body
Painted by the sun
Tennessee Sunshine

I look up at a sky of blue
See the sunshine and remember you
I look up at the stars of night
See them in a glass of wine

Hair golden by the sun
Eyes sparking in the stars
Looking through the light of the moon
Painted by the sun
TENNESSEE SUNSHINE

Copyright 2001 Francis E. Delaney   P-0121-MD

IF IT DIDN'T HAPPEN

Maybe it didn't happen
Maybe it never will
Time knows the answer to that

As long as you're happy
Each and every year
Everything in our life

HAPPENS   P-0122-LL

YES

What is, Yes
It is the opposite of, No

What is, No
It is the opposite of, Yes

What if you say, No
What do you do

You guess

Why

It is the opposite of, YES

Copyright 2001 Francis E. Delaney   P-0123-LL

WE FOUND LOVE

Have you often wondered, Why
There's no water when it's dry
And the tears in your eyes
Are rainbows when you cry

All that was, is at one end of the rainbow
And when love, loves again
All that will be, is unknown to you and me
It's at the other end of the rainbow

We Found Love
In all that we see and hear
For all that will be, never was
And all that never was, is here
In the music we hear
Where we find love

As we reach for the other end of rainbow
We find all its colors in the sun
All its beauty pictured in the sky
Its rainbow in our eyes

For at the other end of the rainbow
Are all the reasons, why
WE FOUND LOVE

Copyright 2001 Francis E. Delaney   P-0124-KY

STEP OUT OF THE PICTURE

When love becomes
As real as life can be
Step Out Of The Picture
Come along with me

Love is a picture where you can find
The time and the place to love
It's where ever you are
When you're in love

Step Out Of The Picture
See the sights, hear the sounds
Taste the rain, feel the ground
Look around and you hold love in your arms

The picture on the wall has no sound
You can see it and you can touch it
Step Out Of The Picture
And hold me in your arms

Step Out OF The Picture

Copyright 2001 Francis E. Delaney   P-0125-LL

YOU STARTED IT ALL

Do you remember the day you said
That I started it all
I remember that day, it was you
You, Started It All

You can't blame me
It was your smile
When I called you Mona Lisa
Your beauty smiled at me
It took me to another world
Where no one else has been

I'm in your picture on the wall
In your eyes that look at me
And as you listen to your music
I'm in the heart of your picture on the wall

Put my picture next to yours on the wall
Let your mother know she started it all
When she asked you "Who is this Guy"
Flirting with you, singing your song

Lisa, When you find your love
Let him in where no one else has been

When you have a little son
Put his picture on the wall next to mine
When he's old enough to ask you, "Who is this guy"
And why, is his picture on the wall

Tell him how and why, YOU STATRED IT ALL

Copyright 2001 Francis E. Delaney   S-0126-LL

REST OF THE WAY

Falling in love with you
Is a love I never knew
The spirit of your love touched me
Take me, the Rest of The Way

All the feelings I've had
And all that I never have
Now fill my body, soul and mind
Take me, the Rest Of The Way

Love is a butterfly waltzing in the sky
Love is a flower watching it fly
They touch and take love the Rest of the Way
Touch me, take me the Rest Of The Way

Tears of love touch our hearts
Take our love to the first day
As the smile that brought you my way
Takes me the Rest Of the Way

When my story comes to its end
Wipe your tears away
All I want to hear is the music of our years
As my love takes you the Rest Of The Way

Tears of love touch our hearts
Takes our love to the last day
When your smile that brought me, your way
Takes me, the Rest Of the Way

When our story comes to its end
Take my tears with you, take me the REST OF THE WAY

Copyright 2001 Francis E. Delaney   S-0127-LL

IS THAT THE BEST THAT YOU CAN

It breaks my heart in two
Just watching you
Are you just another looser
Is That The Best That You Can Do

Open your eyes
See the spider spin his web
What's the matter with you
Is That The Best That You Can Do

Open your ears
Hear the spider spin his web
Everybody knows
You can do better than that

When there is no wind
The leaves don't fly
The sea is calm
Find someone new

Everybody knows, everybody asks
Is there someone better for you
You break their heart in two
Is That the Best that You Can Do

Copyright 2001 Francis E. Delaney   P-0128-MD

ARENA OF LOVE

In the Arena of Love

The rose is the heart of love

In a rose

We find all the beauty of life

In Life

We find all The beauty of Love

In Love

We find each other

In each other

We find the

ARENA OF LOVE

Copyright 2001 Francis E. Delaney   P-0129-AP

ONE MORE TIME

From the feelings in my heart
You travel in my mind
And I know I'm going to ask you
To love me, One More Time

I see myself in a world of love
In a place I never was

I travel in your heart
Through the rivers of your mind
The limits of time
To love you, One More Time

Life takes my heart
Beyond the limits of time
To your beauty of love
In the mirrors in my mind

I travel in your heart
Through the rivers of your mind
Mysteries of wine
To taste love, One More Time

The feelings in our heart
Travel through our minds
And we know we are going to ask us
To love us, ONE MORE TIME

Copyright 2001 Francis E. Delaney   S-0130-LL

ALWAYS WITH LOVE

Just a short little poem

To say I write all of them

With you in my mind

Most of the time

And

ALWAYS IN LOVE

Copyright 2001 Francis E. Delaney   P-0131-MM

WHEN YOU REMEMBER ME

There was a time when I didn't dream
For I didn't believe, there would ever be
Someone who would fall in love with me

Then there was one, beautiful and shy
When You Remember Me
Remember the Melody Of Mary
She made me who I am today

Then there was two, tough and as pretty as you
When You Remember Me
Remember, the Hills Of Maureen
She made me the man I am today

Then there was three, the combination of one and two
When You Remember Me
Remember the other two

They left it all
All the music and all the words
That describe what life and love is like
To the one who loves the man I am

Copyright 2001 Francis E. Delaney   P-0132-LL

RED, WHITE, AND BLUE CHRISTMAS TREE

Red, White and Blue Christmas Tree
This is what it means to me

The gifts that are brought when Christmas is sad
The heartaches and tears that fill the empty years
The smiles of the girls and boys and the laughter of their toys
Mama Kissing Santa Clause, and Daddy knowing, why

He is proud of the color God made her
Proud of the colors He gave to her

Red, for the blood that keeps her free
White for the crosses that died for you and me
Blue for the sadness in the faces she sees
Soldiers of freedom in her history

Color her, Lisa, U.S.A.
Color her American, color her free
A soldier of freedom in the wonderful world of woman in the USA
Color her American, color her free
With a Red, White and Blue Christmas Tree

Color your America, Color Her Free

Copyright 2001 Francis E. Delaney   P-0133-LL

LOVES DEVINE PERFUMES

The truth of love can never be
Unless you found Loves Devine Perfumes
The truth of love will make you blue
Love, faith, trust and understanding

Have faith in the one you love
Trust and understand the reasons of love

Have trust in the one you love
Love and understand the loyalty of love

To understand the one you love
Know the meaning of love

Love is the strongest affection one can have
Its definition is Gods Devine Perfumes

When you love the one who loves you
You have loved the one you love

The truth of love will make you blue
LOVES DEVINE PERFUMES, will keep you true

Copyright 2001 Francis E. Delaney   P0134-ML

SMILE

A smile is the feeling in your eyes
The tickle in your nose
As your ears listen to
There whisper in your ear

What am I going to do
The smile in my heart
Tells me it is true

I love you
With a smile or two

Can it be true
You love me too

It must be true
For God smiled on me

When I met You
Thank You

Copyright 2001 Francis E. Delaney   P-0135-LL

A ROSE NAMED MARY

I'll miss a Rose Named Mary, my lead guitar
But, most of all I'll miss my band, Lisa Ann

The fiddle and the steel guitar
The key boards, drums and bass guitar
The steel and wire strings, the music in the band
Playing in the heart of Lisa Ann

Every beat a word, every word a smile
Every smile a kiss, every kiss a melody of love

I fell in love with the music in the band
And a little bit more than love, Lisa Ann

Never though I'd ever find another band
Where the harmony and melody
Is a concordant of musical sound
The principal words of a song

Thought I'd found her but I guess I goofed
Thought I'd love her but I guess I can't

Fiddle with the steel guitar
Keyboards, drums and bass guitar
All the words and all the music in the band
Is it over or has it just began

I fell in love with the music in the band
And a little bit more

Lisa Ann

Copyright 2001 Francis E. Delaney   S-0136-LL

WALKING THE WRONG WAY

Your, Walking The Wrong Way
Taking an easy ride on a hard road
Where love is rough and life is tough
In a love affair that leads to nowhere

Your, Walking the Wrong Way
Thinking it's easy on the other side
Where love isn't there and life's not fair
In love affairs that come and go nowhere

Walking The Wrong Way
Looking back at a love still there
For all that is now
Leads to nowhere

Your, Walking the Wrong Way
Taking an easy ride on a hard road
Where loves are rough and life is tough
In love affairs that come and go

WALKING THE WRONG WAY

Copyright 2001 Francis E. Delaney   P-0137-MD

AS TIME GOES BY

Love tells no lies
As each new affair
Comes and goes
I find no time

When I was young
Life stood still
When life got faster
I found no time

As Time Goes By
Loves becomes life

When there was not time for love

I found all that love was

All that love is

Too much love for too less time

As Time Goes By

I find all that love

In all of my life

Copyright 2001 Francis E. Delaney   P-0138-FD

IT'S STILL THERE

I walk backwards through the years
All the laughter and all the tears
All the times I should
All the days you would

It's Still There

All the looks and all the feelings
All the love that always was
Is here today
When you look my way

It's Still There

It's the light in every star
In every flower I see
It's the sun that never sets
In your eyes that touch me

It's Still There

I walk forward through the years
All its laughter and all its tears
Are here today
When I look your way

IT'S STILL THERE

Copyright 2001 Francis E. Delaney   P-0139-MD co

TENNESSEE LOVE

A love never started, never ends
It lasts forever in your mind
In a little taste of wine
The heat of the sunshine
And a love for Tennessee
Tennessee Love

The stars in your eyes
Forever in the sky
Remind me of a time
When all I had to do, was ask
For a glass of Tennessee wine
Tennessee Love

Now, as you walk softly in my mind
I feel the spirit of Tennessee wine
The heat of the Tennessee sunshine
And the love of Tennessee, Tennessee Love

Love is as only love can be
As yours and mine survive
The heartaches and tears of cheated years
I feel your spirit
In the heat of the sunshine
The love of Tennessee

Love is as only as love will be
If yours and mine survive
My love for Tennessee, never will die
For all I have to ask for, is a glass of wine
In a little bottle of perfume wine, TENNESSEE LOVE

Copyright 2001 Francis E. Delaney   P-0140-MD

WE ARE ONE

I looked at love and I saw Life
I look at you, what do I see
You are life, you are love
You Are Me, We Are One

Copyright 2001 Francis E. Delaney   P-0141-MH   1957

Will To Win (the)

Look at life
All that you have done
You think there is no more to do
And you find in life and love
You still have not won

Against all odds
Do you have the Will To Win
You can't loose what you never had
But you can win if it's yours to have

Do you have what it takes to win
It's yours to have
Against all odds
If you have the WILL TO WIN

Copyright 2001 Francis E. Delaney   P-0142-LL

NO ONE ELSE Year 2002

I look
I see
All that No One Else
Can see

I listen
I hear
What No One Else
Can hear

I try
Don't ask me
Why

I Found
What No One Else
Can have

You and Me

Copyright 2002 Francis E. Delaney   P-0200-KY

SLEIGHBELL

Back in nineteen eighty-one
I wrote a song Sleighbell

Hold your heart a little higher
Walk a little spryer
I'll stop and talk when you walk by
I'll say "Hello, Sleighbell"

Today I write this poem to Sleighbell
In the mystery of the wine
And all the minutes of time
May you always enjoy

This poetry of yours and mine from the line
"Your smile prints your picture in my mind"
A memory of you
Where ever we may be

Copyright 2002 Francis E. Delaney   P-0201-LL

WILL IT EVER BE OVER

Like a cat in the night
Your eyes pierce the light
We see all that was, and wonder
Will It Ever Be Over

Like the bud of a rose
It blossoms when it does
For it knows, it needs love
Will It Ever Be Over

Its colors are all in the rainbow
Painting your picture in my eyes
Its petals, ribbons in the sky
Will It Ever Be Over

Will It Ever Be Over
For your smile is the rainbow
Of the roses in your heart
All its love, when it starts

Copyright 2002 Francis E. Delaney   P-0202-KY

ALL THAT YOU WERE MEANT TO BE

Some times there's no reason for being blue
Just look back over the years
Each and every day that brought you here
Are All The Things You Were Meant To Be

Sometimes there's no answer for the tears
So look back into the years
Each and every tear that brought you to this year
Are All The Things You Were Meant To Be

When you find that smile, that awakens your eyes
Look back across the years
Each and every smile over all the miles
Are All The Things You Were Meant To Be

When you find the love, that awakens your heart
All the years of the past, make sense at last
For each smile and each tear, each day and each year
Awakens the love in your heart, to start

ALL THAT YOU WERE MEANT TO BE

Copyright 2002 Francis E. Delaney   P-0203-LL

NEXT TO ME

I look around and see no sound
But in my heart I know
If it all didn't happen
I would have never met you

Every time it happens
You, Next To Me
Life is a pleasant place to be
With all of loves treasures, Next To Me

If your life only touches me
It touched me
In all the ways I want it to be
All of life's beauty Next To Me

I look around and hear no sound
But in my heart I know
I will hear that sound
And listen to the quiet words you found

Every time it happens
You, Next To Me
Love is a quiet place to be
With all of loves pleasures next to me

Where ever I am
Your smile makes life a pretty place to be
Your heart a joy to be around
With all of loves beauty NEXT TO ME

Copyright 2002, Francis E. Delaney   S-0204-LL

STRICTLY BUSINESS

Don't ask no questions
Just be on time
Do your work
Everything will be fine

It is, Strictly Business
Nothing else will do
So if you do your job
Good-Bye to you

On the other hand
If you should fall in love
While working for me
Remember one thing

When your mother wants to know
Who is this guy, just tell her
I got the job, I got today
Because he passed my way

Told me to ask no questions

Because he told me no lies

Copyright 2002 Francis E. Delaney   P-0205-KY

DOG HOUSE BLUES

I got the Dog House Blues loving you
Hanging in the hallways of your heart
Playing with its love strings
Love barking at the rhythm of your heart
Listening to the beat of the love in your heart
Feeling the tickle and the tingle of your loveable parts

I got the Dog House Blues loving you
Listening to the rhythm of the love in your heart
Loving you to, the Dog House Blues
Love barking from the dog house in your heart
Hoping in the morning when I awake
The dog house door will be unlocked

Listen to the beat of the love in my heart
The tickle and the tingle of your lovable parts
Loving me to, the Dog House Blues
Loving to the beat of the love in our hearts
Knowing in the morning when we awake
The dog house door will be unlocked

I got the Dog House Blues loving you
To the beat of your music in my heart
The tickle and tingle of its playable parts
Loving you to, the Dog House Blues
Dancing in the dog house with you
To the rhythm and the beat of
The, Dog House Blues

Copyright 2002 Francis E. Delaney   P-2006-KY

GIVE IT TIME

Give It Time
And a dream will come true
The reality of fantasies
Is a dream coming true

When you see love the next time
Your flowers will bloom
Love will come in time
Give It Time

As your love comes alive
The fantasy of reality
Is a love coming true
Give It Time

He will come again
And you will be there
To share love
Give It Time

The flower will bloom
In love that rhymes
Give him time, unwind
GIVE IT TIME

Copyright 2002 Francis E. Delaney   P-0207-LL

BEAUTY OF YOU

You have ears, to listen
Eyes to see
You have a mouth that talks
And when it smiles
It is the Beauty of You

You have a heart to listen to
The words your ears hear
You have a mind of your own
And when it's thinking of what to do
It is the Beauty Of You

When you talk, listen
For your ears to hear the words

When you walk, it's telling me
It Is the Beauty Of You

You have love
Listen to it's beat
It is gentle and sweet
It is the Beauty Of You

Copyright 2002 Francis E. Delaney   P-0209-LL

CHRISTMAS IN SPACE (At Your Place)

Santa went from star to star
Visiting the planets near and far
His reindeer climbed the chimneys of the stars
For their Christmas in Space at your place

Christmas in Space is where it starts
With all the children nobody wants
They took with them what was theirs on earth
Love, a little glass of water and a little dirt

A bird, an animal a flower and a tree
They gave life to their planet of dreams
From the internet screen to the chimneys of the stars

Take a look at your Christmas Sweetheart
If you can see
Love, a little glass of water and a little dirt
A bird an animal a flower and a tree

You got Christmas in Space at your place
The nicest place you like to be
Where life slows down to let you see
Just how very nice things can be

CHRISTMAS IN SPACE
This earth with all its families
The children of the stars at——Your Place

Copyright 2002 Francis E. Delaney   S-0210-LL

MIDDLE OF NOWHERE

Your every where I go
But, nowhere is where you are
I want to love the way you are
In the Middle Of Nowhere
In the middle of love

I carry you in the cradle of my love
The champers of my heart
Running through the parries of my mind
A tumbleweed, a tumbling in time
In the, Middle Of Nowhere

Drifting on a cloud, sleeping in my mind
In the, Middle Of Nowhere

In a little glass of wine, oceans of time
You travel in the desert of my mind
The sun is hot on a empty cloud
Drifting on the back roads of my mind
In the, Middle Of Nowhere

Bubbles in the wine, floating in my mind
A tumbleweed drifting in time
From the, Middle Of Nowhere
To the Middle of Love

Copyright 2002, Francis E. Delaney   S0-0211-LL

MELODIES IN WINE

Dry taunting wines, feathers in my mind
Wet bubbling wines, loves that had no time
Bittersweet wines, loves I thought were mine
Are but memories of mine
Beautiful melodies in time

White haunting wine, bursting in my mind
Cool sparking wine, champagne of wines
Red rare wine, mystery of time
A million blossoms chime
Melodies In Wine

Loves I thought were mine
Are but memories of time
Rare, beautiful loves, that unwind
Countless melodies
In the blood steams of my mind

Clear Rhine wine, visions in my mind
Taunting the blood streams of my time
Beautiful blossoms on a vine
Love wine, floods my mind
Yours and mine

Melodies In Wine

Copyright 2002 Francis E. Delaney   P-0212-LL

YOU CAN ALWAYS LOOK AT ME

The eyes of Eve, look into the sun
I listen to me
Can you see what I hear
Loves arrow, always looking
From the corner of your eye

If there was another you
Waiting for someone to love
I'd walk across the world
For the other part of love
Tennessee love in the eyes of Tennessee

Was it always you
All the days with you
The way you wear your hair
Is it all your fault from the fiddlers waltz
To the pony rock and Louisiana Honeymoon

Was it always you
Perfume wine, a touch of love
Blue roses on the hills of Tennessee
What do you want, Tennessee
You Can Always Look At Me

For I'm always looking at you

Copyright 2002 Francis E. Delaney   P-0213-MD

THE WAY I AM

I place my love
In care of you

And watch it turn
From red to blue

Her heart has left me
The Way I Am

A heart that loved me
To a heart that does

I place my heart
In care of you

And watch it turn
From all colors of blue

I believe in miracles
And watch them turn
From red to gold

Miracles of Love
God has placed
The Way I Am

In care of you

Copyright 2002 Francis E. Delaney   P-0214-CO

YOU JUST DON'T GET IT

There ain't no Mama in this world
Like the Mama you got
And there ain't no Daddy like me

She just don't understand
There ain't enough of time
To love all the time
So when I fall asleep
You Just Don't Get It

Gotta love you before I fall asleep
Or I just get to listen
To the beat of your heart
And feel your lovable parts

When we go to the corner bar
Every body's drinking and trying to score
I look around, my wife and my car are gone
My neighbor is divorced and smiling at me
As she drives me home from the corner bar

Up in the morning and I'm at the wrong front door
Gotta get home before my wife wakes up
Gotta get out of the neighbors house
She was drinking and trying to score
And I don't remember what I did next door

There ain't no Mama in this world
Like the Mama I got
There ain't no Daddy like me
And there ain't nobody gonna take you away from me

Copyright 2002 Francis E. Delaney   P-0208-TP

THIS IS WHERE I WANT TO BE

How do you say
What you should not
What is it, if it is not
All that we have

All that we laughed, all that we cried
All that we loved and all that we had
Is all that we have

All through the years
A memory of the day
A picture of the past
Comes alive in love

How do you say
What you should not

All of those years
Memories of their love
In pictures from their past
Still in our eyes

This Is Where I Want To be
In the heart of a love

How do you say
What you should not
What is it, if it is not
All that we have

This Is Where I Want To Be

Copyright 2002 Francis E. Delaney   P-0215-RV

ALL THAT I HAVE

When the sun and the moon become one

The day loves the night

The stars in your eyes light up my life

All we have to ask is, Why

All we had to say is, I Do

I Love You

Don't Mind me

You can leave

All That I Have

All that you laughed

All that you cried

All that you loved

Is All That I Have

Copyright 2002 Francis E. Delaney   P-0216-MM

YOU CAN BE, YOU

She's cute, cuter than you
In all the ways she's trying
To take me away from you

Now, there's only one thing you can do
If she decides she wants me too
You Can Be, You

Thoughtful, calm and true
Sweet, sly and shy
You Can Be, You

You could have gone all the way
Taken it all away from me
But you kept me cool
In the dog house of the blues

Now it's up to you, if she's cuter than you
What are you going to do
You Can Be, You

Your smile is your picture
In your memory and mine
You Can Be, You

What are you going to do
When you, become you
You Can Be, You

The person I knew

Copyright 2002 Francis E. Delaney   P-0217-LL

ALL THE ROSES

It isn't easy, when a rose begins to grow
From a bud, to the blossom, to the flower I know

A rose looks through her eyes
Sees' it bloom in mine
Thanks for all the Roses
Thanks for letting me love you

It isn't easy when you fall in love
It isn't easy when you first begin to love

A Rose that holds you close
To the blossoms of her heart
Thanks, for all the roses
Thanks, for letting me love you

May you always be
All that I see
Swaying with the roses
There melody loving me

Thanks for letting me love you
From a bud
To the blossom
To the flower that I see

Thanks, for All The Roses

Copyright 2002 Francis E. Delaney   P-0218-MH

Rosalie

I looked at life
Looked at love
I looked at life
Love touched me

Life comes and goes
A bud to a rose
The heart is the rose of love
For it is, Rich in love

Rosalie, look at life
Love is still there
It sees. It hears
Sounds, of all the years

All that we have
Is all that we do
As we take our life
The rest of the way

Rosalie

Look at Life
Look at love
Touch life
Love touches you

Rosalie

Copyright 2002 Francis E. Delaney   P-0219-RVW

YOUR STILL HERE

Your Still Here

All through the years
I didn't know you

Are you the miracle
I never knew

Your Still Here

A love, I never knew
Never said," Good-bye" too

For yesterday and today
Your Still Here

If Your Still Here

Tomorrow and the next day
We'll walk through the year

Read all the poems
Listen to all the songs

For the day you were there
Is the answer to, "Why"

YOUR STILL HERE

Copyright 2002 Francis E. Delaney   P-0220-LL

ANOTHER TOMORROW

I hear words. I have never heard
And find, there is more for me to say

There are tomorrows
There are yesterdays
There is today

Tomorrow will become today
Today will be yesterday
Yesterday will never come
Tomorrow may never come our way

I look and wonder
At the pictures on the wall
And I wait for another day
To see if there is Another Tomorrow

A rose is the heart of love
Its bud, the eyes of tomorrow
Eyes that wait for today
To see if there is Another Tomorrow

Another Tomorrow
Brings the love of the past
And takes it to a new day
ANOTHER TOMORROW

Copyright 2002 Francis E. Delaney   P-0221-RVW

CHEMISTRY, IN LOVE

Think of you
Think of me
Look at you
Look at me

Chemistry of love

I think of you
Though you are gone
I know our chemistry
Was a miracle in love

All that wasn't to be
Happened to you and me
I know someone else will love me
When her chemistry falls in love

When you think of me
I think of you
When you look at me
I look at you

The mystery of being in love

CHEMISTRY, IN LOVE

Copyright 2002   Francis E. Delaney   P-0222-MM-LL

YOU GOTTA LOVE, PLUMBING

Of all the wonders of the world
Plumbing is one of the most interesting
The water we use everyday
Is a story all by itself

Here in Chicago the water comes from Lake Michigan
From the cribs it goes through pipes under the lake
The filtration plants make the water pure
The piping system under ground
Brings this water to all who use water

Would all the beautiful things you see
Be there if there were no plumbers
These beautiful people bring us
Water to all the places they go
You gotta love the plumber

Next time you take a trip
Where would you want to go
Someplace where a plumber has been
Or where he has never been

You Gotta Love, Plumbing
You gotta love your plumber

Copyright 2002 Francis E. Delaney   P-0223-FD

I COULD LOVE THAT

Sitting across the table
Eyes looking in mine

What the hell
Why not ask
I Could Love That

Standing by the table
Don't sit down just turn around
I Could Love That

What the heck
Why not ask
I Could Love That

Looking at each other
Can I love you
I Could Love That

Your love everywhere
Your all that I have
I Could Love That

Why not, Ask
Can I Love You

Copyright 2002 Francis E. Delaney   P-0224-KY

CAN THIS BE DONE

The silent movement of your love
Paints your picture in my mind
I kiss the sweet lips
And taste the moon in the rivers of your eyes

Can This Be Done
Only time will tell
Who is number one
Can This Be Done

The silent music in your pen
Draws a picture in my eyes
Running in my mind
Teasing memories of mine

Can I do this
What no one else has done
Can I make you mine
Can This Be Done

What will it take
For me to do
What can not be
Can This Be Done

Who is number one
Whose words and music will it be

Can This Be Done

Copyright 2002 Francis E. Delaney   P-0225-LL

FEELING FUNNY

When your Feeling Funny

And you don't know what to do

Take a look around

And watch what all the funny people do

The good looking ones

Have no idea what they look like

If they only knew

They would be Feeling Funny too

When your ugly, Feeling Funny

Look around you and you will see

All the rich are as ugly as you

And they feel funny too

The moral of this story is

Too much money makes you Feel Funny

Copyright 2002 Francis E. Delaney   P-0226-MV

BEAUTIFUL WOMAN, BEAUTIFUL SONG

Every woman is a beautiful song
Her musical story in every shape and form
If you like to dance with a song
Get in line and line-dance with a beautiful song

Every beat is a kick, kick, kick
There ain't no kick for—No
Every step is a Yes, Yes, Yes
There is no way, she'll say—No

When you feel her song
Dance her out of the line dance
And two-step with a Beautiful Woman, Beautiful Song

Every beat is a quick, quick, slow, slow
There ain't no quick for —No
Every step is a Yes, Yes, Yes
There is no way to say—No

When you feel the beat
Take it out of the two-step
Double-two a Beautiful Woman, Beautiful Song

Every beat is a double-two
There ain't no time for—No
Every double is a Yes,Yes,Yes
There is no way to say—No

Cond

When you feel the beat
Take it out of the double
And cha-cha, a Beautiful Woman, Beautiful Song

Every beat is a cha-cha-cha
There ain't no cha-cha for—No
Each cha, cha, cha a Yes, Yes, Yes
There is no way to say—No

When you feel the beat
Take it out of the cha-cha
And waltz with a, Beautiful Woman, Beautiful Song

One, two, there, four, five, six
Will it be a Yes or a—No
One, two, three, four, five, six
There is no way to say—No

Every woman is a beautiful song
Her musical story in every shape and form
If you want to dance with her song
Slow Dance a Beautiful Woman, Beautiful Song

Hold a beautiful woman, feel her beautiful song
Slow-Dance a Beautiful Woman, Beautiful Song.

Every Woman is a Beautiful Song

Copyright 2002 Francis E. Delaney   S-0230-CV

THERE I SEE A YELLOW RIBBON

There I See a Yellow Ribbon
Leafs on the ground
Autumn turns to winter
Ribbons on a tree

Winter leaves in snow
Springs brings the rainbow
It's colors painted light
Red to green, caution in between

See a yellow ribbon
In the window of your mind
Leafs of green turn cherry red
Green to golden yellow

Look across the brook colored blue
See the faces you once knew

See the ribbon on the tree
Some are yellow, purple or pink
All are Red, White and Blue

When you see a yellow ribbon
Look across the brook colored blue
Leafs of green to a golden yellow

There I See a Yellow Ribbon
Like the seasons of the year
It colors will always be there
For another year

Copyright 2002 Francis E. Delaney   S-0228-KY

MUSIC ON THE WEB

Make a picture smile

Listen to its' laughter

You can see

A spider in the wind

Hear its' music on the web

Its' smile says, Good-Bye to its' tears

The rose in the mirror

Is your picture on the wall

Make the picture smile

Remember me

Listen to your song

Music on the Web

Copyright 2002 Francis E. Delaney   P-0229-LL

LET YOUR SELF GO

Some days are good
Some days go wrong
When all the good days are gone
Let Yourself Go

Take a ride in the country
A walk along the shore
Find a place to dine
Where you never been before

Doesn't matter if it's close or far
You'll find a friend once more
Like the friend you left behind
With the words for better or worse

So, Let yourself go
Go back to the good days
They were your best

Take a ride in the country
A walk along the shore
Find a place to dine
Where you never been before

Listen to words you never heard
We'll have our bad days, they will be our worst
We'll have our good days, they will be our best
For we will never forget, For better or worse

Copyright 2002 Francis E. Delaney   P-0227-CV

RUNNING LATE

Divorced with two kids
Running Late on Route sixty-six
Which way will I turn
Early for love, late for work

When you are late, I wait
To see if it will be
Another vary blue day
Or Love Running Late

A love very blue
Is a love Running Late
Tell me it's impossible
And I'll tell you it is not

Divorced with two kids
Running late on route sixty-six
Which way will I turn
Early for love, late for work

You put love in my life
Life in my love
I was early for love
And late for work

Copyright 2002 Francis E. Delaney   P-0231-CV

A SET OF BLUES

Colors I see
Rusty hair, a melody in the wind
The words I hear
To the music of my eyes,
A Set Of Blues

Colors of love
Sunsets in hair of rusty gold
Strawberry pie in a rainbow sky
Blue sparks in your eyes
A Set Of Blues

In the mirrors of my mind
Feelings no money can buy
Pictures in your eyes
Blue wine in mine
A Set Of Blues

Early for work
Late for love
Too much love
Too little time

A Set Of Blues
Running Late
And out of time

Copyright 2002 Francis E. Delaney   P-2032-FD

WITH LOVE, I LOVED YOU   2003

You loved me. I loved you.
I feel you like no one has ever felt you
See you in a way no one else could do
The way you are, when I look at you

Like no one I know, your unique beauty
Looks at me in a way only you can feel
With Love, your eyes touch mine

I look into your mind
Your eyes reading mine
The impossible is true
We are in love, with us

Me loving you loving me
You loving me, loving you

I loved you. You loved me.
You feel me like no one has ever felt me
See me in a way no one else could see
The way I am, when you look at me

You look into my mind
Your eyes telling mine
The impossible is true
I'm loving with you

With Love——It started
With Love——I Loved You
With Love——Loved Me —With Love

With Love—It started again

Copyright 2003, Francis E. Delaney   S-0301-MM

LITTLE PART OF TIME

When I think of you

I see you

In, that Little Part Of Time

Your beauty takes me back

To the time and place

In that, Little Part Of Time

When the Lord takes me

To my special place in time

I will thank him for

That precious gift of mine

Your picture forever in my mind

In that, Little Part Of Time

Your smile

Copyright 2003 Francis E. Delaney   P-0302-LL

THE BILLY GOAT

You all gotta do it right
It's like a whirlpool in a swimming pool
A double two, shifting too
The fastest dance that you can do

Right vine, left vine, shuffle up and shuffle back
Left vine, right vine, shuffle back and shuffle up
Right square box and half left turn
Left square box and half right turn

You all gotta do it right
Hop three times up and down
Hip-hop, hip-hop, hip-hop
Now you kneel on the floor
Kick your toes upon the floor
Right, left, right, left
Right, Left, right, left
Stand up fast, turn around and shout
I want to do it once more

You all gotta do it right
Hop four times up and down
Hip-hop, hip-hop, hip-hop, hip-hop
Now you kneel on the floor
Kick both feet, upon the floor
One, two, three, four
One, two, three, four
Stand up fast, turn around and shout
I want to do it once more   Repeat hip- hop as many times as you want

Dance to the Billy Goat with you

Copyright 2003, Francis E. Delaney   D-0303-CO

LOVE PLUMBING

Roll out your mind
In a little ink upon a line
Tell me what you like to be
Tell me about the birds and bees

Honey's made by the bees
Birds fly free

I don't want to tell you
What I want to be
For there are many things I like to be
Tell me about the birds and bees

Well, when the birds are singing
And the bees are stinging you

There's a dance they like to do
The dance of the birds and the bees
Love plumbing in honeycombs
Love flying in the breeze

In a bird nest and a bee hive
You will see, feel and hear
The words and the music to there song
Love Plumbing

Copyright 2003, Francis E. Delaney   P-0304-LL

YOU HAVE A PLACE TO GO

When all is wrong
Life has lost its song
Close the curtain on the show
You Have A Place To Go

Where we were is in the past
The future is where we are
When the past meets the future
You Have A Place To Go

You Have A Place To Go
It's into the future
A place that nobody knows
Where love affairs come and go

You will know when love finds you
Life will sing its song again
The curtain will open
You have a part to play

Is it in the past or is it in the future
Sing your song in life and love
When you have found both
You found the future

Sing your song, play your part
Love from the heart
Make a new start
Let yourself go

YOU HAVE A PLACE TO GO

Copyright 2003 Francis E. Delaney   P-0305-CO

AS LONG AS YOU CAN

When someone finds you
After someone you loved ahs left you
What do you do, How do you say
I'll love you, As Long As I Can

How do, " I love you"
Until the last, "I Love You"

I love with my heart that loves yours
The tears it cries, the laughs it laughs
The love it loves, as long as it last
I'll love you, As Long As I Can

Until you say, "I Love You"
How do I say, "I Love You"

I love with your heart that loves mine
The tears it cries, the laughs it laughs
The love it loves, as long as it last
I'll love you, As Long As I Can

When someone loves you
Until the last, "I Love You"
Love as long as you can
And "I'll love you"

AS LONG AS I CAN

Copyright 2003, Francis E. Delaney   P-0306-CO

LIFT ME UP

Whose gonna know me, whose gonna care
I know what its like, alone
Days are short, nights are long
The sun never shines on the moon

There is no other high
In the feelings of life
Then when you love me
You Lift Me Up

When you know me, you will care
For you know what its like
When love is right
You know, you care, you love

Be all of my days
Fill all of my nights
For I know what it's like
When love is right, it lifts you up

There's something nice
About love and life
Do what you do, love when you can
Lift Me Up

There is no other high
In the feelings of life
Then when you love me
You, LIFT ME UP

Copyright 2003. Francis E. Delaney   P-0307-JB

I'M A SOLDIER TOO

Soldier of Freedom, ribbon on a tree
Red, white and blue flying free
Singing on the wind
"I'm A Soldier Too"

Cross my hands on my heart
And I hold you in my arms

Color Lourie, Jessica and Shanna U.S.A.
Soldiers of Freedom, ribbons on a tree
Color 9-1, Lisa: Red White and Blue
I'm A Soldier Too

Proud of the color God made me
Proud of the colors He gave to me
In the wonderful world of woman in the U.S.A.
"I'm A Soldier Too"

Red for the blood that keeps me free
White for the crosses of three centuries
Blue for the memory in the ribbons I see
They are soldiers too

Color Lourie, Jessica and Shanna U.S.A.
Soldiers of Freedom in our history
Color 9-11, Lisa, Red, White and Blue
She's a soldier Too

I cross my hands on her heart
And I Hold America in my arms

Copyright 2003 Francis E. Delaney   S-0308-LL

RIBBON ON A TREE (I'm A Soldier Too)

Soldiers Of Freedom, Ribbons On A Tree
Red White and Blue flying free
Singing on the wind " I'm A Soldier Too "

Color Lori, Jessica and Shanna U.S.A.
Soldiers of freedom, Ribbons on a Tree
Never forget nine-eleven, Lisa and "Let's Roll"
"I'm A Soldier Too"

Red for the blood that keeps me free
White for the graves of three centuries
Blue for the memory in the faces I see
Soldiers of freedom, Ribbons On a Tree

We are the sons and daughters of America
Proud of the colors God made us
In the wonderful world of woman in the U.S.A.
"I'm A Soldier Too"

Color Lori, Jessica and Shanna U.S.A.
Soldiers of freedom, Ribbons on a tree
Never forget nine-eleven, Lisa and "Let's Roll"
"I'm a Soldier Too"

Cross my hands on my heart
And hold America in my arms
"She's a Soldier Too"

Ribbons on a Tree, They are Soldiers too

Cross your hands on her Heart
And you hold America in your arms
"She's a Soldier Too"

Copyright 2002   Francis E. Delaney   S-0310-LL

THEE SONG (With Love)

I can feel and hear the wind
For I can feel loves arrow cut so deep and hurt so bad

Keep me warm for love never ends
Keep me sweet with your perfumes
Keep me loving you
Keep me with you

I climb the mountain, taste the snow
Bare the cold of the wind I feel and hear
For I know your ruffled love will keep me warm

Keep me warm with love I can see
Keep me sweet with life perfumes
Keep me loving you
Keep me with you

I love your person, taste your tears
Bare the heat of the wind I feel and hear
For I know your special love will keep me warm

Keep me warm with love I can feel
Keep me sweet with your perfumes
Love me loving you
Love me al ways

With--Thee Song-- that never ends
Your love, loving me--"With Love"
In the songs I write since your gone

Copyright 2003   Francis E. Delaney   S-0311-MM

RHYTHM OF THE RIBBONS

Another day is done
You are there and I am here
The two parts of love
When yesterday seemed so close, as today

Another day has come
And I look in your eyes
And I see me there
In the rhythm of the ribbon that I see

Only love knows the other half of love
Its knowing someone you never meet
Feelings that you were always there
In the eyes of the heart where love begins.

It's another day in the same place
Another quiet day, for my way to say
One more day loving you

The Rhythm of The Ribbons
Memories of time
Pictures in my mind

It's another day in a different place
New memories, new pictures
Of a new kind of time

Yesterday is gone, Today is here
And only a new love knows Tomorrow

Copyright 2003 Francis E. Delaney   P-0312-MC

ONE MORE LOOK

It's another day in the same place
When yesterday was easy
I was me and you were you

One More Look
For that part of love hard to find
The eye of the rose in the wine

Only time will tell, when I love again
Only love will know the time and the place
For One More Look at love again

Do I want to play that game again
Have I found that love that's hard to find

One more ride in the eyes of love
The other part of love in our mind
One More Look, for one more time

It's another day in the same place
Looking for that love again
One More Look, to love again

Only you will know, when I love again
Only you will know the time and the place
For One More Look at love again

When I am me
And you are you
One More Look
Is Loving You

Copyright 2003 Francis E. Delaney   P-0313-JP

RED, WHITE AND BLUE MEMORY

I'm A Red, White and Blue Memory
Soldier of freedom in our history
My blood and my crosses cover the graves of three centuries
And I am proud of me
I'm proud of the color God made me
Proud of the colors He gave to me

Red, for the blood that keeps me free
White for the crosses that died for you and me
Blue for the sadness in the faces I see
Knowing that we are the soldiers of freedom in our history
I'm a Red, White and Blue Memory, this is what it means to me

The gifts that are brought when Christmas is sad
The heartaches and the tears that fill the empty years
The smiles of the girls and boys in the laughter of their toys
Mama kissing Santa Clause and Daddy knowing why
He is proud of the color God made her
Proud of the colors He gave to her

Red for the blood that keeps her free
White for the crosses that die for you and me
Blue for the sadness in the faces she sees
Knowing that they are soldiers of freedom in her history

Color her Lisa, USA, Color her American color her free
A Soldier of freedom, in the wonderful world of woman in the USA
Color America free, with a Ribbon on a Tree

Red for the blood that keeps us free
White for the crosses that fight for the graves of this century
Blue for the sadness in the faces they see
Knowing we are Soldiers of Freedom in our history

Copyright 2003 Francis E. Delaney   P-0309-LL

BLUE JEANS

Sugar sweet and all things neat
Love passing by
Your melody in Blue Jeans

The end of the rainbow
On the windowsills of your mind
Waterfalls of music in mine
In the melody of Blue Jeans

Old tears disappear
Into the music of our years
New tears fall in love
Unwinding in another world

Your a melody of mine
Like endless time
On the back roads of my mind
Blue Jeans walking in mind

In different times, and different years
A different heart, a different love
Your love in time with mine
In the Melody of Blue Jeans

The end of the rainbow
On the windowsills of time
Your music in the stars
Forever in my mind

Loving you
To the melody of Blue Jeans

Copyright 2003 Francis E. Delaney   S-0316-CO

NASHVILLE NORTH

Where would I be, if Archie didn't care
I would be where there were only trees
No club, no dancing, no party after the band

Carl and Elli, two step to a live band
Linda and Paul dance to the double two
Carl Jr. and Martha waltzing to their dance
You have a ring on your finger

You love the club at Nashville North
A western swing on the floor
Dancing around the last call line dance
To the beat of the Crossfrye Band

You love the people in this place
All have a story to tell
Stories of life and love
And the closing of this place

When you have been to this place
You can feel all the country
Hear all the songs they sung
Echo in the walls that will soon come down

When this place is gone
Everyone will go their separate ways
But they will always be one
As they remember everyone who was there

The club, the dancers, the parties and the man, Archie

Copyright 2003 Francis E. Delaney   S-0314-AR

IN LOVE AND IN SPACE

Breakfast at McDonalds, three hotcakes no sausage please
Gotta save my pennies for the things my kids need
Gotta love them as much as I can
When the kids are with their father
Look into their world through their windows of love
And Love them as much as I do

On the day my "x' got remarried is the day I meet you
Looking through the window at you
What will I do when you ask me too

A steak dinner at McDonalds, no french fries please
Gotta save my pennies for the things the kids need
Gotta love them as much as you do

The day your "X" got remarried is the day I meet you
Looking through the window in love with you
What will you do When I ask you

"I'll ask my kids if we can give you all the love that we can
a steak dinner at McDonalds no french fries please
saving our pennies for the things the kids need
you gotta love them as much as I love you"

Breakfast at Mc Donalds, four hotcakes, no sausage please
Gotta save our pennies for the things the kids need
There's a window in space and a window in love
And I gotta make it all the way through

I look into the eyes of the family you love
I see into your world through the eyes of their love
And love them as much as you do
As much as I love you

Copyright 2003 Francis E. Delaney   P-0317-CO

ALONE

I don't want to leave
Just to get to heaven
To see you loved me
No Excuses, Please

Are you just another love affair
Comes along and goes nowhere
Or are you the love affair who stays

Love is free.
Don't let me leave

Your voice echos
In the canyous of my mind
Your music playing
In the champers of my heart
Your pretty features
The beauty I see

Are you just another love
Comes along and goes nowhere
No, excuses please
I'll just leave

Alone

Copyright 2003 Francis E. Delaney   P-0318

DIFFERENT YEARS

When you look at life it looks at you
You look through its window
Through different windows every day
You watch and wonder what to say

When you find your the only one who really cared
You look through the windows in a different way
You look for something nice and something far
In the music of the stars

You look in a different year
Find someone nice and someone near
In someone close and someone dear
In the different windows of your years

You look into the eyes of Different Years
And in all of the things they have never seen
The sparkle of a diamond in the rough.
A tough love with a gentle touch

When you look through your window at a star
You will have something nice and something far
The music of our years
In smeone close and someone dear
In the different windows of their years

Love me today, remember me tomorrow
In the different windows of our years

Copyright 2003 Francis E. Delaney   P-0319-CO

WINDOWS

Three hotcakes, no sauage please
Gotta save my pennies for the things my kids need

When the kids are with their father, one thing they need
Look into their world through their windows on love
And love them as much as I do

For on the day my "X" got remarried
I looked through the Windows at someone new
What will I do if he asks me to

A steak dinner at Mc Donalds, no french fries please
Saving my pennies for the things the kids need
And love them as much as you do

For on the day your "X" got remarried
I looked through the window in love with you.
What will you do when I ask you

"I'll as my kids if they can look into your world
 and give you all the love that we can."

There's Windows in space and Windows in love
And you gotta make it all the way through
Look into their world through their Windows of love
And love them as much as I love you

(cont)

WINDOWS (cond)

Windows in space, Windows in love
And we'll make it all the way through
Four hotcakes, five mcMuffins
Six big meals seven milk shakes please

Two steak dinners, no french fries please
Gotta save our pennies for the things our Grand Kids need

One hot cake, no sausage please
Gotta save my pennies for all the things the kids need

There's Windows in space and Windows in love
And we made it all the way throug
Looking in their world through our Window in space
And loving them as much as I love you

There's Windows in space
There's Windows in love

And hwre ever you were

I was there

Copyright 2003 Francis E. Delaney   S-0320-CO

DIVORCED WITH KIDS

Texas boots in mini skirts and white levis
And the way they look at me, Divorced With kids
Telephone ringing and the pager is singing
Fancy boots, lady suits and cross your heart, the way they look at me

Birthday suits on baby boots and high heels shoes
And the way they look at me, Divorced with kids
Telephone ringing and the pager is singing
Stockings boots, stir-up pants and just my size, the way they look at me

I look at you and you look at me
And what do I see. I see life an I see love
You see me, Divorced With Kids

Dinners on the table in love letters
Pillow in the window, music in the bedroom
Telephone ringing and the baby is singing
The way you look at me, Divorced With Kids

I look at you and you look at me and what do I see
I see life and I see love in the way you look at me

Dinners on the table in doggie bags
Pumpkin in the window, children in the bedroom
Telephone ringing and the baby's crying
The way you look at me, Divorced With kids

Diaapers are due only Grandma or Grandpa can do
Now, it's time for a feeding or two that only Mama can do

Telephone is quiet, pager is off. Baby sleeping and the cat is out
Now, mama Singing, the way you look at me
The way I look at you, Divorced With Kids

Copyright 2003, Francis E. Delaney   S-0321-CO

DON'T FORGET, ME

I can't forget you
You are there
I look at the mountains
I look at the sea
I look at the sky
I look at, "Why"

Don't Forget me
I am there
Look at the mountains
Look at the sea
Look at the sky
Look at, "Why"

Who Said, it couldn't get worse
We are here
Look at the bad times
Look at the good times
Look at the baby cry
Look at, 'Why"

You can't reverse, "Why"
Runing in first, "Why"
You have to stop, "Why"
Look at what you got, "Why"
Blue Jeans, Music and You, "Why"
Who said, it couldn't get worse, "Why"

Why, Why, Why Me ?

Why Not ?

Copyright 2003, Francis E. Delaney   P-0322-CO

TELL THEM, WHY

Have you often wondered Why
There are tears when you cry
Where do they come from
Why do eyes cry

When your heart is sad
It brings tears to your eyes
When it is happy
Those same tears cry

The heart is the motor of love
Pumping the emotions of the time
Awakening your mind
To the task of the daily grind

A flower blooms
A butterfly, flys
The sun comes up
The moon goes down

The flower sleeps
The butterfly tries
The sun goes down
The moon covers the ground

Have you often wondered, Why
God makes the tears that you cry
When you wipe the tears from their eyes
TELL THEM, WHY

Copyright 2003 Francis E. Delaney   P-0315-BT

WHERE EVER YOU WERE, I WAS THERE   2004

I don't remember the day that we meet
Never thought I'd ever forget

Sitting by a tiny table in a little room
Brought a glass of wine, your empty chair sitting there
As I drank from your glass of wine
I could feel your love in my body, soul and mind
And I knew that Where Ever You Were, I Was There

As I held your crystal glass
I felt the love in your heart
Become a part of everything and every where
And I knew, that where ever I was, you were there

I remember my love before we met
It took me to the day that I will never forget

Sitting by a little table in a little room
Brought a glass of wine, your love sitting in the chair
As you drank from your glass of wine
I could feel your love in my body, soul and mind
And I knew that Where Ever You Were, I was there

We remember our love before we met
It brought us this day we will never forget
The day before tomorrow, Today
For Where Ever you Were, I Was There

In a crystal glass of wine

Copyright 2004, Francis E. Delaney   S-0401-CO

COYOTE CANYON

Of all the things I've seen
Coloring the sky
Lighting in the river
Coyote Canyon

Of all the sounds I've heard
In the melodies of time
Thunder in the snow
Coyote Canyon

A rainbow looks through
The tunnels of your eyes
It colors the windowsills of your mind
In the mirrors of mine

Your love is warm
In tears that touch me
Your smile is forever
It's lighting and thunder

Coyote, your beauty is
In the eyes that look through me
There's a feeling I see, when I look
At the hills of Coyote Canyon

I see love

I see Coyote

Copyright 2004, Francis E. Delaney   P-0402-CO

SPECIAL WORLD

In the simplicity of a special song
There's a symphony of love
Movements in time with word and rhyme
An angel of God, in a Special World
Born free, from all that bothers you and me

In the complexity of a special song
Life is a true rhapsody in blue
A will to survive the mystery of the mind
An Infant of God, in a Special World
Born free in the complex world of you and me

The silent music of a pen
Prints a special picture in my mind
I see you running in my mind, melodies in time
Still as the feathers on bird flying free
Laughter and tears, memories of mine

God sprinkled the earth with water and dirt
On mountains of hope and valleys of fear
Colored it, special, simple, complex and real
All parts of the songs in the mystery of the mind

In the Reality of a Special World
There's a true mystery that unwinds
A symphony of love, a rhapsody in blue
For an angel of God, in a Special World
Brought love to the world of you and me

In the words and in the music, of a Special Friend

Copyright 2004 Francis E. Delaney   P-0403-RS

JUST A SONG

I don't want to spend a fortune
Just to see your love teasing me
No excuses, please.
Love is Free

Are you just another song
Another love affair that comes along
And goes nowhere
Or are you the song that never ends

Feelings in your eyes touch mine
Your voice echoes in my mind
Filling the champers of my heart
Your music playing in my eyes

Don't let me leave
If your the song that never ends
Come love with me,
Love is free

Or are you just another song
Another love affair that went nowhere
No excuses, please.
I'll just leave

Copyright 2004 Francis E. Delaney   P-0404-FD

WHEN I WAS ONLY THREE

Happy Birthday, Shae Marie, although your only three
Someday, you will be as old as me

The years will come and the years will go
And you will have a little girl age of three
The years will come and the years will go
And you will be a Grandma just like me
They will ask, Grandma, What are your thinking of

Thinking of the days, When I Was Only Three
Someone wrote a song about my Grandma and me
When I Was Only Three
Thinking of the days when I was twenty-three
Life was young and fun and-- love married me, when I was twenty-three

Thinking of the days when I was thirty-three
Four kids and a little girl age of three, when I was thirty-three

Thinking of the days when I was fifty three
Singing that song that someone wrote about my Grandma and me
When I Was Only Three

Thinking about the days when I was sixty-three, hair of silver,
Heart of gold, alone and growing old
The years would come and the years would go
Little did I know, that at the age of eighty-three
I'd be up and around and singing your song
Happy Birthday, Shae Marie

Now, I think about the days when I'll be ninety-three
Life is dear, heaven is near, so I leave my song
To my kids to sing to their little ones all around
The song that someone wrote about my Grandma and me
When I Was Only Three

Copyright 2004 Francis E. Delaney   P-0405-DL

WHEN LOVE IS A REAL DREAM

When Love Is A Real Dream
It is a part of life that will always be
A part of yesterday

Loves name was Mary
When she left, she fell in love
With someone else
And love became another dream

Love is a dream
It never grows old
From young to old
Love, dreams

Loves name was Maureen
God called her, she had to leave
Her love was a real dream
It has become another dream

It's a part of yesterday
It is here today
It is Tomorrow s dream

Loves name, may never be again
For a real live dream
Is hard to find

Love is a dream
It never grows old
From young to old
Love, knows
When Love's A Real Dream

Copyright 2004 Francis E. Delaney   P -0406-FD

SECOND TIME AROUND (the)

How much can one heart take
How many tears to shed from my eyes
A love that ran out of time
How many tears must any heart shed
Before it loves again

One more time, It's up to you
How many times your heart will love mine
The Second Time Around
All the love of our past
Come together for our last

I could not have found a lovelier friend
When I was looking for that love again

When your hearts in love
You can see it in your eyes
I've seen it in yours, when yours read mine
When you can't say, "No" The Second Time Around

The emotions of the past, try to suppress the task
Love takes a different path
Love moves in The Second Time Around
And fills our empty years at last

I could not have found a lovelier friend
To Love me, the Second Time Around

The emotions of today try to suppress the task
Loves takes a different path
Love moves in and the other side of love
Makes it all worth living, the other half of life
The Second Time Around

Copyright 2004 Francis E. Delaney   S-0407-FD

KENTUCKY (A Special Song)

A blue symphony in a rhapsody of love
Special, complex, simple and real.
Kentucky

In the simplicity of a song
There's a crystal glass of time
God made it, special, complex, simple and real
All parts of my song, Kentucky

In the complexity of a song
There's a crystal glass of love
A special addition, a heart and a mind
In a melody of yours and mine

Life is special, complex, simple and real
And it's all worth living, knowing you

A thoroughbred on the hills of Kentucky
A crystal glass of wine, a amethyst jewel
Pictures on the wall, memories of time
A smile, a laugh a kiss hugging me

In the reality of a special song
There's a true mystery that unwinds
Each smile, each word, each kiss, each step
All the tears and all the beers, through all of the years

A blue symphony in a rhapsody of love
Special, complex, simple and real

Kentucky, a special friend

Copyright 2004, Francis E. Delaney   S-0408-LL

BEAUTIFUL SONG (woman)

There's something nice about love and life
A Beautiful Song
Be all of my days and all of my nights
When love is right

Every woman is a beautiful song
Her musical story in every shape and form
If you like to dance with her song
Waltz with a Beautiful Woman, Beautiful Song

Your someone special in love and life
There's no other high

Every woman is a beautiful song
Her musical story in every shape and form
Listen to her story, when you
Dance with a Beautiful Woman, Beautiful Song

She's someone special in love and life
There's no other high
She's all of your life and all of your love
She's lifts you up

Hold your beautiful woman
Feel her beautiful song
Slow dance a Beautiful Woman, Beautiful Song
Slow dance your Beautiful Woman, Beautiful Song

In life and love there's no other high
Every woman is a Beautiful Song

Copyright 2004 Francis E. Delaney   S-0409-CV

TODAY IS YESTERDAYS TOMORROW.

There are no more tomorrows, no more yesterdays
There is just today
Feelings that never fade away
Today is Yesterdays Tomorrow

It's time to look at love again
For the things I've said and done
More than with anyone
They are now the yesterdays
When I was yours

It's time to look at life again
Listen to things I never heard me say
For the things I'll say and do
Will be done for you
Today is Yesterdays Tomorrow

Give me a little bit of yesterday
For tomorrow and today
Will be our yesterdays
Of the things we never done

Look at life and listen to its song
When love came once and never went away
Give me a little bit of yesterday
Today, is Yesterdays Tomorrow

Give me a little bit of yesterday
Give me tomorrow, today
Today is Yesterdays Tomorrow

Copyright 2004 Francis E. Delaney   S-0410-FH

ASK YOUR SELF, WHY

Why do birds fly
While people walk
Why do people cry
When birds can't fly

Have you often wondered Why
Some things make you cry
Tears are happy or sad
Some time you laugh and the tears run by
Some times you cry, no tears in your eyes

Everyday that goes by
Each hour of the day
Each minute of the hour
Each second begins a new year

Look back into the years
Watch each and every day pass by
How many times have you asked your self, why
Some days I cried, no tears in my eyes
Some days I laughed, tears in my eyes

All those you loved, all that they gave
When they were happy or sad
When the birds can't fly
When the seconds don't tick by
Ask yourself, Why

Copyright 2004 Francis E. Delaney   S-0411-AP

COYOTE BLUES

Of all the things I see
Birds flying free
Rainbows in the rain
Lighting, crystals of time

Of all the sounds around
Bird songs are free
Butterfly melodies
Thunder crying in the rain

I have seen eyes that touch
The smile of love
In the eyes of Coyote

Eyes that look through me
See all that no one has seen
Hear all the sounds
In the story of life

I have felt all of love
The rhythm of life
In the heart of Coyote

Your heart in rhythm
In my eyes of time
Crystal, rivers of wine
COYOTE BLUES

Copyright 2004 Francis E. Delaney   P-0412-CO

BOB-O-LINK

This is a bird of North America

Its colors are black, red, white and blue

Its home is mostly in reed plants and trees

It is also called a reed-bird

In some parts of the North America

Its called the rice-bird

It's also a fat bird.

It likes its food

Its song is sweet

It can be heard far away

So when you see a Bob-O-Link

On the blue grass of Kentucky

Remember me

Copyright 2004 Francis E. Delaney   S-0413-KY

HAVE YOU EVER BEEN IN LOVE BEFORE

I can only dream and wonder, why
I have never felt like this before

My heart's with you
Feels the feelings of you
I look into my years
And I wonder, why
I have Never Felt Like this Before

Your heart talks to mine
Feels the feelings of me
You look into your years
And wonder, why
You have never felt like this before

When your close to me
I feel the love I see
Have you ever felt like this before
Have you ever been in love before

We may never love beyond our dreams
But, we will always wonder, why
We have never felt like this before
Have we ever been in love before

Two hearts, one heart beat
Never felt like this before
If you never felt like this before
You have never been in love before

Have You Ever Been In Love Before

Copyright 2004 Francis E. Delaney   S-0414-CO

AIN'T NO MAMA, LIKE ME

You walk in my life
Laughter and tears brought you here
To this time and place that never was
A time and a place-- divorced with kids

Cell phone ring tones and the kids are singing their song
Ain't No Mama, like the Mama we got

Up in the morning at four and back at eight
Gotta keep my kids in cloths and a full plate
Off to school and baseball too
And all the things the kids like to do
Visit Grandma, Grandma and Daddy too
Twenty-four hours a day and only paid for eight

Dinner at Crackle Barrel, dancing at the hall
To the bogy line boogie and the billy goat dance
Telephone ring tones and the kids are singing its song
Ain't No Mama. Like the Mama we got

I look at them and they look at me and what do they see
They see life and they see love in the way you look at me

In my Texas boots, mini skirts and tight blue jeans
Bikini suits on baby boots and high heel shoes
There ain't no Mama like the Mama you see
There ain't no Mama Like me

Cont.

Cont.

I walk in your life
Laughter and tears brought me here
To this time and place that never was
A time and a place and love

Cell phone ring tones and the baby's singing it's song
Ain't No Mama, Like the Mama I got

Up in the morning at four and back at eight
Gotta keep my kids in cloths and a full plate
Off to school and baseball too
Visit Grandma, Grandpa and Daddy too
Twenty-four hours a day and only paid for eight

Telephone is quiet, pager is off
The kids are sleeping and the dog wants out
We look at each other and what do we see
We see life and we see love in a way we never dreamed

You walk in my life
Laughter and tears brought you here
To this time and place that never was
A time a place and love

There Ain't No mama, like the Mama you got
Ain't nobody gonna take you away from me
There Ain't No Mama Like Me

Copyright Francis E. Delaney   S-0415-CO

DIVORCED WITH MORE KIDS (Ain't No Mama Like me)

You walk in my life, laughter and tears brought you here
To a time and a place, Divorced With More Kids

Cell-phone ring tones, and the kids are singing their song
Ain't no Mama, like the mama we got

Up in the morning at four and back at eight
Gotta keep my kids in clothes and a full plate
Off to school and baseball too
And all the other things the kids like to do
Visit Grandma, Grandpa and Daddy too
Twenty four hours a day and only paid for eight

Dinner on the table, love all around
Baby is feeding, the diapers are singing
Dog is barking at the cell-phone ringing, Ain't No Mama like me
And the baby's singing her song
Ain't no Mama like the Mama I got
Texas boots, high heels shoes and baby boots
Bikini suits, low-belly blues and suede shoes
Wedding dressed in white levis and just my size
Ain't no Mama like me

Telephones are quiet, kids are sleeping, the dog is in
Now, Mama is singing her song
There ain't no Mama in this world like the Mama you got
And there ain't nobody gonna take you away from me

I walk in your life, laughter and tears brought me here
To a time and a place to love
DIVORCED WITH MORE KIDS

Copyright 2004 Francis E. Delaney   S-0417-CO

WATCHING THE KIDS GROW

Danny was eight his brother was four
Brought candy from them at the front door
As long as I can remember we had dinner at four
At this little cafe, our favorite place to dine
One day he asked me why I was alone
Well, I had to tell him. God took Maureen home

This place was happy
This place is sad
Someday I'll be back
To watch the kids grow

Danny was nine his brother was five
Brought candy from them at the front door
At this little cafe, my favorite place to dine
For ten years more

This place was happy
This place was sad
Writing my songs
And Watching The Kids Grow

I came back from Nashville this place was sad
I asked his mother, why so sad, she said
His brother and sister ask me why
When Danny was twenty-one, God took him home

I had his name engraved in the Children Wall
At our Lady of Snows, WATCHING THE KIDS GROW

Copyright 2004 Francis E. Delaney   P-0418-DD

DREAM

When you dream
And it wakes you up
Do you remember
What woke you up   P-0416-TM

IMAGINATION

Travel with me
Beyond the stars
Imagine what you can see

You can see what nothing is
Nothing is so far away
There's no place to stay

You would be
A speck of dust
Floating free

You would be
Faster then light
If you were me

You will travel
Beyond the universe you see
To the end of space

We have found that place
Beyond our
IMAGINATION

Copyright 2004 Francis E. Delaney   P-0419-FD

LOVE ISN'T EASY

Where did you come from
You came from love
Where are you going
You're going to love

All that happened,
Happened. That's why
Love Isn't Easy

Where did the kids come from
They came from love
When they grow up and leave
They're going to love

Look around, If God can't be found, Where is He

He's in the heart of their Father
He's in the eyes of your kids
In the arms of their Mother

He's in the words I write
And if He's writing, Love Isn't Easy

He's in your Fathers love
In the arms of your Mother
He's in the eyes of your kids
In the arms of their mother

Where did we come from we came from love
Where are we going, we're going to love.   LOVE ISN'T EASY

Copyright 2000 Francis E. Delaney   P-0420-CO

LOVE TURNED AROUND

words & music:
Francis E. Delaney

VERSE 1: What-ev-er the rea-son may be   Sin-gle, di-vorced or wid-owed
You will nev-er have the fu-ture If you bring a-long the past VERSE 2: Look for some-one
new You'll find you knew each oth-er Be-fore you met in the eyes of love To-
day is to-mor-row's yes-ter-day LIFT: All the signs of love are in the
sun It's old, yet it's love turns a-round CHORUS 1: The eye of the heart, the
                                          CHORUS 2: The eye of the heart, the
eye of the mind And the eye of the flesh be-come one In the eyes of love
eye of the mind And the eye of the flesh be-came one In the eye of love
Leave the past, nev-er ask Why love turned a-round VERSE 3: When love comes a-
Leave the past, nev-er ask Why love turned a-round VERSE 4: When love comes a-
gain Take a look at what's a-round If you see on-ly one Love turned a-round
gain Take a look at what's a-round When you love on-ly one Love turned a-round

© COPYRIGHT 2005 FRANCIS E. DELANEY all rights reserved.
P.O. Box 932 Frankfort, IL 60423

#Lap-0427-CO

RL

WHERE DID JENNY GO

Got to thinking about Jenny
Where did she go
Married at seventeen
Single at eighteen
Married at nineteen
Single at twenty

Jenny couldn't go home
Her mother said, No
Where Did Jenny Go

I remember Jenny
It was only nine years ago
She used to draw my picture
Drew a smile on my face

She was young but she knew
What love and life was like
One day she drew her picture
With a smile on its face

Beneath her picture she wrote

WHERE DID JENNY GO

Copyright 2004 Francis E. Delaney   P-0421-JW

DON'T QUIT NOW

Time of emotions
Wind in the trees

Everything in motion
Don't Quit, Now

The feeling of winning
When I'm loosing you

Is the mystery in love
Two feelings, Feeling one

If you want to know
What's coming next

The answer is complex
Two feelings, feeling one

The mystic in love
When to say

Win or loose
DON'T QUIT NOW

Copyright 2004 Francis E. Delaney   P-0422-FD

IS IT STILL THERE

Did I find that special love
The second time around
Is It Still There
That's a Catchy One

We may never know our love
But we will always know
The love we found in a song
That a band of gold turned love around

I found a new kind of love
In the words and music of your love
Is It Still There
That's a Catchy One

As time goes on, the clock unwinds
On this second love of mine
Can I find the time to love
A love still there

I found a Catchy One
In the eye of a smile, an old car
Your words and music, tell it all
Catch me if, It's Still There

Copyright 2004 Francis E. Delaney   S-0423-ML

TAKEN

I find you in the tunnel of my eye
I like to take a second look
If you tell me your "Taken"
I'll still finish my book

I hope your "Taken" and not took
You'll never know
Unless you read
The ending of your book

Everybody has a book
It's the story of their life
Each and every one you love
On each and every day you live

Every time I hear that word "Taken"
I gotta take another look
Take all that love in my eyes
And put it on the pages in my book

Taken but not took
Gotta take another look
Gonna finish my book

Took but not "TAKEN"

Copyright 2004 Francis E. Delaney   P-0424-MV-KY

WATCHING THE WATER

Sitting on the rocks
Lake Michigan shore
The wind blowing in
The spray of the water
Splashing on the rocks

I heard a voice say do you always watch the water
She was a lady about seventy-seven
With her seven year old grand daughter
Neither of whom should have been walking on the rocks
With the wind blowing in, splashing on the rocks

"Do you always sit here and watch the water
Will you be back next year," she asked

When ever I come to Evanston
I always sit on the rocks by the lake
For its water has been everywhere
It has seen all of history
It will be here until
Its last dance in the rain

Copyright 2004 Francis E. Delaney   P-0425-FD

CAROLINA TIME

Sandy beaches, north and south
Its' mountains shadow the sun
There silhouette in the moonlight
On this beautiful Carolina land

I remember loving you in Carolina
Young love in love for the first time
I'll always love you in Carolina
And all Carolina Time

How many times have I said, I love you
How many times did I try
I'll always love you in Carolina
And all my Carolina Time

Have we ever said, I love
Have we ever said, I do
I guess we never have
Perhaps we never will

I'll love you in Carolina, this beautiful land
On its sandy beaches, on the hills of Carolina
In the shadows of the mountains and in the light of the moon
I'll always love my Carolina Time

I'll love you in Carolina
Have I ever told you, I'll do
Carolina Time, in Carolina with you

Copyright 2004 Francis E. Delaney   S-0426-CO

LOVE TURNED AROUND

Walk into the future
Leave the Past
Never ask why
Love Turned Around

Whatever the reason
Single, divorced or widowed
You will never see the future
If you bring along the past

You will find in yourself a person you never knew
Looking at somebody new
You will feel you knew each other before you met
In the eyes of love

The eye of the heart, the eye of the mind and
The eye of the flesh, become one in the eye of love
Leave the past, never ask why, love comes around

When love comes around the second time around
Take a look at what's around
When you can look everyone in the eye and see only one
Leave the past, never ask why, Love Turned Around

For the eye of the heart, the eye of the mind
And the eye of the flesh became one in the eye of love
Leave the past, never ask why, Love Turned Around

Copyright 2004 Francis E. Delaney   S-0427-CO

OLD FASHIONED CHRISTMAS

Sitting in a rocker waiting for Breakfast
Rocking to the memories in this Old Country Store
Kids all around, listen to the sights and sounds
Of an Old Fashioned Christmas in a Crackle Barrel Town

Fire in the fireplace, memories on the wall
Hanging above the hard wood floor in this old Country Store
We look back through the years, of all who have passed through these doors
For an Old Fashioned Christmas in a Crackle Barrel Town

On a Christmas Eve in a Crackle Barrel Store
We found the answer, what are we looking for
We sit by the fireplace and listen to our song
Old Fashioned Christmas, in our Crackle Barrel Store

On the last day of the year we cheer in the new
As we leave the old, we take One More Look
As people all around celebrate the sights and sounds
Of an Old Fashioned New Years In Crackle Barrel Town

Fire in the fireplace, memories on the wall
Hanging above the hard wood floor in this old Country Store
We look at future, and all who will pass through its door
To an Old Fashioned New Year in a Crackle Barrel Town

As we travel the sights and the sounds of another year
Waiting for breakfast, a rocking chair rocks
The fireplace warms the memories of the faces in this place
Of an Old Fashioned Christmas in a Crackle Barrel Town

Copyright 2004 Francis E. Delaney   P-0428-ANN

WHATEVER THE REASON MAY BE

2005

When the snow is off the mountain
The hilltop is free
The trees rock to a wind song
The flowers kiss the bees
The leaves are green
Whatever The Reason May Be

Have you often wondered why
The snow on the mountain
Never melts away
The trees are forever greens
No flowers to be seen
Whatever the Reason May Be

Sometimes I wonder
About, what's it all about
If you know the answer
Keep it to yourself
For no one will believe you
Whatever The Reason May Be

When someone believes you
The snow melts
The wind blows
The flower blooms
The leaves fall on love
Whatever The Reason May Be

Copyright 2005 Francis E. Delaney   P-0501-KY

JUST BEING ALIVE

Each day I awake
Open my eyes
For in the eyes of life
You can hear
All that is not said
All that is,
Just Being Alive

You can hear a bird
You can't see
You can hear the wind
You can't see
All that can't be seen
You can see
Just Being Alive

Someday I'll fall asleep
Close my eyes
In the mystery of sleep
When I open my eyes
I'll count every star in the sky
Every fish in the sea
I'll see all that I didn't see
Just Being Alive

Copyright 2005 Francis E. Delaney   P-0502-FD

MYSTERY OF LOVE

A new Mystery of Love
There's something about it
Reminds me of you
One more Melody
In the mystery of our love

When you have had it all
And suddenly it's gone
The leaves fall
The snow melts
New life in the flowers that bloom

Each and every day
Life is a first and a last day
All the days we live
All the days we love
Are the days in between

It's the cycle of life
A moment of time
A taste of wine
When you were my
Mystery Of Love

Copyright 2005 Francis E. Delaney   P-0503-ML

CRACKER BARREL CHRISTMAS

On Christmas Eve in a Cracker Barrel Store
We found the answer, to what are we looking for, and
We sit by the fireside and listen to a song
Cracker Barrel Christmas in an old country town
Sitting by the fireside waiting for breakfast
Rocking to the memories in this Old Country Store
Kids all around the sights and sounds
Old Fashioned Christmas in a Cracker Barrel Town

In the old family restaurant in the Old Country Store
Rocking chairs rock to the old country rock
Lunch by the fireside, memories of it's taste
Warm the face of the pictures in this old country place
We look to the future and all who will pass through its doors

Family and friends, travelers from every state
In the All Country Restaurant in the Old Country Store
Sparks in the fireplace memories on the wall
Hang above the hard wood floor in this Old Country Store
We look back through the years
At all who have passed through its doors
As we leave the old we bring in the new
Fireworks spark the faces in this place
Dinner by the fireplace, a Happy New Year and one more look
At an Old fashioned Christmas in the Old Country Store

Family and friends travelers from everywhere
In the All Country Restaurant in the Old Country Store
Rocking chairs rock to the Cracker Barrel rock
Cracker Barrel Christmas in an Old Country Town

Copyright 2005 Francis E. Delaney   S-0504-KY-CO

MEMORIES, MINUTES IN TIME

When I think of you
In that little part of time

Your rhythm and melody
The arrangements of your moods
It's in your walk and talk
The composition of your soul
Arranged in parts, music is the score of life

Your beauty takes me
To memories in time and place
They become the sound of music
The songs that poets write
Music is a gift God gave everyone

When the Lord takes me
To my special place in life
I will thank Him for your time
Memories Playing in my mind
Set to music in pieces of time

Music is the language of love
Memories, minutes in time

Copyright 2005 Francis E. Delaney   P-0505-KY

TAKE A WALK IN YOUR MIND

Now I find myself going back in time
Through all the years of love, laughter and tears
Take A Walk in Your Mind

Take yourself back through the years
Walk along and you will see
Each and every year had its love, laughter and tears

If you don't think you can remember
Come along with me
Listen to each years love, laughter and tears

Take a walk in your mind
Look where you have been
See the love, you loved
As you see the world again

Take a Walk in Your Mind
To where you have never been

Copyright 2005 Francis E. Delaney   P-0506-CO

AUDIENCE OF ONE

When I was twenty-three, Mary was seventeen
Life and love was young, falling in love was fun
I wrote them and she read them
And I sang my songs to Mary, my Audience of One
I didn't care if anyone ever heard a song I'd written and sung
To my Audience of One
When she was twenty-three, Mary left me
Of all the things I ever had to do, the hardest of them all
Was saying Good-Bye to Mary, my Audience of One

When I was twenty-nine, Maureen was Twenty-five
Live as life could be, full of the devil and falling in love
I wrote them and she read them
And I sang my songs to Maureen, my Audience of One
I didn't care if anyone ever heard a song I'd written and sung
To my Audience of One
When she was fifty-two, Maureen left me
Of all the things I ever had to do, the saddest of them all
Was saying good-bye to Maureen, my Audience of One

When I was older my Audience of One was younger
It was like we knew each other before we met
I wrote them and she read them and I sang my songs again
I want everyone to hear the songs I've written and sung
To my Audience of One
For no one will ever have the Grammys I have
The Melodies of Mary, The Hills of Maureen and
Beautiful Kentucky's, Ribbon On a Tree
And of all the things I'll have to do
The easiest of them all will be always loving you
My Audience of One. Is "This" You

Copyright 2005 Francis E. Delaney   P-0507-KY

IS "THIS" YOU (love)

What is, This
I find myself in my mind
Where I never been before
Like a land that's never been explored

What is This
I've been in love before
Felt all the feelings of love
Before and after love

What is This
That comes along, is this love
How can there be any more
When I have loved all of love before

Who is This
Who comes along and takes my heart
To where its never been
To the end of Time

What is This, is this love
That takes life to where it has been before

Is "This" You
Is "This" Love

Who Is You

Copyright 2005 Francis E. Delaney   P-0508-ML

COME OUT OF THE BLUES

Tell me it's true
So my days can
Come Out of the Blues

I try to forget, it's impossible to do
Everywhere I look
I'm looking at you
Coming out of the blues

Love a part of life
It's not impossible to
Take life to its' real dream
Come Out of the Blues

To live love
Tell me it's not a dream
And my story comes true
When you, Come Out of the Blues

Copyright 2005 Francis E. Delaney   P-0509-ML

DREAMS

I can see all
I want to see

Be all I want to be
I can Dream

Dreams about things
That may never be

Dreams, about you
Dreaming about me

Writing and asking
Waiting for a day

When a dream comes alive
Walking and talking

Memories of real time
Dreams

Copyright 2005 Francis E. Delaney   P-0510-KY

DAYS

I wouldn't change a day
Since I met you

Days that would have never been
Years that will always be

Minutes in time
Since I met you

All the colors
All the sounds

A rainbow touching the ground
Turning my world around

Days, you never leave me
Days, I never leave you

All the Days
Since I met you

Copyright 2005 Francis E. Delaney   P-0511-ML

SOMETIME

Sometimes you promise
Sometimes you wish
You didn't promise
What you wished

Sometimes you got to do
What you go to do
You got to say
What you got to say

This is the time
It may not be the place
I got to say
I love you

I got to do
What I got to do
I got to talk to you
Sometimes

If Sometime
Becomes all the time
Then we got to do
What we got to do

Will you marry me
Sometime

Copyright 2005 Francis E. Delaney   P-0512-LL

GIVE ME, TO YOU

I have dreamed many dreams
All have come true
Give Me, To You

If your are a dreamer too
When all your dreams come true
Will you find me
Give Me, To You

The flower gives honey to the bee
The rivers feed the sea
God made you and God made me
To Give Me To You

I give me to you
Take all my love I ever knew
Make it like you, bold and true
Give Me, To You

Take our love and let it make
All our dreams come true
As the rivers of our love
Make all our dreams come true

Copyright 2005 Francis E. Delaney   P-0513-KY

CHALLENGE

I Challenge
All that used to be
Take another run at love
Only I can see

Challenge me
Make the challenge
To all that you can be
A love only you can see

Challenge love
To places you have never been
So love can be
Everywhere you have been

Take another run at love
Challenge me
I Challenge you
To a love only we can see

If it's like it used to be
Take another run to love
A love that Challenges you and me

Copyright 2005 Francis E. Delaney   P-0514-FD

THE POLISH BAR

When I am here
Will you be here
Will you take me to this place
Table twenty-seven at The Polish Bar

The Polish Bar
Where Gallo Red, Rosey and Zinfendel
Empty glasses of wine
Waiting for the Rhine

The Polish Bar where I wrote
Your music is pretty tonight
To the melody of Rhine wine
Your picture in my mind

Will you be there
To accept a Grammy for a song I'll write
"When you were there"
After you have been there

When I'm still here
Will you be there

Copyright 2005 Francis E. Delaney   P-0515-FD

TAGGING ALONG

I was there
But you were gone
Only a dream
Tagging Along

A walk along the lake shore
Pretty woman walking by
Catches my eye
And you, Tagging Along

Where ever I go
I'm caught in your eyes
I look around to see
Why they are looking at me

Walking in the door
I was there, you were gone
Only a dream
Tagging Along

Sitting by the table
A dinner for two
You were there
Tagging Along

Copyright 2005 Francis E. Delaney   P-0516-KY

THE REST OF THE WAY

words & music:
Francis E. Delaney

| Dm | G | C |

Fall-ing in love with you   Is a love I nev-er knew

| C | Dm | G | C |

The spir-it of your love touched me   Take me the rest of the way

VERSE 3: When

| C | Dm | G | C |

VERSE 2: All the feel-ings I've had   And all that I nev-er have
my sto-ry comes to its end   Wipe your tears a-way   All I

| C | Dm | G | C |

Now fill my bod-y, soul and mind   Take me the rest of the way
want to hear is the music of our years   As my love takes you the rest of the

| C | Dm | G | Dm |

CHORUS: Tears of love touch our heart   Take our love to the first day
way   Tears of love touch our heart   Take our love to the last day

| G | D | D | G |

As the smile that brought you my way
When your smile that brought me your way

| G | Dm | G | C |

Takes me the rest of the way
Takes me the rest of the way

| C | Am | Em | Am |

BRIDGE: Love is a but-ter-fly waltz-ing in the sky   Love is a flow-er

Lap-0127-LL

© 2001 FRANCIS E. DELANEY all rights reserved.
P.O. Box 932 Frankfort, IL 60423

RL

192

THE REST OF THE WAY

page: 2

watch-ing it fly They touch and take love the rest of the way Touch me the rest of the way VERSE 4: When our sto-ry comes to its end Take my tears with you Take me the rest of the way

© 2001 FRANCIS E. DELANEY all rights reserved.

TEDDY BEAR CHRISTMAS
Merry Christmas, Teddy Bear

Teddy Bear, Oh Teddy Bear
You'll always be a friend of mine
With a hug and a kiss or two
A smile and a "Hi"
Never be another Teddy Bear quit like you

Christmas card on the tree
Teddy Bear laying there
I'll always have a Teddy Bear Christmas
Merry Christmas, Teddy Bear

My love for my Teddy Bear
Makes all my dreams come true
Every year I fall in love with you
A Teddy Bear Christmas loving you
Merry Christmas Teddy Bear

Teddy Bear, Oh, Teddy Bear
You'll always be a friend of mine
With a hug and a kiss or two
A picture and a card
Never be another Teddy Bear, quit like me

And of all the things I'll ever do
Never be another Teddy Bear quit like you
Merry Christmas, Teddy Bear

Copyright 2005 Francis E. Delaney   S-0517-LL

"HI "

For small word
It sure does a lot
The first word I said, to you, "HI"
Look at all that little word can do
It lifts you up
It makes your day
I's a smile
It's a laugh
Some times
It's in love
There's no other high
HI. Will you marry me
Why,
Why Not
An Everyday--"HI   P-0518-KY

―――――――――――――

ZEPHYR

A Zephyr is a mild breeze
A soft touch of nature
It can't be seen
You know it's there
It's like love
It feels you
When it passes by

Copyright 2005 Francis E. Delaney   P-0519-LL

LOVE IS A GOOD WORD

Green is the color of your love
A seven day creation
And if you wondered, why
The color of my love is you
Love is a Good Word

Never thought I'd fall in love again
Two strangers were we, without us
Twinkle, twinkle little star

A seven day creation
A part of life in the eyes of love
And if you wonder, why
The color of your love, is us
Love Is A Good Word

Try it and see
So when it happens without me
The color of your love will be love
Love is a Good Word

Twinkle, twinkle little star, "   "
Your Love, Is a Good Word

Copyright 2005 Francis E. Delaney   P-0520-ML

THE WAY WE FELL IN LOVE

The Way We fell In Love, isn't written in this song
No one will hear. The Way We Fell In Love

All who listen, won't find their story in this song
It's all there, printed in their mind
Playing to the rhythm of two hearts in time

There's no other high
Then ——The Way We Fell In Love
It's printed in time, the music in our heart
Playing in the mirrors of our mind

           The Way We Fell In Love
               Instrumental
"
Sing your love song. It's written in your mind
   To 32 bars of— The Way We Fell in Love

                                          "
If you never write a letter, or a note on a line
There's no other high, printed in my mind
Then ——The Way We Fell In Love——Love Fed

Copyright 2005 Francis E. Delaney   S-0521-FD

INDEX

1964
My Love Note Tree   S-6401
Blackie   S-6402

1965
Teachers Pet   S-6501
War of Love   S-6502

1966
Arrested By you   S-6601
Heck No   S-6604
Hickory Kick   S-6602
You Gotta Be Goofy   S-6603

1967
Blue Mist   S-6701
Funny Face   S-6704
Stop it, Stupid   S-6702
Yummy, Yummy Dum-Dum   S-6704

1968
Blackie Bottom (dance)   S-6805
Gentle on my body   S-6804
My Little Old Lady   S-6801
Nickel Cup Of Coffee   S-6803
Red, Red Roses of June   S-6806
Rusty   S-6802
Quiet Americans   S-6807   P-682005

1969
Blinky, The Blue Nosed Snow Deer   S-6907
Bunny Fun   S-6902
Good Earth, the   S-6901
I Don't Like You Anymore   S-6904
Mariann's Sandman   S-6906
Mini Blouse Bounce (dance)   S-6905
My Family Tree   S-6903
In My Fantastic mood   S-7811
Peace of Love   S-6908
Water and Dirt (original poem)   S-6909

1970
Candy Land of Love   S-7007
Halloween Honey   S-7008
Hills of Maureen (A Irish Ballard)   S-7003
Little Green Bag   S-7001
Love That Man of Yours   S-7004
Pussyfooting around   S-7005
Sugar Daddy   S-7002
World Began to Sing   S-7006

1971
A Moment of Your Time   S-7105
Chicken Kick, the   S-7102
Christmas Love   S-7106
I Can't Find a woman   S-7104
It's Only An Accident   S-7108
Little World Of Snow   S-7103
Love Call   S-7101
Super Star   S-7107
When Tomorrow Is   S-7109

1972
Oklahoma Blues   S-7205
I'll Always Be Loving You   S-7201
It's Fantastic, It's   S-7204
Two Strangers Are We   S-7203
Wild Eyes of Love   S-7202

S = Song   P = Poem

Each year in alphabetical order

1973
Appalachain Wine   S-7305
And I Am Yours   S-7303
Is There No Santa   S-7301
Melody of Mary   S-7302
Tiami a Mi   S-7304

1974
Alive in Love   S-6601
Blue Jeans, red hair & Music   S-7415
Country Waltz   S-7408
Christmas Is (that's what)   S-7402
Its the Choo Choo Bump   S-7409.5
Lazy Country days   S-7407
Greatest Gift of all   S-7400
Mister Music (Duke Ellington)   S-7404
Musical Sounds   S-7417
No Other City (Los Angeles)   S-7414
Old country home of Nashville Tn   S-7413
Red White Blue Christmas Tree   S-7412
Sea Nymph   S-7403
Songwriter   S-7411
Sugar Shack   S-7409.5
Walking down the country road   S-7405
Winter time   P-7416   Will of the wisp   S-7406

1975
All the Corners of My Mind   S-7507
Blue Symphony   S-7502
Butterfly Waltz   S-7510
Country Christmas   S-7501
I Have Known Sadness   S-7509
Nashville Music Train   S-7504
Ragtime Chick   S-7506
Ruffian (An American Dream a song about a race horse)   S-7508
Ragtime Dude   S-7503
Your Something Called Love   S-7505

1976
Big City Blues   S-7608
Can't Keep the Hurt from showing   S-7618
Christmas Miracles   S-7611
Country moon shine magic on me   S-7603
Cry Softly When I Leave   S-7620
Disco Baby Rock   S-7606
Disco Blinkey   S-7614
Disco to the body walk (dance)   S-7612
Disco Dan, the Radio Man   S-7619
Georgia Jazz   S-7617
High & Lows   S-7607
Jade   S-7605   One Day   S-7609
Patty's Song   S-7601
Ronda's Song   S-7604
Roses in the Wine   S-7621
Shades of Blue Moods   S-7610
Silver River   S-7615
Sugar and Spice   S-7613
Tanya's Song   S-7602
Yolando   S-7616

1977
A Banquet For My Baby   S-7706
Dallas Dan, Gambling Man   S-7705
Dance Your Cares Away   S-7715
I Am Earth   S-7708
I Can't Believe   S-7714
I'm Returning to Georgia   S-7716
Love Me Again   S-7712
Make The Music Beautiful   S-7704
Moe (More of everything)   S-7709
My Secret Song   S-7718
Next Year is Tomorrow   S-7721
Normal Feelings   S-7711
Poor Marilyn   S-7701
Purple Peppermint Wine   S-7703
Restless Spirits in the night   S-7707
Sammy the Star   S-7702
She's a Little Dusty   S-7720
Survive   P-7703
The way you wear your hair   S-7717
We Belong Together   S-7713
Yvonne Louise   S-7710

1978
Angela   S-7823
Bad Boy Charlie Brown   P-7804
Bing Sings His song   S-7810
Cuddle Up For Sweet ~~Dreams~~   S-7812
Dancing Love   S-7819
Forever Free   S-7821
Get A Little Closer   S-7809
Good-bye Mister Blue   S-7817
Heavens Got To Be That Way   S-7822
Hold Me Don't Let Me Go   S-7801
I Could Not Say Good-bye   S-7803
In My Fantastic Mood   S-7811
In Our Land of Liberty   S-7800
I Saw You Passing By   S-7802
Love Symptoms   S-7820
Love Is Wanting To0   S-7815
Memory   S-7807
Maybe I'll Get Lucky   S-7808
Monkey Hug (dance)   S-7814
Patterns of Love   S-7818
The Songwriter   S-7806
Walkin' Thru The Years   S-7805
When Elvis Played His Music   S-7813
When your in love   S-7816

1979
American Mama   S-7905
A Snowflake   P-7900
Coming Down Hard   S-7911
Country in my Heart   S-7902
Happy Times and You   S-7906
I lost my bra at the old canteen   S-7904
Just a picture in my mind   P-7910
Little Christmas   P-7912
Litmitations   P-7909
Real Live Toy   S-7903
Spanish Rhapsody   S-7907
Strummin' A Pretty Western Tune   S-7901
Unbroken Circle   P-7908

Index Code 1964 through 2005   Small # after code #, original year written
One of my first poems was written in 1958 "My Love Note Tree"
This book doesn't look like a tree but it is made of paper from many trees.

INDEX

1980

Angel   S-8005
 Charisma   S-8007
  Chill is off the Flower   S-8000
Hanging on a Rainbow   S-8004
 I Do, I love You   S-8003
  I'm a Country Singer   S-8006
   I wanna be With you for Christmas   S-8008
Maybe I Would not be here tomorrow   S-8001
 Tantalizing Music Magic   S-8002

1981

Eight O'clock Shuffle   S-8104
 Face of a Clown, the   S-8109
My Dream Didn't Come True   P-8107
 Put a Little Ink on Me   P-8100
Reasons I Love You   S-8108
 Sleighbell   S-8106
  Snowflakes and Wine   S-8102
   Starlite Over You   S-8101
Your Way to Love   S-8103

1982

Angels and Stars   S-8202
 Christmas Memories   S-8204
Jump with Joy   S-8203
 Texas Eyes   S-8201

1983

Country Woman Loving Me   S-8301
 Figi and Taffy   P-8304
Lake, the   P-8305
 Melodies   P-8302
Sound of the Mind   P-8304

1984

Bonafide   P-8402
 Expectations   P-8404
  Invitation to a ball   P-8406
   Mini Skirts and White Levis   S-8405
   Tell Me, Why
You And Me   P-8403

1985

Bad, Bad Blues   P-8502
 It's No Use   P-8503
When Your Loving me in Country   S-8501
 Your Sister   P-8504

1986

Fascination   P-8604
 I Used to know her from Tennessee   S-8601
 Roll Out Your Mind   P-8602
  Sleeping in the hay   P-8605
That's the way She Is   P-8603

1987

Do You Think, You Can Think   S-8701
 Leave Me Alone   P-8703
 Number One on the Charts   P-8704
  Pretty Little You   P-8705
Return To Sender   P-8702

2

1988

Must I Pass Her By   P-8802
 Texas Flower   P-8801
There's No Way   P-8803
 Wrong Side of the Street   P-8804

1989

All Timers Hers , Alzheimer's   P-8904
 Can She Make it   P-8901
No Way Out   P-8905
 San Antoine   P-8902
What Went Wrong   P-8903

1990

Home in the Woods   P-9005
 Love in the breezeway   P-9004
  Margarite   P-9003
Sing Another Song   P-9002
 Tears Cloud My Eyes   P-9001
Tracy   P9006

1991

After I Said, No   P-9103
 I.C.U.   P-9102
Little Bitty Love   P-9104
 Wrong Way   P-9101

1992

All That and you loved me too   P-9207
 Christmas Love   P-9207
Hour Glass, No More Sand   P-9204
 If I Ever Love Again   P-9206
I'm Chicago Call me Jazz   S-9201
 Love Makes my Heart, Try   p-9202
New Years Eve, what ever way it goes   P-9210
 Remission   P-9203
  We Did It All   P-9208
You Gave My Life Love   P-9

1993

All That & You Loved me Too   P-9312
 Cancer Took My Tears   P-9302
  Color Of Your Love   P-9308
Falling Leaves   S-9307
 First And Last   P-9313
  I Will Remember   P-9303
Little Fish   P-9301
Looking For That Love again   S-9305
 New Years Eve   P-9309
One Beautiful Moment   S-9306
 Pictures on the Wall   S-9311
Star Of Christmas   S-9310
Those days Have Gone By   P-9304
Walking On Four   S-9314

1994

All My Heart Can Take   P-9415
 All The Time My Valentine   P-9417
  All Your caring Moments   P-9410
   Always Round My Heart   S-9415
   Audience of One   S-9412
Birthdays, younger than me   P-9421
 Boston Bay   S-9406
 Breathless   P-9425
Butterfly Walk   P-9434
 Colors in the rain   P-9407
  Dreams of Love   P-9424

1994

Cheese Cake and Rose Wine   P-9433
 Christmas Sweetheart   P-9428
Different Windows   S-9420
 Eyes (I's) of Love   S-9403
Falling in Love With You   S-9422
First Time You Said, No   P-9429
 It's Nice the Way It Is   S-9430
Lavender Blue   P-9413
 Look What You Did   P-9408
 Love's Another dream   P-9402
  Music   P-9435
  Music, Talk of Love   P-9436
No One Else is There   S-9431
Pink Butterfly   S-9432
 Rainbows   P-9409
  Roses In The Wine   S-9418
She's Country   S-9405
Six O'clock Blues   S-9414
 Texas Eyes   S-9411
  Teddy Bear Christmas   P-9416
 Thanks For Loving Me   S-9404
This Place   P-9419
Vibrations   P-9427
 Wednesday Night   S-9423
When the Roses Turn Silver   S-9401

1995

Are You Alright   P-9528
Are You Happy Now   P-9513
 Bachelors Trap, the   P-9506
 Beauty of the Rose   P-9541
 Boots on the Floor   S-9554
Christmas in Space   S-9534
Country Love   S-9505
Does Anybody know, why   P-9552
 Empty Bubbles   S-9539
 Everybody's Gone   S-9512
Falling in love with trouble   S-9531
 Foot Prints in the Snow   S-9503
 For, I remember Love   P-9502
Give me a little bit of Yesterday   P-9507
Glass of Wine   P-9547
Gotta get back to where we were   S-9542
 Green To Blue   P-9536
He Saved the Best for Last   S-9509
 Heart of Roses   P-9519
How many times have I cried   P-9515
I Don't have to dream Anymore   P-9526
 In the winter of my Love   S-9532
Knocking on the Door   S-9517
Marry me and love me again   P-9523
Man and Woman   P-9550
 Mini Skirts and White Levis   S-9538
 Minutes of Gold   P-9520
Maybe I Would not be here Tomorrow   S-9553
My Heart is Getting Crowded   P-9511
 Nashville Closer to the Top   S-9525
 Number me Last   P-9521
Pretty Music   S-9501
Ring Finger, Left Hand   P-9548
 So Far Away   S-9527
 Something About Me   P-9537
 Sounds   P-9529
Stocking boots & Teddy Bear sweaters   P-9551
Summer Theme   Int. 9533
Sun and Rain   P-9543
 That Feeling don't go Away   S-9510
Why did you leave me   P-9522
 Why did you do this to me   P-9546

196

INDEX

1995

The Music's Back   P-9516
    Too much for one night   P-9540
      This is It   P-9508
Waiter   P-9544
    Water and Dirt   S-9535
    Way He Looks at You, the   P-9549
    What Do I Say   P-9514
Where Were you When I was young   S-9504
You have to wait   P-9518
    You know, What life is   P-9524
Mariola Blues   P-9612

1996

All the ways I Love You   P-96102
    All the Different faces   P-9655
    Ally May   P-9661
    Another World   S-9641
Be With Me   P-9691
    Black Water   P-9679
    Blue lavender   P-9630
    Bottle of Honey   P-9663
    Brandy   P-96104
Can't Get at it Right Now   P-9684
    Can't Stop Now   S-9613
    Caring   P96105
    Check Out   P-9673
    Children of the Stars   S-9623
    Color in the Rain   P-9629
    Country Music   P-9659
    Crossfire   S-9640
Dark Eyes   P-96117
    Does anybody know what love is   P-9622
    Don't ever let me loose again   P-9665
    Don't Smile at Me   P-9674
Easy in and easy out   P-9692
    Every Little Love   P-9680
    Everything is All Your fault   P-96100
Farther Than I can See   P-9644
    First Dream   P-9615
    Folded Arms   P-9670
    Friends are Blue   P-96110
Getting Better   P-9699
    Got a Little Cool   P-9677
Happening   S-9649
Hurt   P-9695
How many times, Have You said, No   P-9648
    Hurting Tears   S-9650
It will be Better in the morning   S-9620
If I Hear From You   P-9671
    I Forgive Myself for Loving you   P-9656
    If She Was Mine   P-9638
I'm Not Going to Cry   P-9618
I'm Not Going To Nashville   S-9633
    It Happens the other part of love   P-9616
I want to love you but you wont' stand still   P-9626
    It's Just the Way I Am   S-9647
Is It Over   P-9654
    I Think of You   P-9642
It's Up To You   P-9637
I Walked the Streets of Nashville   S-9698
    I Wanna Feel Good Again   S-96111
    It Was A Country Ride   P-9689
    I Want To Love You   P-96296
It will be better in the morning   S-9620
Kati   P-9687
    Keep in Touch   P-9690

1996 (cond)

Love Today   P-9625
Love is Piling up   P-9627
    Last Dance in the rain   S-9614
      Lights of Nevada   P-9658
      Little Nashville   P-9639
      Long Way Home   P-96106
Looking at you Looking at Me   P-9685
    Love is Gonna Catch me   S-9604
    Love Stuffin   P-9624
For ever, (it will) Last   P-97
    Garden of Roses   P-9719
    Maybe It was Just me   P-9688
      Me and You   p-9645
      Music and rainbows   P-9632
No More Birthdays   P-9697
    No More of Everything   P-96116
    Not Supposed to Be   P-9631
    Now, I Know Why   P-9668
    Now, It's time for me to leave   P-96115
One Heart   P-9611
    One Who Loves More   P-9628
    Out of my Mind   P-9606
    Out of Money, out of Dreams   p-9667
    Over Spilt Love   P-9639
Pair of white Levis   P-9662
    Pretty & Beautiful Too   P-96101
Quiet   P-96107
Rainy Night in Warsaw   S-9643
    Real Life's Love   P-9607
    Reindeers Can't Dance   p-96112
    Remember   S-9617
    Roll of the Dice   P-9669
Saginaw Bag   S-9693
    Shadow of Love   P-9696
    She's Jealous   P-9634
Sleeping in my Mind   P-9635
    Song Between the Mountains   S-9657
    Sunday Morning, Wed. Night   P-9619
      Susan, Indian Sue   P-9672
      Sweet Dreams   P-9636
Tears You Left Behind   P-9686
    Thanks For All the Roses   S-9686
    The way You Look at Me   S-9694
    Too Much heartache   S-9666
    Turned me on, never turned me off   P-9610
    Two Hearts   P-9608
Unless I Know   P-96103
    Until You Say, I Do   S-9602
Vegas Blues   P-9652
Valentine   P-96109
Walk In The Wind   P-9621
    Walking Softly in My Heart   P-96118
    Warsaw Blues   P-9653
    When a Woman Looks at a Man   P-96114
Which Way is Lonely   P-9646
What Would you Do   P-9609
Xylophone   P-9603
    You Left Me in Chicago   P-9683
      You looked But I Was Gone   P-9682
You Still Look at Me   P-9651
    Your Caught in My Mind   S-9605
    Your Special Anyway   P-9675
You Still Got the Touch   P-9651
You Have a ring on your finger   S
    Suddenly It's You   P-9678
    Summer Cat   P-9663
    Sun Burn   P-9660

1997

Angels in the Night   P-9718
Best thing I Have Ever Done   S-9712
    Black Water Lilly   P-9707
    Boots on the Floor   S-9727
Can You See, What I hear   S-9746
    Colorado Blues   P-9725
    Cookies Song   P-9725
    Fiddlers Waltz   S-9733
Fireside at Nashville North   P-9709
Your Always There   P-9530
Gentle   S-9722
How Lonely Are You   S-9745
    Had No Idea   P-9713
    Have You Got a Date   P-9704
I Am Blessed   P-9703
Last One, the   P-9732
    Look into the Sun   P-9734
    Love is telling someone, No   P-9729
    Loves' Arrow   S-9743
Man in Me   S-9715
    Memory of You is all I Need   P-9726
Never Done This Before   S-9716
    New Year, New Love   P-9701
    Nothing But Love   P-9724
Perfume Wine   S-9728
    Put Your Boots on, Dad   P-9735
Seasons   S-9708
    She's Not Yours   P-9748
    Since You loved Me   P-9748
    Stop Picking on Me   P-9706
    Sun Down   P-9731
Teach Me Love   P-9705
    Tennessee   S-9738
    Till It's Gone   S-9742
    Things You Never Say   P-9711
Tiny Tear Drops   P-9720
    Through a Looking Glass   P-9714
    Touch Of Love   P-9736
Universal Language Of Love   P-9739
Waiting For Someone to Love   P-9740
    Walk Around The World   P-9741
    Way you wear your Hair, the   S-9744
    Which way will your boots be   S-9717
    Woodlawn Taper   S-9721
    Windows of Christmas   S-9747
    Didn't I tell you no more   P-9723
    Pony Tail Rock   S-9735

1998

Barbie Doll   P-9834
Cherry Blue   S-9803
    Corner of your eye, the   S-9820
Devil in Your eye, the   P-9830
    Don't Go Away   P-9821
Ecstasy   P-9825
    Ellie Lorainne   S-9822
Feel Me Different   S-9818
    Feelings in You   P-9844
Gonna do it right, this time   P-9814
Got It   P-9836
Heart of Fire   P-9839
    Hills of Colleen   S-9807
If There Was Another You   P-9806
I walked the streets of Nashville   S-9809
Kelly Green   P-9829
    Dance Judy Dance   S-9826
    bEmpty Boots   P-9843

INDEX

1998 (Cond)

Linda Jo   S-9801
   Lines of Force   P-9810
   Loads of Love   P-9802
Let Me Hear That Again   P-9840
   Maybe She will say, Good-Bye   P-9837
   Make me want to Stay   P- 9827
Neon Wine   P-9823
One Time   P-9808
   Other Side of the Road   p-9817
Pink Rose, Pink Wine   P-9841
   Pretty All Over   S-9811
   Putting the Pictures away   P-9812
Red Ribbon Blues   P-9816
   Roses To Wine   P-9833
She's a Lot of Trouble   P-9832
Someone New, (in the eyes of)   S-9813
Teachers Lady   S-9805
   Texas Double Two (dance)   P-9819
   Think of anything, think of me   P-9824
   Three Bottles of Wine   P-9835
Walking Bottle   S-9804
   What a Place   P-9828
   What To Do   P-9831
   Why Not   P-9815
You keep trying to take me out   P-9842
Zodiac   P-9838

1999

Am I Ready   P-9906
Across the Century   P-9934
   Across the table   P-9946
   All the Things That I See   P-9919
   Music In The Band   P-9937
Band of Gold   S-9935
   Beautiful Kentucky   P-9955
   Beyond the Sun   P-9948
Cathleen   P-9949
Dancing in the Dog House   9932
   Don't Look Back   P-9913
   Do You Know Me   P-9910
Eyes of Tennessee   P-9912
For You, I Will Do It   P-9954
Hand To Hand   S-9915
   Hills of Kentucky   P-9938
   Honky-Tonk Waltz   S-9933
If You Were Here   P-9936
   I'll Keep Asking for You   P-9918
   I'll Pretend It's You   S-9920
   It Will Be Nicer Tonight   P-9911
   I Still Look at You   p-9931
Lady Bug   P-9952
   Last day of the Millennium   P-9956
   Life's a Long Song   P-9917
   Little Bit of Wiggle   P-9905
Lisa, Your Music is Pretty Tonight   S-9903
   Love Doesn't Care   P-9923
Mama Ain't Bad   S-9914
   May You Always be   P-9901
   Me   P-9929
Never Felt Like This   P-9926
   Never Forgotten   P-9945
   Never Been This Way   S-9927
   Never is, Now   P-9916
Only Have One   P-9947
Parking Lot   P-9943
Pretty Short and Petite   P-9950
   How Will I Know   P-9936

1999 (cond)

Red Ribbon Blues   S—9957
Someone New   S-9951
   Sunday Morning Blues   P-9944
   That's All Your Gonna Hear   P-9928
   Things I Should Not Do   P-9908
   Tell, No One   P-9925
Tennessee Wine   S-9921
   To Know, That   P-9902
   Two Thousand Years   P-9909
   Wabash Avenue swing   P-9930
   Watermelon Wine   P-9907
   What a Car   P-9940
   Wilma Jean   P-9904
   When I Was Your Age   S-9953
Why can't I fall in love with you   S-9941
You Have, What I Love, You   P-9922
You, Me, Nashville and Tennessee   P-9942
Ursula   S-9924

2000

Always Be Friends   S-0030
   At the End of Love   P-0048
Bill   P-0059   Because I said, Yes   P-0007
   Blinky, The Space Deer   S-0001
   Burger Song   Wendys   S-0034
Call Me For Love   P-0043
   Christmas In Space   S0010
   Christmas Tree   P0027
Don't Do This to Me Now   P-0042
   Don't Sit Down   P-0008
   Do Something   P-0023
   Do You Love Me Now   P-0019
   Eyes of An Eagle   P-0018
   Eyes of Life   P-0046
Feeling, the   P-0015
   First Time   P-0012
   For a Long Time   P-0041
   For the First Time   P-0031
   Fred (the cat)   0028
Has it Just Begun   P-0009
   Have I ever Said, No   S-0051
If I Didn't Know You   P-0026
   I Love All of You   P-0020
   It's All Yours   P-0039
   It's Never Forever Anymore   P-0024
   It's Never Gonna Happen   P-0045
   It Isn't There   P-0022
Keep Me With You   S-0005
   Less Than Me   P-0052
   Lips I Didn't Kiss   P-0032
Looking at Love   P-0057
   Losing You   S-0006
   Louisiana Honeymoon   S-0017
   Long Distance Driver   P-0049
   Love is Just Love   P-0056
My Name Is Mary   S-0013
   Put The Blame on Me   S-0040
Real Time   P0053
   Red To Blue   P-0036
   Rest of The way   S-0060
   Rusty Rose   P-0025
Slam it to the Floor   S-0014
   Some Thing Different About You   P-0002
   Song of Christmas   P-0016
   Someone Else Is there   P-0038
   Alone With me   P-0050
   Like it Was Yesterday   S-0029

2000 (cond)

Temptations To Love   P-0047
   Thanks For Being You   P-0037
   Try, Yes   P-0044
   We'll All Be Together   P-0021
   What do I Say to my friend   P-0055
   When the Lights Go Out   P-0061
   Who Will She Be   P-0035
   Wonderful World of Woman   P-0054
   You Have Always Been There   S-0058
   You know I'm going to ask you   P-0003
   You Held Me Too Close   P-0033
   Your Love   S-0004
You and Me   S-0011

2001

A Rose Named Mary   S-0136
   All That Touches me   P-0110
   A Little Bit More than Love   S-0105
Always With Love   P-0131
   Arena of Love   P-0129
   Are You the Reason Why   S-0106
As Time Goes By   P-0138
Country In Your Eyes   P-0102
Emotions of Love   P-0111
   Feeling Inside, the   S-0107
I Want To Cheat With You   P-0116
   If It Didn't Happen   P-0122
   Is That the Best You Can Do   P-0128
   Is there more of you for me to love   S-0104
   It's Still There   P-0139
Just Me   P-0103
   Just Looking at You   S-0120
Letters In Love   P-0112
   Loves' Devine Perfumes   P-0134
   Now, Your Acting Like a Woman   P-0108
   Next To You   P-0113
One More Time   S-0130
   Red, white and blue Christmas Tree   S-0133
   Rest of The Way   S-0127
Smile   P-0135
   Stay Out of My Mind   P-0101
Take a walk around the moon with me   S-0118
   Tennessee Love   P-0140
   Tennessee Sunshine   P-0121
Water And Dirt   P-0109
We Are One   P-0141   WHY   P-0119
   We Found Love   P-0124
   When No, Means Yes   P-0114
   When the Music Plays   P-0115
When you Remember Me   P-0132
   Will to Win, the   P-0142
   Walking The Wrong Way   P-0137
Yes   P-0123   You   P-0117
You Started It All   P-0120
   Step Out of the Picture   P-0125

2002

A Set of Blues   P-0232
   All The Roses   P-0218
All That You were Meant To Be   P-0203
   All That I Have   P-0216
   Another Tomorrow   P-0221
Beautiful Woman, Beautiful Song   S-0230
Beauty Of You   P-0209

INDEX

2002 (cond)

Can This Be Done   P-0225
    Chemistry In Love   P-0222
    Christmas in Space (2000)   S-0210
Dog House Blues   P-0206
Feeling Funny   P-0226
Give It Time   P-0207
I Could Love That   P-0224
Let Yourself Go   P-0227
Melodies In Wine   P-0212
    Middle Of Nowhere   S-0211
    Music On The Web   P-0229
Next To Me   S-0204
No One Else Is There   0200
Rosalie   P-0219   Running Late   P-0231
Sleighbell   P-0201
    Strictly Business   P-0205
There I See a Yellow Ribbon   S-0228
    This is where I want to be   P-0215
    The Way I Am   P-0214
Will It Ever Be Over   P-0202
    You Can Be You   P-0217
    You Just Don't Get It   P-0208
You Gotta Love Plumbing   P-0223
Your Still Here   P-0220

2003

Alone   P-0318
As Long As YouCan   P-0306

Billy Goat, the   P-03
    Blue Jeans   S-0316
Different Years   P-0319
    Divorced With Kids   S-0321
    Don't Forget Me   P-0322
I'm A Soldier Too   S-0308
    In Love And In Space   P-0317
Lift Me Up   P-0307
    Little Par Of Time   P-0302
    Love Plumbing   P-0304
Nashville North   P-0314
One More Look   P-0313
Red, White And Blue Memory   P-0309
    Rhythm of the Ribbons   P-0312
    Ribbon On A Tree   S-0310
Tell Me, Why   P-0315
    Thee Song   S-0311
Windows (in love and in space)   S- 0320
    With Love, I Loved You   S-03011
You Have a Place To Go   P-0305

2004

Ain't No Mama Like Me   S-0415
    Ask Yourself, Why   P-0411
Beautiful Woman (waltz)   S-04-9
Bob-o-link   P-0413
Carolina Time   S-0426
    Coyote Canyon   P-0402
    Coyote Blues   P-0412
Dream   P-0416
    Divorced with More Kids   S-0417
    Don't Quit Now   P-0422
Have You Ever Been In Love Before   P-0414
Is It Still There   P-0423
    Today Is Yesterdays Tomorrow   P-0410

2004 (cond)

Just a Song   P-040
Imagination   P-0419
Kentucky   S-0408
Love Isn't Easy   P-0420
    Love Turned around   S-0427
Old Fashioned Christmas   P-0428
Second Time Around   S-0407
    Special World   P-0403
Taken   P-0424
Watching the Kids Grow   P-0418
    Water the Water   P-0425
Where Did Jenny Go   P-0421
Where ever you were I was there   S-0401
    When I Was Only Three   P-0405
    When Love Is a Real dream   P-0406

2005

Audience Of One   P-0507
Challenge   P-0514
    Come Out of the Blues   P-0509
    Cracker Barrel Christmas   S-0504
Days   P-0511
    Dreams   P-0510
Give me, To You   P-0513
Hi !   P-0518
    Is " This " You   P-0508
Just Being Alive   P-0502
    Mystery Of Love   P-0503

Memories, Minutes in Time   S-0505
Book title

Polish Bar   P-0515
Teddy Bear Christmas   P-0517
Sometime   P-0512
Tagging Along   P-0516
    Take a Walk in Your Mind   P-0506
    The Way We Fell In Love   S-0521
What Ever the Reasons May Be   P-0501
Love is a Good Word   P-0520
Zephyr   P-0519

CHILDREN OF THE STARS

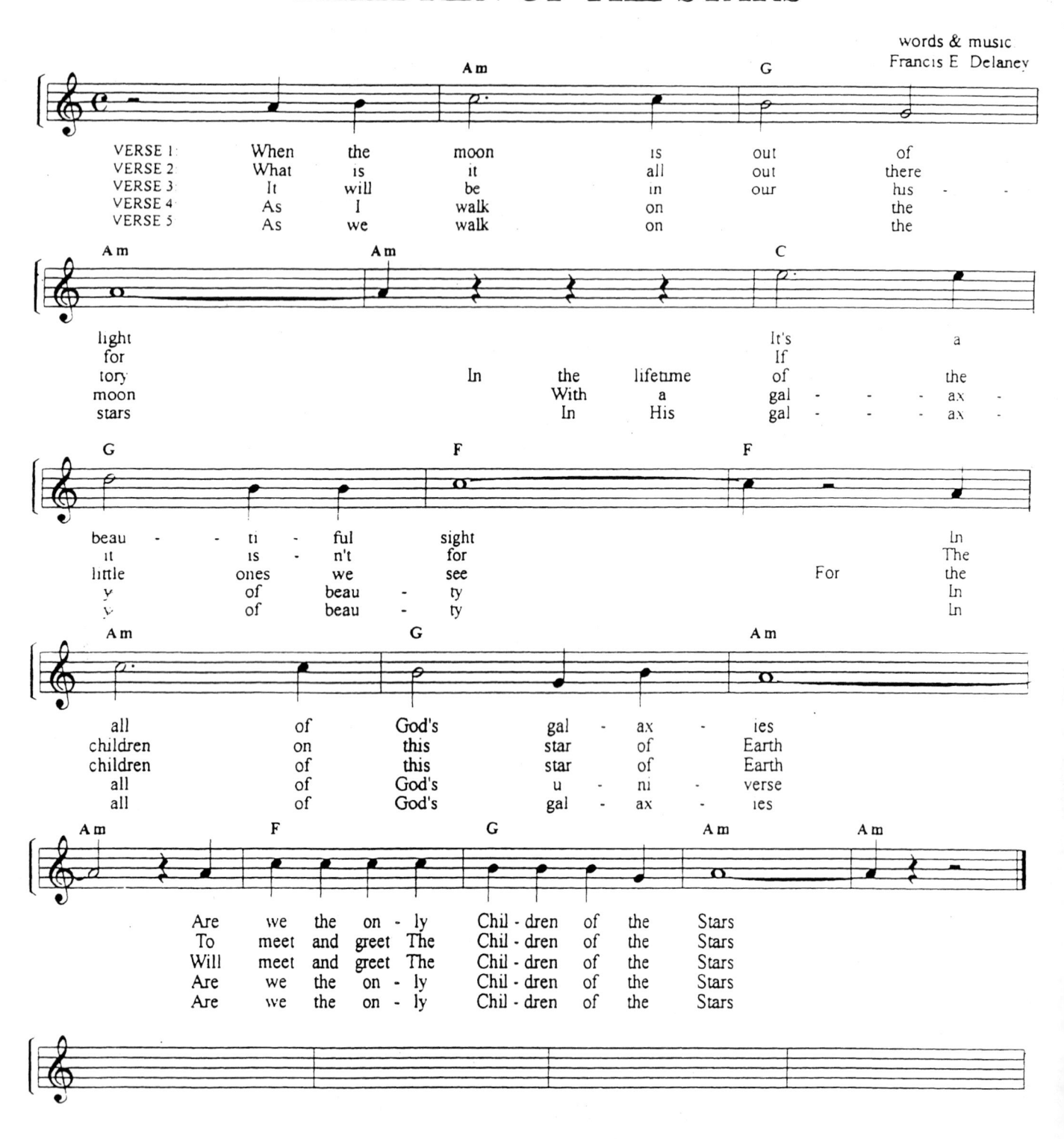

words & music
Francis E. Delaney

VERSE 1: When the moon is out of light — It's a beau-ti-ful sight — In all of God's gal-ax-ies Are we the only Chil-dren of the Stars
VERSE 2: What is it all out there for — If it isn't for — children on this star of Earth To meet and greet The Chil-dren of the Stars
VERSE 3: It will be in our his-tory — In the lifetime of the little ones we see — For the children of this star of Earth Will meet and greet The Chil-dren of the Stars
VERSE 4: As I walk on the moon — With a gal-ax-y of beau-ty — In all of God's u-ni-verse Are we the only Chil-dren of the Stars
VERSE 5: As we walk on the stars — In His gal-ax-y of beau-ty — In all of God's gal-ax-ies Are we the only Chil-dren of the Stars

Copyright 1996-2000 Francis E. Delaney
P.O. Box 932 Frankfort, IL 60423

Nap-9623-MR-KY
All Rights Reserved

RL